MAKING THEIR DAYS HAPPEN

Monika Mitra

MAKING THEIR DAYS HAPPEN

Paid Personal Assistance Services
Supporting People with Disability Living
in Their Homes and Communities

LISA I. IEZZONI

TEMPLE UNIVERSITY PRESS
Philadelphia • Rome • Tokyo

TEMPLE UNIVERSITY PRESS
Philadelphia, Pennsylvania 19122
tupress.temple.edu

Library of Congress Cataloging-in-Publication Data

Names: Iezzoni, Lisa I., author.
Title: Making their days happen : paid personal assistance services
  supporting people with disability living in their homes and communities
  / Lisa I. Iezzoni.
Description: Philadelphia : Temple University Press, 2022. | Includes
  bibliographical references and index. | Summary: "Most Americans, even
  with significant disability, want to live in their homes and
  communities. Without adequate supports from relatives or friends, people
  with difficulties performing basic activities of daily living (ADL)
  require paid personal assistance services (PAS) to remain at home.
  Nearly 8 million Americans need in-home ADL supports, and roughly 15%
  receive paid PAS. With aging 'baby boomers' and other demographic
  trends, the numbers of people needing paid home-based PAS will grow
  significantly in coming decades. But a mismatch between this rising
  demand and the paid PAS workforce has been widening for many years and
  now nears crisis proportions. This book reviews the health, civil
  rights, and labor policies affecting paid PAS (Chapters 2-4); draws from
  in-depth interviews to explore the characteristics and complex
  interpersonal dynamics of PAS consumers and providers (Chapters 5-12);
  and offers recommendations for improving future experiences of PAS
  consumers and providers (Chapters 13 and 14)"—Provided by publisher.
Identifiers: LCCN 2021022993 (print) | LCCN 2021022994 (ebook) | ISBN
  9781439920756 (cloth) | ISBN 9781439920763 (paperback) | ISBN
  9781439920770 (pdf)
Subjects: LCSH: Home health aides—Employment—United States. | Home health
  aides—Government policy—United States. | Home health aides—Supply and
  demand—United States. | Home care services—United States. | Home care
  services—Employees—Government policy—United States. | Home care
  services—Employees—Supply and demand—United States. | People with
  disabilities—Home care—United States.
Classification: LCC RA645.35 .I39 2021 (print) | LCC RA645.35 (ebook) |
  DDC 362.14—dc23
LC record available at https://lccn.loc.gov/2021022993
LC ebook record available at https://lccn.loc.gov/2021022994

Printed in the United States of America

9 8 7 6 5 4 3 2 1

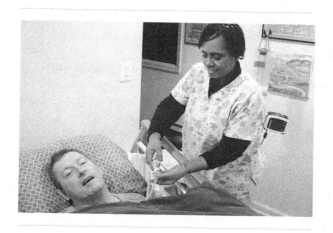

To Michael and Nelita

I MET MICHAEL in the late afternoon of October 29, 2009, the day my scooter died. I had started using this scooter in 1988, as my multiple sclerosis (MS) progressed and walking became unsafe and unreliable. Since then, the scooter had carried me many miles and on numerous business trips, and it lasted well beyond its expected lifespan. I had flown to Newark Airport that day from Boston, my hometown, en route to a business meeting in Princeton, New Jersey. As I rolled from the airport gate to the nearby train station to take New Jersey Transit to Princeton Junction, the scooter stopped, never to roll on its own again. Train conductors pushed me onto and off the train. At Princeton Junction Station, a fellow passenger came up to me, offering to help. He stayed with me 45 minutes, as the sun sank and evening chill fell, providing primarily moral support until the car sent by the meeting organizers arrived to take me away.

That man was Michael. He operated his wheelchair's joystick with his right hand, his spastic left arm tightly gripping his chest. His head twisted rightward with torticollis, and his lower limbs were still,

Top: Nelita giving Michael his evening tube feeding on December 29, 2019. The bag of feed hangs on the pole behind Nelita's left shoulder; below that is the small device that pumps the feed. (Photo credit: Hanniel Dossous)

unmoving because of primary progressive multiple sclerosis. Without hesitancy, he claimed kinship—one wheelchair user to another. Within months, we became great friends, and over the years we have rolled hundreds of miles together—sometimes Michael taking the lead, other times with me out front. Michael was born in England, and the saying "stay calm and carry on" seems his unspoken motto. Life has thrown much at him, but he carries on.

I met Nelita late in the evening of March 9, 2010. Michael had been hospitalized for what turned out to be a stage 4 pressure injury, and I had promised to be his advocate. Once again, I flew from Boston to Newark Airport, taking two New Jersey Transit trains to finally reach Princeton. Following Michael's directions in pitch-black darkness, I rode my new scooter with grim determination through town, up Witherspoon Street past the Princeton Cemetery, and eventually reached what was then a community hospital. Michael appeared gaunt, unshaven, and ill—but at least now his wound was recognized, and treatment could begin. He planned for me to stay at his fully accessible home during my brief visit and had arranged for his long-time personal care assistant Nelita to drive me there in his ramp-equipped van.

After loading me into the van, Nelita's brother-in-law drove the several miles to Michael's small home. I entered through the garage, which has a ramp into his house. As I rolled into the garage with its musty smell and shadowy light, I saw two racing bicycles hanging from the rafters—one sky blue, the other silver. I learned later that Michael had ridden those bikes throughout the United States and Canada from the early 1980s until around 2000, when multiple sclerosis intervened. With gentle kindness, Nelita made sure I settled into the unfamiliar surroundings, and over the ensuing few days, she offered any help she could. Since then, I have seen Nelita often when I visit Michael, watched her son grow into a fine registered nurse, texted and called periodically to keep in touch, and witnessed her devotion to Michael's well-being across many rough times. Their relationship started as professional, but it is now also personal. Nelita has assisted Michael to live his life as he wishes.

December 22, 2020

Contents

IV EXPERIENCES AND PERCEPTIONS OF RECEIVING AND PROVIDING PAS

V   MAKING PAS HAPPEN

14 PAS in the Future   233

    Epilogue   265

    Notes   273

    Index   297

Acknowledgments

Over the years while visiting Michael, I met dozens of paid personal assistance services (PAS) workers supporting him in his home. Many I saw only once; others were present across multiple visits, some over several years. During moments together, in the kitchen or during periodic down times, I asked them about their stories. Virtually all worked multiple jobs. The vast majority were women. Some were born in the United States, and others had come to the United States as children or immigrated as adults. Many adult immigrants had extensive education in their home countries, some with professional health care degrees; others had well-respected jobs before leaving their homelands. I vividly remember a conversation late one hot summer afternoon, while peeling corn on the cob on Michael's back deck with a woman, trauma etched deeply on her face, recounting her escape from the sexual violence of war roiling her country. Some people hesitated to talk, but even this reticence was eloquent. My thanks go to these many PAS providers for giving me insights into their working lives and impetus to do this project.

The Gordon and Betty Moore Foundation (GBMF) provided generous financial support for this work. Their grant allowed me to spend 18 months diving deeply into federal and state (Medicaid) policies affecting PAS in the United States and to link these policies to the personal stories of both PAS consumers and providers. GBMF Project Officer Sutep Laohavanich supported my insistence on interviewing PAS consumers and workers. The words of these interviewees, present throughout this book, underscore my belief that PAS policies have direct personal consequences. I am grateful to the 21 consumers and 20 PAS workers who spoke with me for this project—their experiences and perspectives convey both the complexity and urgency of the imminent PAS crisis confronting the United States. I also thank a college student I call Fred (his pseudonym choice), whom I Skyped with later to hear the perspective of a young person facing decades of needing PAS supports. Finally, GBMF also supported reviews of our draft project reports by fifteen interdisciplinary experts, who provided incisive critiques, which greatly informed and improved our work.

I could not have done the GBMF project without the tireless and enthusiastic efforts of project manager Naomi Gallopyn, M.S. We had tight time deadlines, and Naomi plunged headlong into the work, which we divided between us. For the GBMF policy review, she focused on the many demonstration projects conducted by federal and state agencies to explore models of PAS over the last 50 years. Naomi also identified most interviewees, obtained their informed consent for my interviews, and organized the audio recordings. She combed the verbatim transcripts of the 41 interviews and took the lead on writing up results from the PAS workers for the research report we submitted to GBMF. I borrowed liberally from the GBMF policy and interview reports in preparing this book and am thus truly grateful to Naomi for her foundational work.

Over the course of the GBMF project, Naomi and I benefited from the wise and deeply informed insights provided by our collaborators and consultants. Kezia Scales, Ph.D., director of policy research, and Jodi M. Sturgeon, president of PHI (formerly known as Paraprofessional Healthcare Institute), were collaborators from the start and provided critical assistance at many points, whether clarifying core realities of PAS work, assisting with identifying PAS provider interviewees, or reviewing draft reports. I cite PHI publications, produced by Dr. Scales and PHI's first-rate research team, liberally throughout this book. Robyn I. Stone, Dr.P.H., senior vice president of research at LeadingAge and codirector of the LeadingAge LTSS Center at University of Massachusetts–Boston, and Natasha Bryant, M.A., managing director and senior research associate at the UMass-Boston LeadingAge LTSS Center, also provided critical ongoing guidance throughout the project. Their collective experiences encompass this complex field, with the authority of many decades of direct, often hands-on, involvement.

Nicole D. Agaronnik spent 15 months with me as a stellar research assistant before matriculating at Harvard Medical School in August 2020. Nicole brought exceptional personal insights about disability and an incredible work ethic—emails arrived from her about research issues night and day! At my request, she sought and synthesized the literature for book chapters, found numbers to populate tables, and took the lead on fact checking. This book could not have happened without Nicole's tireless but always willing and witty efforts. She will make a wonderful doctor!

Finally, I thank my friends and colleagues throughout the disability community for speaking with me about this project and teaching me about PAS. Dennis Heaphy, in particular, has been a true north for me on all things disability. Charlie Carr, whose story appears in Chapters 2 and 3, kindly read those pages and corrected one small factual error. Despite having had multiple sclerosis for 44 years, I do not yet need PAS; my husband, Reed, frees my time by doing daily tasks—cooking dinner (I often drop things, so probably a good idea), grocery shopping, laundry, and many other chores. Finally, the novel coronavirus pandemic upended some plans, especially for photographs. Social distancing demands prevented me from capturing certain images I had envisioned, and I cajoled friends, family, and PAS workers into taking photographs at my virtual direction. I date some of these pictures to distinguish the premask from the postmask era. In these uncertain times of COVID-19, I thank them for assisting in making this book happen.

Lisa I. Iezzoni
December 22, 2020

MAKING THEIR DAYS HAPPEN

1

What's Needed?

Bob and Dan, brothers in their sixties, live full and active lives in their community despite progressive, lifelong functional limitations from muscular dystrophy. They have quick, intelligent minds; Dan is renowned for excelling at the quiz show *Jeopardy*. Both have severe mobility disability. Bob can move his hand sufficiently to operate his power wheelchair's manual joystick, but Dan must use a chin-operated miniature trackball joystick to direct his power wheelchair. The brothers need assistance with all activities of daily living (ADLs)—bathing, toileting, dressing, feeding, and basic mobility—and various instrumental ADLs (IADLs), such as meal preparation, shopping, and housework. They also periodically need suctioning of mucous secretions to keep them comfortable and reduce risks of aspiration.

The brothers live in their family home, where they have made many modifications over the years to improve accessibility. Bob can be transferred safely using a standard Hoyer lift, but Dan cannot because his neck is unstable. To accommodate his transfers, Dan devised an ingenious pulley system secured to ceiling beams and operated by a single personal assistant (PA). This pulley apparatus functioned well until Dan started feeling unsafe. Now Dan needs two—or sometimes three—PAs to lift and transfer him safely.

Their mother had been the primary caregiver for Bob and Dan for most of their sixty-plus years. She is now in her late eighties and has dementia, requiring assistance with her own ADLs and IADLs. A complex team currently supports Bob, Dan, and their mother in their home. One man has provided personal assistance services (PAS) for the brothers for almost 15 years, working nearly 80 hours per week. Lifting Dan, after he abandoned his jerry-rigged pulley contraption, requires concerted strength. Devoted to Bob and Dan, this male PA feels he cannot cut back his hours because he has the greatest physical strength of all the PAs and is therefore needed frequently.

Mona, in her early fifties, organizes the multimember PAS team that provides round-the-clock, in-home support for the brothers and their mother. She began her career as a certified nursing assistant in hospitals, but about a dozen years ago, she decided to move into home-based direct care providing PAS. Mona worked for a home care agency until Bob and Dan recruited her to work under their direction. She views herself as "case managing for the whole house. . . . I provide personal care, medicine, reminders, house cleaning, of course, shopping, you name it." She works hard but finds meaning in her work. As Mona explained about Bob and Dan,

> Even though they're disabled, and they can't do very much for themselves, they still want to be a part of the world. . . . I want to be able to help them achieve their goals of being a part of society. . . . The caregivers who work in the house, we all feel like *we are part of making their days happen*. And at the end of the day, when I come home or the other caregivers leave, we heave a sigh of relief. . . . It's not a sigh of relief like we're glad the job is done. We heave a sigh of relief that we've completed the task for them. . . . It makes me feel like I'm doing something. I'm being of service.

———

Americans overwhelmingly want to live in their homes and communities, even when they have significant disability. Only 4% of Americans prefer to enter a nursing home if they become unable to care for themselves.[1] However, like brothers Bob and Dan and their mother, people with substantial disability often require daily assistance with ADLs, their most intimate physical needs. Without basic ADL supports, people with significant disability cannot live safely, comfortably, and with dignity in their homes, maximizing their overall health, general well-being, quality of life, and hope for the future.

Over three-quarters of Americans who need in-home ADL supports receive this assistance from family members or friends, a vast unpaid workforce.[2] As a shorthand, unpaid family members or friends are often called informal caregivers, although the word *informal* fails to "capture the complexity of what family caregivers do or their connection to the older adults they are helping."[3] In 2020 an estimated 53.0 million adults in the United States—21% of adult Americans—reported being an informal caregiver to an adult or child in the prior year, with 24% of these caregivers saying they assisted two or more people.[4] On average, informal caregivers were 49 years old, 61% were female, about 61% were non-Hispanic White, 17% were Hispanic, 14% were non-Hispanic Black, and 5% were Asian American or Pacific Islander.[5] The racial and ethnic distributions of informal caregivers thus reflected the U.S. population overall in 2020—and the family members and friends that these caregivers served. Most informal caregivers (89%) took care of a relative, 50% cared for a parent or parent-in-law, and 12% assisted their spouse or partner.[6]

Assisting family members or friends offers rewards, including the intangible but deeply meaningful satisfaction of serving a loved one: 51% of informal caregivers find personal meaning or purpose in this role.[7] Nonetheless, informal caregiving can exact a heavy toll. Many informal caregivers feel they have no option but to serve. When other informal help is unavailable, 66% of those caring for a spouse or partner feel they have no choice about becoming caregivers, as do 61% supporting a parent or parent-in-law, 45% assisting other relatives, and 21% serving friends or neighbors.[8] Among informal caregivers providing high-intensity care, 32% report worse personal health because of their caregiving activities,[9] 29% experience high physical strain,[10] 49% admit high emotional stress,[11] and 29% describe financial problems because of caregiving.[12]

In contrast to the unpaid informal caregiver workforce, paid PAS workers provide approximately 16% of the total hours of in-home ADL support to Americans nationwide.[13] For consumers with limited social networks and more complex needs, paid PAS is a lifeline.[14] The percentage of paid PAS—so-called formal caregivers—will likely rise in coming decades. According to a 2016 report, "While the need for caregiving is rapidly increasing, the pool of potential family caregivers is shrinking. Families have fewer children, older adults are more likely to have never married or to be divorced, and adult children often live far from their parents or may be caring for more than one older adult or their own children."[15] Even if family members are around, they often have competing demands on their time and cannot fully support their relative needing assistance.

Paid PAs, like Mona and the staff providing 24/7 support for Bob, Dan, and their mother, increasingly assist Americans with severe disability living in their homes and communities. In 2018 approximately 1.55 million workers provided paid in-home PAS, an increase of 242% over the approximately 452,000 paid PAS workers in 2008 (Figure 1.1).[16] Formal PAS providers look different from informal caregivers. The vast majority (almost 90%) are women, 60% are people of color, and roughly one in four is an immigrant.[17] Paid PAs also supplement the efforts of informal caregivers: about 31% of informal caregivers report assistance from paid workers—aides, housekeepers, or others—in caring for their family members or friends in the prior year.[18]

Despite rising demand for their services, paid PAs earn low wages. In 2018 in-home PAS workers earned an average of $11.40 per hour, an increase

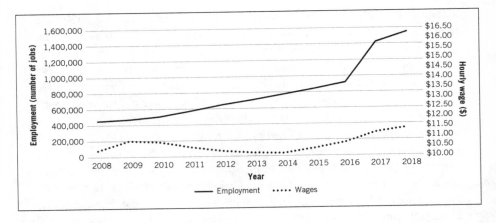

Figure 1.1 Personal Care Aides: Number of Jobs and Average Hourly Wages, 2008–2018

Source: U.S. Bureau of Labor Statistics, Division of Occupational Employment Statistics (OES). 2019. May 2008 to May 2018 national industry-specific occupational employment and wage estimates. https://www.bls.gov/oes/current/oessrci.htm; analysis by PHI (July 2, 2019). In 2018, the U.S. living wage was $16.14/hour (Massachusetts Institute of Technology Living Wage Calculator: https://livingwage.mit.edu/articles/37-new-data-up-calculation-of-the-living-wage).

of only $1.07 over the hourly wage in 2008 of $10.33.[19] Approximately one-fifth of in-home PAS workers have incomes below the federal poverty level.[20] Nonetheless, home-based supportive care is one of the fastest growing jobs in the United States today. According to the U.S. Department of Labor Bureau of Labor Statistics, demand for home-based PAS jobs will rise an estimated 36% from 2018 to 2028, much higher growth than for most other occupations in the United States.[21] The Bureau of Labor Statistics lists personal care aides as the occupation with the highest projected numeric growth in its workforce, expected to have added 881,000 jobs from 2018 to 2028.[22] In many regions across the United States, however, too few people are available or willing to take paid PAS jobs; thus the demand for paid PAs far outstrips the supply. Without this essential in-home support, individuals with disability who lack informal caregivers face the risk of institutionalization.

The Impending Crisis in Home-Based Paid Personal Assistance Services

For more than 40 years, health care professionals, policy makers, and advocates for consumers and formal caregivers have warned of this impending PAS crisis, with widening gaps between the available workforce and rising numbers of Americans needing in-home ADL supports. Confluent demographic and workforce trends have generated an almost perfect storm, and projections of insufficient numbers of qualified workers to meet home-based PAS needs are increasingly troubling. On the consumer side, demographic forces include the following:

- The U.S. population is aging. Not only are individuals from the World War II generation reaching very advanced ages, but also the 78-million-person baby-boom generation, individuals born between 1946 and 1964, began turning 65 in 2011. Baby boomers have fewer family members available to become informal caregivers than prior generations did.
- The World War II generation had substantially better health and functional status than their parents' and grandparents' generations, thus reducing their need for home-based PAS until very late in life. But the baby boomers are reversing those favorable trends. Despite their lower smoking rates, baby boomers have higher rates of obesity, less frequent exercise, and other risk factors that increase disability rates.[23]
- With medical advances, people born with significant disability now survive into middle and older ages; similarly, people who develop a disability in early adulthood are also living longer. Of 8.4 million people currently receiving long-term services and supports, 37% are younger than 65.[24] This population of younger adults requiring home-based PAS is growing.
- Racial and demographic population trends might also increase demand for home-based PAS. The rapidly growing Hispanic and Asian populations typically use more home and community-based supports and less institutional long-term care than do White or Black populations.[25]

For paid PAS providers, factors contributing to widening gaps between consumers' in-home support needs and the available workforce include the following:

- Women comprise nearly 90% of the paid PAS workforce; by 2024, however, the number of women 24–64 years old in the United States will grow by only 1.9 million.[26] This pool of potential PAS job candidates will be too small to meet the growth in demand.
- Paid PAs typically earn low incomes. Between 2009 and 2019, median hourly wages, adjusted for inflation, for home care workers rose from $11.21 to $12.12, only by 8%. In 2018, nearly half (47%)

of home care workers earned less than 200% of the federal poverty level, with median annual incomes of $17,200.[27]

- From 40% to 60% of paid PAs quit after less than one year on the job, largely because of low wages compounded by meager benefits, heavy workloads, poor supervision, little upward career mobility, and high transportation costs.[28]
- Some regions have worse PAS workforce shortages than others, primarily because of entrenched structural factors. With their aging populations, sparsely inhabited rural areas are especially vulnerable to PAS workforce shortfalls. Greater travel distances between PAS clients and lack of public transportation also cause problems in rural regions. Nearly a quarter of PAS workers are foreign-born, but 96% of them live in cities.[29]

Thus, powerful demographic and societal trends suggest that paid PAS consumers and providers may look very different in the future. The changes have critical implications for long-term care delivery systems, public and private health and long-term care insurance, housing and other community policies, and society more broadly. As a 2008 Institute of Medicine report summarized,

The future elderly population will be different from today's older adults in a number of ways. The demographic characteristics of older Americans will differ from [those of] previous generations in terms of their race, family structure, socioeconomic status, education, geographic distribution, and openness regarding their sexual orientation. All of these factors can affect health status and utilization of services. Trends in illness and disability will influence the need for services among the future older adult population. . . . Finally, older adults in the future may simply have different preferences for care than their predecessors.[30]

Nonetheless, one preference seems immutable: consumers' strong desire to remain home. "It amazes me that nobody's gotten this notion yet: the 'boomers' are coming," said a woman in her mid-fifties with multiple sclerosis (MS). "Despite MS and other diseases, they're going to live longer. We're not going to warehouse them in nursing homes. These 'boomers' simply won't do that. They're not going to go quietly into the night."[31] A widow living alone, she was determined to remain at home despite severe mobility problems necessitating personal assistance with toileting, bathing, and dressing. She constantly struggled to find PAs but had recently identified a young woman, an immigrant from eastern Europe, who seemed reliable and a good match. Communicating in English was challenging, but each seemed determined to make the situation work. Having an enduring, positive, supportive relationship would benefit both the woman with MS and her new PA—the reciprocity or win-win for both consumers and PAs that underlies long-term PAS success.

The growing mismatch between consumers' needs for paid PAS and the available PAS workforce has numerous implications, including those for population health, societal expectations about aging in America, health care and other social costs to governments and individuals, community-based social service agencies, and policy and regulatory systems that must respond to this looming threat. At the heart of this crisis are individual people with significant disability and their paid PAs, interacting generally daily—sometimes around the clock—in intimate ways in the privacy of consumers' homes. The interpersonal dynamics of PAS consumers and PAs are complex, complicated by wage and payment policies, job training and oversight, differences by gender, race, ethnicity, language, immigration status, culture, structural racism, and myriad other human factors. How consumers and PAs respond to the dynamics determines the durability of these consumer-PA dyads, with critical implications for the satisfaction and well-being of both.

The Goals of This Book

Finding sustainable solutions to the looming paid PAS crisis requires understanding the intertwined and complex policy, personal, and interpersonal factors affecting in-home ADL supports. This book therefore explores both the policy context of paid PAS and the experiences and attitudes of PAS consumers and PAs, real people. Policies and structural factors directly affect people's lives and well-being along multiple dimensions and largely determine whether people requiring ADL supports can continue living in their homes as they wish or need to enter a nursing home.

To examine how policies affect actual people, this book draws on narratives from paid PAS consumers and PAs, describing their lived experiences and perspectives about paid in-home PAS. Many publications have addressed PAS for people at very advanced ages. As the Institute of Medicine notes, however, "older adults in the future may simply have different preferences for care than their predecessors."[32]

Therefore, this book focuses on people in middle age or at the leading edge of the baby boom—people in their early seventies. In 2018 I interviewed 21 in-home, paid PAS consumers in these age ranges and 20 PAS workers; for Chapters 13 and 14, I later interviewed a 20-year old college student with a severe disability to introduce the perspective of someone who will need paid

PAS well into the future. I audio-recorded all interviews, which were then transcribed verbatim. This book uses interviewees' own words, stories, and viewpoints to explore paid in-home PAS. I did not edit quotes for grammar or syntax in order to retain authenticity. With several exceptions, I refer to interviewees using pseudonyms and change small details to protect their confidentiality. With their permission, I use real names for Michael and Nelita, to whom I dedicate this book, as well as three new PAs introduced in the epilogue.

The novel coronavirus pandemic hit the United States in late February 2020, when I had written nearly half of this book, and it continues ablaze, killing thousands of Americans daily, as I review the final manuscript. The pandemic carries enormous and life-altering consequences for both consumers and PAs. Early in the pandemic, although home-based PAs were considered essential workers, their pay remained unchanged, they still often lacked health insurance benefits, and they generally worked without adequate personal protective equipment (PPE).[33] Nonetheless, in the upswelling, heartfelt emotions of those initial months, these PAs were called heroic—and in many cases they were. But understandably many left the PAS workforce. Just as the pandemic laid bare long-standing inequities within the U.S. health care system, it also heightened the impending crisis affecting home-based PAS.

Although all interviews long predated the tragic COVID-19 pandemic, throughout the book, I briefly suggest implications of COVID-19 and any future pandemics for PAS consumers and PAs. As elsewhere in U.S. society, the novel coronavirus pandemic will likely have long-term consequences for paid PAS that remain unforetold. The epilogue does tell one story from the frontlines of early COVID-19, about how three PAs saved the life of their consumer who became deathly ill, Michael.

Notes on Language

In the United States, roles of PAS workers are evolving rapidly, as policy makers aim to shift long-term support services away from nursing homes and other facilities into homes and communities. Looking across institutional and home-based settings, workers who provide personal assistance are often grouped with other so-called direct care workers. According to the 2008 Institute of Medicine report,[34] direct care encompasses three categories of paraprofessionals:

1. **Nurse aides**, also known as certified nursing assistants (CNA), geriatric aides, orderlies, and hospital attendants, work primarily in institutions—hospitals, nursing homes, and residential care facilities. On-site nursing staff supervise nurse aides. Typical activi-

ties include answering patients' call lights; serving meals and helping patients eat; making beds; assisting patients with bathing and dressing; escorting patients to medical appointments; and taking vital signs, administering medications, and performing other supervised medical tasks (e.g., wound care, urinary catheter management).

2. **Home health aides** generally work for home health care agencies or residential care facilities. They assist clients with ADL needs in their homes and can also prepare meals and perform light housekeeping tasks. Supervision typically involves periodic checks with nurses, physical or occupational therapists, social workers, or case managers. Some state regulations allow home health aides to also perform clinical tasks under the supervision of a licensed professional.

3. **Personal assistance services workers** are employed either by an agency or directly by consumers (or the consumer's family). They work in homes and assist with ADLs and IADLs. With some employers, PAS providers may have little or no supervision by a health care professional.

Today boundaries are blurring between home health aides, who perform tasks addressing consumers' health conditions among other duties, and PAS workers, who often cannot provide health-related services because of state regulations. Home- and community-based service (HCBS) initiatives increasingly bring PAS workers into interprofessional care teams, working alongside licensed health care professionals to keep consumers as healthy as possible and prevent hospitalization.

The language used to refer to both PAS consumers and workers varies substantially across and within regions. PAS consumers are sometimes called employers or supervisors when they directly hire and manage their in-home workers. Home care agencies that provide and oversee PAS workers sometime call consumers clients or use clinical terminology—"patients" or "cases"—language eschewed by many disability rights advocates wary of medicalizing their daily lives.

Terminology for PAS workers also varies widely, including PAS worker or PAS provider; home care worker or aide; personal care assistant, attendant, or aide (all with the acronym PCA); paid or formal caregiver; and other local, regional, or regulatory nomenclatures. In parallel, other words and phrases to describe PAS include attendant care or services, home care services, support services, or a mélange of these terms, such as home support services or PCA work. With evolving roles, some PAS workers now refer to themselves as home health aides (HHAs), although as noted above, this phrase historically applied only to workers with nurses or other health care professionals as supervisors.

Here, when referring to individual workers, I generally use personal assistant (PA), although in discussions of specific policies, I use terminology (e.g., PCA) employed by the relevant policy makers. The acronym PA is preferred by Natalie, a consumer in her early fifties with spinal muscular atrophy, who had eight PAs providing in-home ADL supports each week. Over her lifetime, Natalie estimates she has had over 100 PAs:

> I'm using about 14 hours a day. . . . A lot of people [refer to these workers as a] PCA, personal care assistant. I'm not fond of the idea that they take care of me. I like the idea that they assist me in caring for myself. So, I tend to use personal assistant, or the older term, attendant. . . . My friend's in the UK. He uses the word "carer." . . . I have my personal preference, but I actually couldn't care less in the bigger picture, as long as people know what we're talking about.

Embedded within language are implicit assumptions about the value and merit of the work and the person receiving this support. Some observers avoid calling PAs workers, viewing the term as demeaning and disrespectful of the skills and effort required to perform PAS. Here, at the outset of this book, it is critical to emphasize that consumers with significant disability who lack informal caregivers could not survive in their homes and communities without the support of paid PAs. Often PAS work requires astute observation, quick thinking, unerring judgment, manual and physical dexterity, and understanding of health conditions and their complications. At all times, PAS demands skill in negotiating complex interpersonal relationships between people—consumers and their PAs.

In-home PAS has a valid claim to being lifesaving. This work is also essential for preserving the dignity, self-respect, and quality of life of consumers with disability who require ADL supports. Appreciating these complexities, this book celebrates both PAS work and PAs for supporting people with disability to live their lives as they wish in their homes and communities.

I

POLICY AND
SOCIAL CONTEXTS

PART I examines broad policies and their social contexts that affect paid
PAS. Chapter 2 discusses where people with disability live and the
laws and regulations that protect their civil rights. Consumers receive
most PAS in their homes; consumers' homes are therefore PAs' workplaces. In
1999 the U.S. Supreme Court ruled that people with disability have the civil
right to live in homes and communities rather than institutions, if they wish.
Chapter 3 reviews policies relating to paying for PAS, focusing on Medicaid, the largest public payor for home-based PAS. Chapter 4 addresses labor
policies that affect home-based PAs. Although policies—and laws, regulations,
and judicial rulings that implement or enforce these policies—seem like distant and dry topics, they directly affect the lives of real people. Policy is personal.
To make this point, Part I tells stories of two people whose lives were disadvantaged by policy and who advocated for change in high-profile ways. Charlie Carr was institutionalized in his teens after a spinal cord injury; he later
became a prominent champion of consumer self-directed PAS and served as
commissioner of the Massachusetts Rehabilitation Commission from 2007
to 2015. He still conducts grassroots disability advocacy in Massachusetts.
Carr's story, which he recounted for a disability oral history project housed
at Bancroft Library, University of California, Berkeley, wends throughout
Chapter 2 and continues in Chapter 3. Chapter 4 tells the story of Evelyn
Coke, a home care agency PA who went to court to protest long work hours
without overtime pay. Coke's lawsuit reached the U.S. Supreme Court in
2007. She died in 2009 at 74 years of age. Her lawsuit catalyzed fundamental
changes in labor policies to protect home-based paid PAs.

2

Where People with Disability Live and Recognizing Their Civil Rights

C harlie Carr was born in 1953 in Revere, Massachusetts, a working-class town on the Atlantic coast a few miles from Boston, but he grew up mainly in Everett, the next town over.[1] His father, a U.S. Navy corpsman, was often absent, serving long deployments on submarines. During Carr's childhood, his family moved several times but always lived near water. "I had a good childhood," recalled Carr, the oldest of four boys. "But now looking back at it . . . we lived a spartan existence. But I never thought of myself as poor." At the age of eight, Carr lost hearing in his left ear from mumps, and his school required him to attend weekly lip-reading classes in case he ever lost hearing in his other ear. Nonetheless, Carr never thought of himself as disabled.

One hot afternoon in June 1968, Carr took the bus from Everett to Revere to join other boys swimming at the beach. He arrived about 3:00 and saw his friends in the distance diving off the retainer wall into the waves. Carr didn't realize it was low tide—his friends were carefully timing their dives as waves peaked, when water is deepest. Running up to his friends and pulling off his shirt and shoes, Carr dove off the wall into shallow water.

> I was not unconscious. I remember my teeth crumbling in my mouth and . . . thinking to myself, "Oh my God, I broke my teeth." So, as I went to swim to the top to get out—and there was no pain—I wasn't going anywhere. . . . I was swimming in my mind, but I noticed my arm floating out next to me. . . . I'm face down in the water and . . . thinking to myself, "Well, I can't hold my breath anymore, so my next

breath is going to be a mouth full of water, and I guess I'm going to drown." It was a very peaceful feeling.

As Carr was about to inhale water, someone grabbed his hair, wrenching his head back, and he vividly remembers next breathing air. One boy fetched a policeman, and they transported Carr on the floor of a police paddy wagon over Boston streets, notoriously in disrepair—"All the way, it was, bump, bump, bump, bump"—to Massachusetts General Hospital. There he lost consciousness, and a priest gave him last rights. Carr lived but with a high cervical spinal cord injury. Multiple severe complications followed, keeping him hospitalized for many months. "I was kind of like a miracle quad to survive," Carr said. "The physical therapy and the occupational therapy folks wrote me off. They said, 'There's nothing we can do for you or with you. You're just basically going to live your life in an institution, and there's no need for us to work with you, because there's nothing you can do.'"

Carr's father refused to accept this bleak prognosis. In early 1969 he finagled his son's admission to the Chelsea Naval Hospital nearby. Carr shared a 24-bed open ward with severely injured soldiers who had returned from Vietnam, and staff treated Carr just like the wounded soldiers. He received intensive rehabilitation to improve his arm and hand function. Carr attributes regaining enough hand mobility to operate his power wheelchair joystick to "their aggressive therapy. The military people are like, 'We're going to work you like a dog.' And it paid off. But all the while, I was missing school. I was still fifteen years old."

Behind the scenes, Carr's mother fought with his former school to let him return. At the time, Chapter 766 of Massachusetts law—which guarantees education suited to their needs to youth with disability from 3 to 22 years old—did not yet exist. His school refused to readmit Carr. To continue his education, in April 1969 Carr moved from the Chelsea Naval Hospital to the Massachusetts Hospital School, an institution in Canton about 25 miles south of his Everett home.

Having a Home

To receive home-based PAS, people needing ADL supports must have a home. For everyone, housing represents more than simply a place to live. Where and how people live reflect social status, kinship and other sociocultural relationships, economic class, political forces, and legal rights. For millennia, dominant groups within human societies have shunned stigmatized subgroups, spurring their migration, segregating them in ghettos, or constricting them within institutions. Governmental and private entities have deployed specific strategies to marginalize certain populations. For instance, starting in the late 1960s and early 1970s, banking institutions in some U.S. cities began a practice called redlining, overtly discriminating against poor and racial minority neighborhoods in making loans and providing other financial services, thus accelerating their downward economic spiral and perpetuating segregation.[2] For Charlie Carr, institutionalization achieved critical practical goals, supporting both his ADL and his educational needs. Institutionalizing Carr and other youth with disability also kept them hidden, apart from their peers, and out of society's view.

Many people draw distinctions between housing—a roof over one's head—and a home. Common sayings convey the human, emotional, and legal implications of this distinction, such as "home sweet home," "there's no place like home," "home is where the heart is," "home is a shelter from all storms," and "a man's home is his castle." This latter proverb traces back to 17th-century English law (hence the male construction) and metaphorically asserts the rights of inhabitants to restrict who enters their home. The castle imagery reflected beliefs that men could do whatever they wished—with notable exceptions, which have evolved over time—within their home. In the Bill of Rights, the Fourth Amendment of the U.S. Constitution enshrines this concept for Americans, ensuring the "right of the people to be secure in their persons, houses, papers, and effects, against unreasonable searches and seizures." The Fourth Amendment gives Americans the right to privacy within their own homes, unless specific exceptions apply (e.g., legal warrants for targeted searches).

However, as detailed in Part IV, paid PAS upends consumers' expectations about control over their homes and personal privacy even within intimate spaces, like bedrooms and bathrooms. For consumers, jettisoning presumptions of privacy and exclusive dominion over their personal premises is necessary to obtain the ADL supports they need to live—they have no choice. But living without privacy and absolute control over their household possessions, large and small, can exact an emotional toll on paid PAS consumers.

In contrast, for PAS workers, consumers' homes are their workplaces. As the U.S. Occupational Safety and Health Administration notes, PAS workers "have little control over their work environment which may contain a number of safety and health hazards . . . [including] bloodborne pathogens and biological hazards, . . . hostile animals and unhygienic and dangerous conditions."[3] For many reasons, PAs may be unable to improve their workplace safety, such as by making changes to their client's home. In addition, with some exceptions, like the multiple PAs supporting brothers Bob and Dan (see Chapter 1), many PAs are the only employee in the consumer's home at a given time. Without colleagues to share their experiences, PAs' workplaces—consumers' homes—can feel lonely, isolated, and, at worst, unsafe.

As another complexity, many paid PAs are racial or ethnic minorities or immigrants (see Chapter 6). Racial and ethnic segregation of housing, reinforced by redlining and systemic racism, frequently results in consumers and PAs living on different sides of town. PAs who are minorities can feel unwelcome in their consumers' neighborhoods and fear being stopped by the police while driving through these communities. PAS workers might not have reliable and affordable public transportation to and from their workplace, especially outside typical business hours (e.g., early mornings, later evenings). PAS consumers in wealthier, White neighborhoods might therefore face difficulties recruiting willing PAs who can reliably arrive on time.

Since the nation's founding, shifting laws and policies have affected where and how people with disability live and thus, by extension, the workplaces for PAS workers. The last half-century has brought transformational changes for people with disability, moving away from institutionalization toward community-based living. The desire of people with disability to participate actively in their communities propelled the disability civil rights movement, culminating in the 1990 Americans with Disabilities Act (ADA). The history of how federal disability rights legislation eventually passed is complex—this chapter only scratches the surface. Fundamental changes and civil rights protections came only after centuries of Americans with disability living isolated lives behind closed doors of private homes or institutions.

Where and How People with Disability Lived in Early America

The daily lives of people with disability in early America—and if or how people received ADL supports—varied substantially with their origins: indigenous people, European settlers, or enslaved people transported from Africa.

Indigenous People with Disability

Before European settlers arrived, tens of millions of indigenous people living in North America led physically arduous lives, within distinct and separate communities and speaking nearly 2,500 different languages.[4] Most North American indigenous communities had neither words nor concepts equivalent to today's notion of disability. The history of indigenous people with disability in North American is therefore obscured, not because these individuals were hidden away but because categorizing people as disabled was irrelevant to their worldview. The notion of "able-bodied" also had no equivalent.

Despite heterogeneity across indigenous tribes, native peoples shared some common concepts: "Prior to European conquest, the worldviews of indigenous people understood body, mind, and spirit to be one. These beliefs allowed for fluid definitions of bodily and mental norms, and fundamentally assumed that all had gifts to share with the community."[5] Indigenous people perceived these gifts and thus contributions to communities as inherent within each individual, albeit evolving across the lifespan. In concert with another belief that all bodies alter with time, acquired disability attracted little notice. With aging, the cumulative rigors of daily existence exact a physical toll but offer the valued gift of wisdom.

Analyses of centuries-old skeletal remains suggest that some indigenous populations were healthier than others, likely because of local environmental, nutritional, or lifestyle factors.[6] However, European settlers introduced lethal and debilitating diseases, such as smallpox, bubonic plague, malaria, measles, cholera, typhus fever, influenza, diphtheria, and scarlet fever. Epidemics decimated indigenous populations, virtually eradicating entire communities and leaving others with disease and disability. Although Europeans founded institutions to house individuals with disability, indigenous families hesitated to relinquish their relatives with disability to these facilities. In isolating certain people from their communities, these institutions violated the fundamental belief that all lives have inherent value. However, as rampant disease, malnutrition, and other assaults destroyed indigenous populations, these scourges also upended social conventions that had long integrated indigenous individuals with disability within their communities.

European Settlers with Disability

In the 17th century, early European settlers recognized the physical hardships of transatlantic travel and demands of inhabiting rugged lands with unfamiliar dangers. Many crossed the ocean to pursue wealth by intense physical exertion, like farming or exploring for gold or goods to trade. Organizers of expeditions to North America generally rejected passengers without bodily or mental stamina to endure harsh conditions.[7] In 1701, for example, Massachusetts passed a law requiring ship captains sailing to North America to return, at their own expense, passengers who were "lame, impotent, or infirm persons, incapable of maintaining themselves" when they boarded the vessel.[8] Colonies could deport people with physical or mental impairments.[9]

European settlers expected that families would care for their relatives who needed support. The 1641 Massachusetts Body of Liberties, part of the Pilgrim's legal code, guaranteed that individuals could not be forced into public service if their functioning was limited by "want of years, greatness of age, defect in mind, failing of senses, or impotency of Limbs."[10] However, communities shunned individuals seeking public assistance, enacting laws—with titles like "For the Preventing of Poor Persons"—requiring newcomers to prove they would not become economic burdens.[11] Most colonies followed English poor laws, which explicitly withheld public relief from people with parents, grandparents, adult children, or grandchildren who could shelter them.[12]

Communities did need to deal with people without families or shelter who could not care for themselves. Jurisdictions, towns, and counties adopted distinctly local strategies to address such situations. Boston constructed the first American almshouse in 1662, and many others followed throughout Massachusetts.[13] In contrast, Thomas Jefferson reported in 1781 that Virginians without "strength to labour" were "boarded in the houses of good farmers," supported by tithes from local parishes.[14]

In the early 1800s, diverse institutions arose to house various populations with specific needs. In Charleston, South Carolina, for example, impoverished people with debilitating illness or disability but without relatives were placed in almshouses, following assurances they were not of degenerate or intemperate character.[15] Nursing homes originated in this period to shelter genteel older women who had no other home and could not withstand the misery and hoi polloi of almshouses.[16] The private facilities generally demanded substantial entrance fees and certificates documenting good character. One early facility, Boston's Home for Aged Women (1850), strove to protect the "needy poor" from foreigners who "have taken possession of the public charities."[17]

In 1821 Josiah Quincy chaired a committee that decried the surging Massachusetts pauper population. The committee recognized two distinct subgroups of paupers: "1. The impotent poor; in which denomination are included all, who are wholly incapable of work, through old age, infancy, sickness, or corporeal debility. 2. The able poor; . . . [including] all, who are capable of work, of some nature."[18] Quincy's committee acknowledged that Christian charity compelled assistance to the impotent poor. To provide these supports, in 1824 Massachusetts had 83 almshouses, rising to 180 in 1839, and 219 almshouses in 1860.[19]

Enslaved People from Africa with Disability

Europeans brought the first Africans to colonial shores in 1619. Although transporting slaves to North America was abolished in 1808, by 1800, approximately 893,000 enslaved Africans already lived there, with their numbers rising to almost 3,954,000 in 1860, one year before the Civil War (1861–1865).[20] To justify slavery, Europeans argued that Africans had low intelligence, abnormal bodies, and inferior motor skills and were lazy, shiftless, and defective—in essence, that they were disabled.[21] Europeans believed that

Africans could not care for themselves and therefore slavery was beneficent, with owners overseeing their lives. In 1848 Samuel Cartwright, a physician and prominent proponent of scientific racism, asserted that "[B]lacks' physical and mental defects made it impossible for them to survive without white supervision and care."[22]

In Africa, after abducting people and processing them for shipment overseas, slave traders systematically winnowed out those they viewed as least fit, often outright killing old men and women, many children, and individuals with disability.[23] Africans who became sick or disabled during the Middle Passage, the horrific ocean voyage from Africa to North America, were, in the infamous case of the French slave ship *Le Rodeur*, thrown overboard, weighted with ballast.[24] Once in North America, hard labor, brutal physical punishments, and mental anguish frequently debilitated slaves who had arrived in good health. Traders viewed slaves with seeming physical, mental, or intellectual disability as damaged goods, of low economic value. These so-called refuse slaves had few options. Almshouses serving European descendants were closed to slaves.

While White Americans expected families to care for their relatives with disability, enslaved Africans were often brutally separated from spouses, children, and other family members. Slave communities tried to care for their members who became too debilitated to labor, but owners employed harsh measures to rid themselves of slaves they considered worthless. Despite laws against it, owners sometimes freed slaves who were very old or disabled and then released them to fend for themselves in southern cities. Other owners dispatched old or blind slaves to isolated cabins in the woods, to subsist on their own.

Frederick Douglass recalled his cousin Henny, who had been disabled by severe burns in childhood and could not work as her master insisted despite incessant beatings, being "set adrift to take care of herself . . . a helpless child, to starve and die."[25] Douglass decried the cruelty of his master Thomas Auld. Despite claiming to have had a religious conversion, Auld held "with tight grasp the well-framed and able-bodied slaves . . . who in freedom could have taken care of themselves," Douglass wrote, while turning "loose the only cripple among them, virtually to starve and die."[26]

Institutionalization of People with Disability

The early 19th century brought inventions of revolutionary medical technologies, starting with the stethoscope and followed shortly by the microscope, spirometer, ophthalmoscope, radiograph, and other diagnostic instruments. With these new diagnostic tools, perceptions of disability shifted to biological

---

Box 2.1 Medical Model of Disability

"The *medical model* views disability as a problem of the person, directly caused by disease, trauma or other health condition, which requires medical care. . . . Management of the disability is aimed at cure or the individual's adjustment and behaviour change. Medical care is viewed as the main issue."[1]

[1] World Health Organization. *International Classification of Functioning, Disability and Health.* World Health Organization; 2001: 20.

---

causes and away from prior beliefs about supernatural visitations or punishment by a wrathful divinity. These new technologies gave authority to medical professionals—rather than clergy—to direct treatment and to determine who qualified as legitimately disabled and thus deserving of public benefits.[27] This new understanding produced the medical model of disability (Box 2.1).

In early-19th-century America, local authorities favored institutional solutions for various troublesome populations, constructing not only almshouses but also orphanages, prisons, and reformatories.[28] This strategy extended to disability. With growing recognition of the biological basis of disability, medical and other professionals asserted control over wide-ranging aspects of the daily lives of people with disability. Throughout much of the 19th and into mid-20th century America, many people who were blind or deaf or who had intellectual or developmental disability, mental illness, or significant physical disability were placed in institutions or residential schools.

Proponents believed that institutions and residential schools provided humanitarian custody grounded in science and progressive thinking[29] and "optimistic assumptions about the possibilities of reform, rehabilitation, and education."[30] Funded by philanthropies, voluntary groups, governments, or multiple sources, by 1850 new institutions targeted people by disability type, offering specific educational and rehabilitation programs. "This use of secular institutions as deliberate agencies of social policy, their specialization, and their emphasis on the formation or reformation of character represented a new and momentous development."[31]

New England led this movement, founding new residential schools with lofty and redemptive goals. In 1817 Thomas Hopkins Gallaudet and Laurent Clerc opened the American Asylum for the Deaf in Hartford, Connecticut. Citing himself as an example, Clerc claimed their asylum would transform "those unfortunate beings who . . . would be condemned all their life, to the most sad vegetation" from "the class of brutes to the class of men."[32] The asylum and other schools for deaf people generally did increase residents' educational levels, literacy, and economic opportunities. Samuel Gridley Howe, a physician and abolitionist, aimed to remedy the "ignorance, the depravity, the sufferings of one man, or of one class of men" to relieve broader societal ills.[33] Howe concentrated on educating people who were blind, deaf-blind, or "idiots," in 1829 founding the Perkins School for the Blind in Watertown, Massachusetts (which Anne Sullivan and Helen Keller later attended and which remains active today).

Howe's efforts targeting "idiots"—terminology then used for intellectual disability—had less positive outcomes. Until then, families with adequate resources had housed their relatives with intellectual disability. Howe argued that methods introduced in France in the 1840s could better educate these individuals.[34] In 1847 Howe decried the numbers of Massachusetts residents with intellectual disability who "are condemned to their hopeless idiocy" and "left to their brutishness."[35] He asserted that state-run residential schools could properly educate these people, and their "spark of intellect . . . might be nurtured into a flame."[36] Howe's moral arguments convinced the Massachusetts legislature in 1849 to establish the Massachusetts School for Idiotic Children and Youth. Other states followed, founding similar institutions nationwide.

Despite soaring rhetoric and worthy intentions, these various institutions left a complex legacy. Young people from poor families often could not afford schools for deaf or blind children; although some schools accepted racial minority students, others, especially in the South, were segregated. Howe's much-touted educational methods for people with intellectual disability did not achieve the promised benefits. Residential schools for people with intellectual disability shifted from aspirational educational goals to serving primarily as custodians of their inhabitants.

Dorothea Lynde Dix exposed the horrors of some institutions housing residents with mental illness or intellectual disability.[37] Born in 1802, Dix founded schools for girls in Boston but stopped teaching because of tuberculosis. Dix later visited England and encountered social reformers who exposed her to inhumane living conditions afflicting some people with intellectual disability. Upon returning to Boston in 1841, Dix began investigating the circumstances of women with intellectual disability. In East Cambridge, just outside Boston, Dix discovered women naked in dark jail cells, chained to walls, and abused by prison guards or other inmates.[38] Although the Massachusetts State House generally excluded women, the legislature permitted Dix to address them about her extensive study documenting horrific living conditions of people with intellectual disability. In 1854 she convinced the U.S. Congress to enact legislation allocating federal lands to build institutions for indigent people who were deaf, blind, or mute or who had intellectual disability, but President Franklin Pierce vetoed the bill. In 1881, with failing health, Dix moved into the New Jersey Hospital in Trenton, which she had helped found; she died there in 1887. "Ironically, Dix's achievement in fostering the creation of institutions led to many of the same abuses she campaigned to end: the incarceration of people with disabilities in (now massive) facilities where they were often neglected and abused."[39]

From roughly 1880 through 1925 in the United States, two movements—eugenics and Social Darwinism—further entrenched institutionalization.[40] Eugenics posits that people inherit intellectual and other disability following Mendelian genetic patterns, passing these traits to subsequent generations and ultimately degrading the human species. To Charles Benedict Davenport, a leading U.S. proponent, eugenics represented "the science of the improvement of the human race by better breeding."[41] Social Darwinism argues that society needs protection from the deviance of intellectual and other disabilities (e.g., deafness), facilitated by institutionalizing and isolating these populations.

These twin forces inflamed public fears about women with disability having children. Many states banned women with disability from marrying, some mandated compulsory contraception, and 30 states legalized forced sterilization of women with disability.[42] Courts upheld involuntary sterilization regulations, which particularly targeted people with intellectual disability or serious mental illness. In *Buck v. Bell* in 1927, the U.S. Supreme Court ruled that the Commonwealth of Virginia could forcibly sterilize Carrie Buck, described as "feebleminded." Buck and her mother, also deemed feebleminded, lived in the same institution. In writing the court's decision, Justice Oliver Wendell Holmes Jr. concluded, "Three generations of imbeciles are enough."[43] The ruling asserted that state statutes mandating sterilization of institutionalized people did not violate the equal protection clause of the Constitution's Fourteenth Amendment. As of this writing, the Supreme Court has not yet overturned the *Buck v. Bell* decision.

Racing ahead many decades, in the late 1960s, the media and advocacy groups exposed wretched conditions in institutions housing people with disability, especially intellectual disability or mental illness. These often-graphic stories stoked public outrage. Lawsuits contested keeping people with disability in largely state-run institutions, resulting in the closure or downsizing of facilities nationwide. From 1955 through 1980, the resident populations from mental institutions fell from 559,000 to 154,000.[44] Between 1971 and 1990, the number of Americans institutionalized with developmental disability dropped from 195,000 to 88,000.[45] As this exodus proceeded, the pressing question became whether communities were prepared to absorb the massive influx of deinstitutionalized people with disability.

Charlie Carr and the Massachusetts Hospital School

Despite his mother's pleas, Carr's school refused to readmit him after the spinal cord injury (SCI), which left him quadriplegic. At the age of 15, he therefore entered the residential Massachusetts Hospital School—"in the boondocks," Carr said—about 25 miles from his parents' home. In 1904 the Massachusetts legislature had authorized the hospital school, which opened in 1907 with just over 100 residents.[46] In 1920 the school acquired another 100 acres, expanding its facilities. "It was built to be a self-sustaining farm," Carr explained.

> All of the meat and produce would be grown and raised by the residents. . . . The population at that time were kids with polio or other deformities. They were what I would term today as minimally disabled, but social outcasts. . . . Their families couldn't or wouldn't care for them. So, at five or six years old, they would be left there, and they wouldn't leave until graduation. Some kids . . . would stay on until 19 or 20 because they didn't . . . have any supports in place. But once you reached 18, 19, 20, you had to leave. That was the deal.

The Massachusetts Hospital School had two residential options: a hospital for residents who had significant ADL needs or health problems; and scattered cottages for children needing minimal physical assistance but requiring some structure where they lived. Carr landed on Bradford One, the hospital's SCI floor. "There were no power wheelchairs then, so I had to be pushed around," he recalled. "I was the most significantly disabled quad there." He spent many hours in bed and "attended" school by watching video broadcasts from cameras set up in classrooms. Bedbound students had to answer teachers' questions via a microphone, or else they received demerits. Carr began thinking, "this is my life. . . . I went into a whole different level of depression."

On Bradford One, the nursing staff tightly controlled all activities, giving residents little choice:

> You went to bed when they told you it was time to go to bed, you got up when they told you it was time to get up, you ate when the meals were put on the table or you didn't eat. If you were lucky enough to get a bath or a shower, you got it when they had time to get to you. . . . You could complain, but you were marked as . . . a problem patient. . . . We were given no privacy, no rights, no nothing. So, I started to

evolve in those early days as a radical leader. Somebody who would suffer the retribution of speaking up. . . . I became the spokesperson for the patients.

Carr channeled his hate for the Massachusetts Hospital School into his studies. In 1971 he was valedictorian of his small graduating class and had to give a speech. By tapping with a spoon clenched in his teeth, Carr laboriously typed out no-holds-barred comments. The school's principal demanded to see the speech and tore his paper to shreds, forbidding him from giving his talk. But Carr had made a carbon copy. At the graduation ceremony, after "Born Free," the class song, Carr began reading his speech:

> I watched the look on [the principal's] face as I read. . . . "This is a prison. We're forced to stay here. There's not much difference between prison inmates and us. We're apart from our families and our friends. We're getting a lousy education." She almost passed out. Surprisingly, the auditorium at the end of my speech erupted in cheers, and clapping, and "Yeah!" . . . I remember the curtain went down, and I had Bob, the [wheelchair] pusher, push me out the back door. My family was outside, and I just made a run for it. I never looked back, and I never went back until many years later.

Carr spent the next month at home with his family: "That was probably one of the most disastrous months you can imagine. I spent the whole time in bed." Afterward, Carr and two of his hospital school classmates moved into Middlesex County Hospital, hoping to find some way to attend college.

Living Independently in Communities

As public concerns about institutions escalated in the mid-20th century, harbingers of changing attitudes about people with disability began building. During World War II, while able-bodied men fought abroad, U.S. employers hired previously unemployed people with disability, who labored on the home front alongside women.[47] Employers laid off women and workers with disability when veterans returned home, but World War II veterans with disability received accommodations to attend college and work.[48] The accommodations sometimes carried over to nonveterans with disability. Over the ensuing 20 to 30 years, other forces catalyzed dramatic social changes, including the independent living movement, increasing interest in self-help rather than professional directives, large-scale deinstitutionalization of people with various disabilities, and nationwide campaigns for civil rights and equal

> ## Box 2.2 Social Model of Disability
>
> "The *social model* . . . sees the issue mainly as a socially created problem, and basically as a matter of the full integration of individuals into society. Disability is not an attribute of an individual, but rather a complex collection of conditions, many of which are created by the social environment. . . . The issue is therefore an attitudinal or ideological one requiring social change, which at the political level becomes a question of human rights."[1]
>
> [1] World Health Organization, *International Classification*, 20.

opportunity for racial and ethnic minorities and women. These attitudes coalesced into a *social model of disability* (Box 2.2).

Disability rights advocates rejected control by health care professionals and assumptions that people's functional impairments cause barriers to participation in daily life activities. They dismissed notions that "if one cannot accomplish a task without the help of another person, then one is dependent."[49] Instead, as the social model held, "Problems lie not within the persons with disabilities but in the environment that fails to accommodate persons with disabilities and in the negative attitudes of people without disabilities."[50] Disability is "imposed on top of our impairments by the way we are unnecessarily isolated and excluded from full participation in society."[51] People with disability wanted control over how they led their lives.

Berkeley, California, was ground zero for the independent living concept, and Edward V. Roberts was its visionary leader.[52] Roberts was born in 1939 in San Mateo, California, and contracted polio at the age of 14. He developed respiratory quadriplegia, requiring a respirator to breathe during the day and an iron lung at night. Roberts recalled hearing a doctor tell his mother that letting him die would be best, that he would become "a vegetable."[53] He joked later that, if he became a vegetable, he wanted to be an artichoke—prickly on the outside but with a large heart—and he exhorted "all the vegetables of the world to unite."[54] At the time, however, his doctor's prognosis was no laughing matter. Roberts admitted identifying with "all the stereotypes: I would never marry, have a job, or be a whole person. I tried to starve myself, the only way to commit suicide."[55]

In high school, Roberts was an honor student, but the principal initially refused to let him graduate because he had skipped gym classes and driver education. He attended San Mateo Community College for two years, again excelling. His academic adviser encouraged him to continue at the University of California–Berkeley. Unable to afford Berkeley's tuition, Roberts sought financial aid from California's Department of Vocational Rehabilitation, which rejected him, asserting he was not college material and was unlikely to ever work.[56] Accompanied by his San Mateo Community College mentors, Roberts told his story to the local news media, convincing the rehabilitation agency to approve his financial aid application. The next hurdle was the university, which balked at allowing Roberts on campus and raised alarms about physical access and his health. "We've tried cripples and it didn't work," said one university official.[57] Roberts persisted, and he matriculated at University of California–Berkeley in the fall of 1962.

When Roberts arrived, the campus did not have independent living services. Roberts's younger brother Ron, a fellow university student, provided his ADL and other supports. No dormitory room could accommodate his iron lung, and he therefore lived at Cowell Hospital on campus. Roberts gained celebrity after a newspaper published his story under the headline "Helpless Cripple Attends U.C. Classes," and other students with severe disability gravitated to the university.[58] The disabled students banded together as the "Rolling Quads," and they advocated improving accessibility at the University of California–Berkley campus. Their efforts culminated in creation of the Physically Disabled Students' Program, which provided PAS, community-based living, and advocacy: "it became a prototype for independent living centers and a forerunner of the independent living movement."[59] Roberts received his master's degree in political science in 1966; he completed all requirements for his doctorate except the thesis.

In 1972 in Berkeley, Roberts cofounded and directed the first Center for Independent Living (CIL) in the United States. When Roberts left, the center's annual budget had grown from $40,000 to over $1 million. In 1975 California Governor Jerry Brown appointed Roberts to direct the state's Department of Vocational Rehabilitation. His mother, Zona Roberts, recalled that some department staff resisted having "one of their former clients be their boss. They were used to being the big saviors of disabled people, and here this cripple was telling them what to do."[60] Roberts left the department in 1983, and in 1984 he won a MacArthur Fellowship, honored as a civil rights leader. With the award money, he funded the World Institute on Disability in Berkeley, which he had cofounded with Judith Heumann and Joan Leon, to spread concepts of independent living worldwide. Roberts died in 1995.

Rehabilitation Act of 1973 Section 504

As Roberts and other disability rights advocates advanced independent living initiatives in California, the Rehabilitation Act of 1973 aimed to update federal vocational rehabilitation policies in effect for 50 years. With impetus from disability rights advocates, however, components of the law—notably its Section 504—went much further, aiming to remove barriers to participation for people with disability in programs receiving federal funding. President Richard Nixon refused to sign the 1972 version of the bill, claiming it was too expansive. Disability rights advocates protested Nixon's pocket veto at the Lincoln Monument in Washington, DC; afterward, 150 activists with disability marched down Connecticut Avenue.[61] After testimony from John Nagle, director of the National Federation of the Blind, "that because a man is blind or deaf or without legs, he is not less a citizen,"[62] Congress again passed the law in 1973. Once more, Nixon vetoed the legislation, finally signing it on September 26, 1973, after Congress revised the bill to address his concerns.

Section 504 of the Rehabilitation Act of 1973 presaged the Americans with Disabilities Act of 1990. Despite its monumental implications, Section 504 was a legislative afterthought. "Congressional aides could not even remember who had suggested adding the civil rights protection . . . [with] wording clearly . . . copied straight out of the Civil Rights Act of 1964."[63] For the first time in federal law, Section 504 prohibits discrimination because of disability in federal programs, as well as programs receiving federal funds, federal employment, and employment by federal contractors:

> No otherwise qualified individual with a disability in the United States . . . shall, solely by reason of his or her disability, be excluded from the participation in, be denied the benefits of, or be subjected to discrimination under any program or activity receiving Federal financial assistance or under any program or activity conducted by any Executive agency (29 U.S.C. Section 794).

For four years, successive administrations—first President Gerald Ford and then Jimmy Carter—refused to implement Section 504, fearing its potential costs. Finally, in April 1977, frustrated disability rights activists protested by occupying federal offices in San Francisco for 25 days, riveting national attention. As a counteroffer, one Carter administration official suggested establishing separate but equal facilities for people with disability. This proposal, with its impolitic verbiage, backfired. Although the Carter administration implemented Section 504 regulations, his successor, President Ronald Reagan, tried to repeal or dismantle them, leading to battles about disability rights throughout the 1980s.

The Rehabilitation Act of 1973 has undergone multiple amendments. The 1978 amendments have particular implications for home-based PAS. Title VII of the amended Rehabilitation Act establishes CILs in communities nationwide, overseen by the Administration for Community Living in the U.S. Department of Health and Human Services (Box 2.3). Title VII

Box 2.3 Key Provisions of the 1978 Amendments of the Rehabilitation Act of 1973

Title VII—Independent Living Services and Centers for Independent Living

Chapter 1—Individuals with Significant Disabilities

Part A—General Provisions

Sec. 701. Purpose

The purpose of this chapter is to promote a philosophy of independent living, including a philosophy of consumer control, peer support, self-help, self-determination, equal access, and individual and system advocacy, in order to maximize the leadership, empowerment, independence, and productivity of individuals with disabilities, and the integration and full inclusion of individuals with disabilities into the mainstream of American society.

Sec. 702. Definitions

(2) CENTER FOR INDEPENDENT LIVING.—The term "center for independent living" means a consumer-controlled, community-based, cross-disability, nonresidential private nonprofit agency for individuals with significant disabilities. . . .

(17) INDEPENDENT LIVING CORE SERVICES.—The term "independent living core services" means—
(A) information and referral services;
(B) independent living skills training;
(C) peer counseling (including cross-disability peer counseling);
(D) individual and systems advocacy; and
(E) services that—
(i) facilitate the transition of individuals with significant disabilities from nursing homes and other institutions to home and community-based residences, with the requisite supports and services;
(ii) provide assistance to individuals with significant disabilities who are at risk of entering institutions so that the individuals may remain in the community; and
(iii) facilitate the transition of youth who are individuals with significant disabilities, who were eligible for individualized education programs under section 614(d) of the Individuals with Disabilities Education Act.

promulgates many key concepts and fundamental principles supporting paid PAS programs for people with disability, including consumer control, self-determination, and community-based living. In some states, CILs play major roles in important programs, such as Medicaid, for obtaining and organizing PAS (see Chapter 3).

Charlie Carr Moves into the Community

In 1971, when Charlie Carr first saw the floor at the Middlesex County Hospital where he moved after leaving the Massachusetts Hospital School, he viewed it as "a pit stop to heaven" for most of its long-term patients and "like the Dark Ages." Middlesex County, which opened in the 1930s as a tuberculosis hospital, still primarily served older patients with chronic diseases.

Despite these initial impressions, however, Carr and his two hospital school classmates, who were all moving at the same time, liked the large rooms and adjoining balcony. A young physician had just become the medical director, and he avidly supported their efforts to attend college. Another young leader had recently become dean at nearby Massachusetts Bay Community College, where the three classmates matriculated. Funding from the Massachusetts Rehabilitation Commission covered the costs of transportation, tuition, and books. "If you can get a B or better in each course," the young dean told them, "you can come back next semester, and we'll put ramps on two more buildings, and you can take two more courses."

As happened to Ed Roberts, the *Boston Globe* published an article about "these three young guys living in an institution, going to college," Carr recalled. "That one article sparked hundreds of letters from people around the state and other states who said, 'We want to do this, too.'" Middlesex County Hospital's medical director decided to repurpose Wellington Hall, a vacant wing of the hospital, admitting young people with disability who wanted to attend school or work. When Wellington Hall opened, under strict supervision by a nurse, eight or nine young adults with disability, men and women, moved in. Carr became the residence leader and negotiated various policies, including that workers would wear street clothes, residents could come and go to socialize, and they could have guests in their rooms, although they were not allowed to lock the doors. "We could drink, if we had a doctor's prescription," Carr recounted. "We found out great ways to justify drinking beer."

Carr remembers Wellington Hall feeling like freedom in contrast to a nursing home, where he might have ended up. He met his wife, now of many decades, when she did an internship there as a Northeastern University student. Tragedies did occur: two residents committed suicide, and others died from health problems. Nonetheless, for Carr "and for many people there, it was a chance to catch up on a lot of lost time."

By 1973 or 1974, though, Carr started contemplating his future. He heard about the CIL in Berkeley and telephoned Ed Roberts, learning "about this whole thing called independent living." He had begun thinking that "Wellington Hall, for most people, was going to be the final resting place. This was where we would reach some kind of goal that we figured was acceptable enough. But . . . I didn't want to do that. I wanted to get out of there."

As Carr deliberated how to have a home of his own, he met Fred Fay. Nine years older than Carr, Fay had quadriplegia from a SCI at the age of 17. Within a year, Fay and his mother founded Opening Doors to provide counseling and information to people with disability. Fay earned his doctorate in educational psychology, led advocacy for Section 504 of the 1973 Rehabilitation Act, and mentored many disability rights advocates across the United States.[64] "I looked at Fred and talked to him," said Carr, "and he told me that he was married. He told me that he lived in an apartment, and he told me that he had a son." Fay met privately one night with several Wellington Hall residents to explore their goals. Finally, Fay asked whether they wanted help figuring out how to leave Wellington Hall and live in their own apartments with PAS. That was exactly what Carr and the others wanted.

Before Carr and his floormates could leave Wellington Hall, however, lots of pieces needed to fall into place. Through Fay's connections, they found advocates in Boston to identify accessible housing. They started planning the Boston Center for Independent Living (BCIL), which opened in 1974, the second CIL in the United States. They found a van operator to provide transportation. But before they could move into the community, they needed to organize PAS. They decided to seek support from the Department of Public Welfare.

Ironically, one of the two welfare department officials who met with them had been the Massachusetts General Hospital occupational therapist who had told Carr he would be institutionalized his entire life, making intensive rehabilitation therapy moot. "We went in, about five of us," Carr recalled. "We said, 'We're willing, and we want to move into these accessible apartments, but we need personal care assistants.' So, we fought with them tooth and nail, and they eventually agreed to do something on a pilot basis." Charlie Carr's story continues in Chapter 3.

Americans with Disabilities Act of 1990 and ADA Amendments Act of 2008

Section 504 of the 1973 Rehabilitation Act prohibits discrimination but only in situations involving federal funding. Almost two decades passed before

---

Box 2.4 Definition of Disability under the Americans with Disabilities Act

"The term 'disability' means, with respect to an individual

(A) a physical or mental impairment that substantially limits one or more major life activities of such individual;
(B) a record of such an impairment; or
(C) being regarded as having such an impairment."[1]

[1] Americans With Disabilities Act of 1990, Pub. L. No. 101-336, 104 Stat. 328 (1990).

Congress enacted the Americans with Disabilities Act of 1990 (P.L. 101-336), signed by President George H. W. Bush on July 26, 1990. Fears about high costs, frivolous litigation, and operational burdens to businesses initially blocked widespread support for the ADA, which was written to cover all public facilities and services and private entities that serve the public.[65] Furthermore, lack of unified messages from disability rights advocates—representing diverse and distinct constituencies—diluted public pressure for the law. The ADA poses unusual requirements under civil rights laws. It requires not only that businesses and governments stop discriminatory actions but also that they take proactive steps to provide equal opportunity to people with disability, within the bounds of being "reasonable accommodations" or "readily achievable." Ultimately, the universality of the cause catalyzed the ADA's passage: most people either are disabled themselves, will have disability at some point during their lifespan, or have close family members or friends with disability. Congress passed the ADA with strong bipartisan support.

To be protected under the ADA, people must first prove that they are disabled. The ADA adopted the same broad, three-part definition of disability from Section 504 (Box 2.4). In passing the ADA, Congress intended to view disability broadly. In early years, however, courts often interpreted the definition narrowly when deciding whether litigants were disabled and thus merited protection under the ADA.

The ADA Amendments Act (ADAAA) of 2008 (P.L. 110-325), signed by President George W. Bush, aimed to clarify Congress's broad intent in defining disability for civil rights protection. The ADAAA mandates that "major life activities include, but are not limited to, caring for oneself, performing manual tasks, seeing, hearing, eating, sleeping, walking, standing, lifting, bending, speaking, breathing, learning, reading, concentrating, thinking, communicating, and working," as well as "operation of a major bodily function, including but not limited to, functions of the immune system, normal cell growth, digestive, bowel, bladder, neurological, brain, respiratory, circulatory, endocrine, and reproductive functions."[66]

The ADAAA considers impairments that last less than six months to be transitory and are not covered under the ADA. Nevertheless, the ADAAA indicates "an impairment that is episodic or in remission is a disability if it would substantially limit a major life activity when active."[67] With the exception of ordinary glasses or contact lenses, mitigating effects of medications, equipment, or devices—including cochlear implants, limb prostheses, and other mobility devices—are not considered when determining disability for civil rights protections.

Living in the Community Is a Civil Right

The ADA has had wide-ranging effects and generated numerous judicial rulings delineating civil rights for Americans with disability. The landmark 1999 U.S. Supreme Court case *Olmstead v. L.C.* had profound implications for deinstitutionalization and community-based living. The opposing sides in this case were Tommy Olmstead, commissioner of the Georgia Department of Human Resources, and two women, Lois Curtis and Elaine Wilson, inpatients at the Georgia Regional Hospital psychiatric unit. Both women had mental illness and developmental disability and had agreed to admission to the state-run hospital:

> Ms. Curtis had first been institutionalized at age 13. In 1992, she was again admitted for inpatient psychiatric treatment. Although her treatment team determined in 1993 that her needs could be met in the community, she remained institutionalized and was not discharged to a community-based treatment program until 1996. Similarly, Ms. Wilson was admitted to an inpatient psychiatric unit in 1995. At one point, the hospital proposed discharging her to a homeless shelter, which she successfully challenged. In 1996, Ms. Wilson's treating doctor determined that she could be served in the community, but she was not discharged from the institution until 1997. Both women sued, arguing that the state's failure to provide community-based services, as recommended by their treating professionals, violated the ADA. While both women were receiving community-based treatment services when the Supreme Court heard their case, the Court recognized that the nature of their disabilities and their treatment history made it likely that they would again experience institutionalization.[68]

Georgia argued that the hospital admissions largely resulted from the institutional bias of Medicaid, the joint federal-state health insurance program for low-income individuals (see Chapter 3).[69]

On June 22, 1999, Curtis and Wilson won their Supreme Court case by a 6–3 vote, under Title II of the ADA, which prohibits state and local governments from excluding people with disability from participating in or receiving the benefits of public programs. The late Justice Ruth Bader Ginsburg wrote the majority opinion, asserting that in passing the ADA, Congress took a broad view of what constitutes discrimination against people with disability, including segregating them in institutions. Justice Ginsburg wrote, "The identification of unjustified segregation as discrimination reflects two evident judgments: Institutional placement of persons who can handle and benefit from community settings perpetuates unwarranted assumptions that persons so isolated are incapable or unworthy of participating in community life . . .; and institutional confinement severely diminishes individuals' everyday life activities."[70]

The *Olmstead* opinion recognizes that some people may not be able to live in the community. But for people with disability who, with appropriate supports, can live in the community, the ADA confers that civil right. As described in Chapter 3, however, *Olmstead* does not guarantee that Medicaid will pay for PAS and other supports its beneficiaries need to live in their homes or communities. Thus, although *Olmstead* powerfully asserts the civil right of Americans with disability to live in their homes and communities, having the financial wherewithal—or other resources—to do so remains a persistent hurdle.

3

Paying for Home-Based Personal
Assistance Services

Charlie Carr vividly remembers the day in late 1974 when he saw his first apartment, a two-bedroom in Medford, Massachusetts, just outside Boston,[1] and about 9 miles from Wellington Hall at Middlesex County Hospital, where he had lived for several years. After working with disability rights advocates and various state agencies, Carr was finally moving into his own home (see Chapter 2). A man agreed to be his first live-in personal assistant, and together they drove to Mystic Valley Towers, which housed his accessible apartment.

> I went to the rental office . . . got my keys, we went up, opened the door, and I looked into this place. Compared to my little room at Wellington Hall, it seemed palatial. I went in and it smelled brand new, and there was a big picture window that overlooked a parking lot. There was a kitchen with a stove. I went down the hallway and there was this huge bathroom. There were two bedrooms. And I just looked at it and . . . I had this sort of second epiphany, which was, "I'm never going to go back."

Carr faced some stark realities. "I had no money," he admitted. Middlesex County Hospital took his monthly Supplemental Security Income (SSI) check, giving Carr $35 per month in spending money. Nevertheless, Carr decided to move on December 1, 1974. "We had one hellacious New Year's party in our new apartment," Carr remembered. "Had no furniture. We slept on mattresses on the floor." Over the ensuing weeks and months, his live-in PA and other

PAs worked for free—Carr had no money to pay them. The Boston Center for Independent Living and Massachusetts Medicaid had supposedly worked out arrangements to pay the PAs, but paychecks never came. Finally, after resolving an administrative logjam, Medicaid started paying Carr's PAs, and Carr could relax. With paid PAS, he was finally living in his own home.

A verage Americans who turn 65 years old today will need at least $138,000 to fund their future ADL support needs.[2] Young people in their early twenties, as Charlie Carr was, have considerably higher lifetime costs. In 2018 the national median annual cost of paying privately for 30 hours per week (roughly 4.3 hours per day) of in-home ADL and IADL support was $34,300.[3] People with Carr's ADL impairments need many more PAS hours daily, compounding the costs. Few individuals or families can afford these expenses. Furthermore, few people can buy expensive private insurance to cover long-term services and supports (LTSS).[4]

A 2007 survey found that 39% of baby boomers and older Americans mistakenly believe that Medicare, the federal health insurance program for people ages 65 and older and some disabled adults, covers long-term care costs.[5] Only 11% knew correctly that Medicaid—the joint federal-state program for qualifying people with low incomes—covers long-term care. In 2017 U.S. LTSS costs (including nursing homes and in-home care) totaled $235 billion, with 57% paid by Medicaid, 23% out-of-pocket by consumers, 4% by private long-term care insurance, and 16% by other sources.[6] In fiscal year 2016, Medicaid spent 57% of its LTSS expenditures on community-based care and 43% on institutions,[7] with this distribution varying considerably across states. Medicaid has become a last resort for people needing LTSS who cannot afford it.[8]

People requiring ADL supports have no choice. But such support is costly, and adult Americans with disability on average have substantially fewer resources than do nondisabled individuals (see Table 3.1). People with self-care limitations also have higher rates of other socioeconomic disadvantages, with 28% having less than a high school education and 48% being unable to work, as compared with 10% and 2%, respectively, for nondisabled people. Their incomes are too low to afford extensive PAS: 62% of adult Americans with self-care limitations have annual incomes below $25,000.

No current U.S. policy covers home-based PAS for all Americans who need it (see Chapter 14). Public programs that do fund LTSS have long legacies of favoring institutional over the in-home care that Americans prefer. Local, state-specific factors determine options for covering PAS. This chapter briefly reviews this complex topic, focusing on Medicaid—the leading public

TABLE 3.1 SOCIODEMOGRAPHIC CHARACTERISTICS BY DISABILITY STATUS: NONINSTITUTIONALIZED U.S. RESIDENTS AGES 18 YEARS AND OLDER

Sociodemographic characteristics	No disability	Disability type					
		Any disability	Mobility disability	Vision disability	Hearing disability	Cognitive disability	Self-care disability
		Age-adjusted percentage (%)					
Education level[a]							
Some high school or less	9.7	21.3	24.5	27.6	23.2	23.8	30.3
High school or less	57.3	64.1	62.5	60.5	61.4	63.7	59.3
College graduate	32.9	14.6	13.0	11.9	15.4	12.5	10.4
Employment status[a]							
Employed	66.4	41.8	30.5	39.9	49.4	37.7	22.2
Out of work	4.2	8.8	8.9	9.1	6.8	8.7	8.7
Unable to work	1.7	21.1	34.8	24.3	17.0	25.4	47.9
Other	27.7	28.3	25.7	26.6	26.7	27.1	21.2
Income level[a]							
<$15,000	6.6	20.7	26.6	27.1	18.2	24.9	31.3
$15,000 to <$25,000	12.9	25.5	28.2	27.8	23.3	27.2	30.1
$25,000 to <$35,000	9.5	11.8	11.4	12.5	11.3	11.6	11.5
$35,000 to <$50,000	13.0	12.4	11.1	10.3	13.3	11.3	9.4
$50,000+	58.0	29.6	22.7	22.2	33.8	25.1	17.8

Marital status[a]

Married/unmarried couple	58.3	43.7	43.9	41.5	50.7	39.1	40.1
Divorced/separated	10.8	18.0	21.6	19.5	18.1	19.8	24.4
Widowed	4.7	7.8	8.7	8.9	7.9	8.3	8.6
Never married	26.2	30.5	25.8	30.1	23.3	32.9	26.8

Health insurance coverage[b]

Persons 21 to 64 years of age

Uninsured	12.4	9.8	8.3	12.5	9.8	9.6	6.8
Insured	87.6	90.2	91.7	87.5	90.2	90.4	93.2
Medicare	1.7	23.8	31.7	20.8	17.3	27.4	37.6
Medicaid	11.6	42.1	46.5	39.1	29.1	53.9	56.4
Employer/union	65.4	34.7	29.3	36.0	45.9	25.3	24.1
Purchased	11.4	10.6	10.7	11.3	10.9	9.1	9.7
Military/Veterans Affairs	3.3	6.9	7.0	5.5	11.2	6.7	5.9
Indian Health Services	0.4	0.8	0.8	0.9	0.9	0.7	0.7

[a] Source: National Center on Birth Defects and Developmental Disabilities, Division of Human Development and Disability, Centers for Disease Control and Prevention. Disability and Health Data System (DHDS) Data [online]. Accessed May 26, 2020. https://dhds.cdc.gov

[b] Source: Erickson W, Lee C, von Schrader S. Disability statistics from the American Community Survey (ACS). Cornell University, Yang-Tan Institute; 2017. www.disabilitystatistics.org

payor for in-home PAS. While the Department of Veterans Affairs and other programs (e.g., through the Older Americans Act of 1965) also fund home-based PAS, they serve specific populations and far fewer people than Medicaid. Although dollars paid privately out of pocket cover an unknown fraction of in-home PAS costs, little information is available about such payments—some are off the books (i.e., paid informally to PAs, without employer tax payments or other documentation—see Chapter 12). This review starts with the New Deal of the early 20th century, which set the national direction for public funding of LTSS.

Social Security Sets the Course

In 1880 roughly half of Americans lived on farms. Agrarian family-based social networks typically supported family members across their lifespans, within their own homes or with nearby relatives. In subsequent decades, industrialization fractured these familial networks, upending lifelong expectations of support. New social structures in this industrial economy were fragile, risking breakdown when income fell from unemployment, retirement, disability, or death of the family breadwinner.[9] By 1930, only 21% of Americans worked on farms. Between 1920 and 1924, unemployment rates of nonfarm workers ranged from 4% to 20%; in 1932—at the height of the Great Depression—nonfarm unemployment was 34%.[10] Public desperation stoked by widespread poverty accelerated moves toward a broad federal social insurance program.

On August 14, 1935, President Franklin D. Roosevelt signed the Social Security Act (SSA) into law.[11] The SSA created four major programs that, despite evolution over time, remain as the core of basic income security for Americans of all ages (Box 3.1). Enacted in 1935, SSA old-age insurance benefits did not begin until the 1939 SSA amendments, which modified the initial benefit formula (basing benefits on average wages rather than cumulative wages, as originally planned). These 1939 amendments also added benefits for dependents (wives and children) and survivors of insured individuals. (Men received spousal and survivor benefits later.) Benefits initially went only to people employed in industry and commerce, leaving out agricultural and domestic workers and thus excluding many people of color. The 1950 amendments extended Social Security benefits to farm and domestic workers and most self-employed people. The 1957 amendments expanded coverage to disabled workers between 50 and 64 years of age, and 1960 amendments included coverage for disabled workers of all ages and their dependents.

Although multiple complex factors contributed, income security of Americans did improve in the years immediately after enactment of the SSA. As described in Chapter 2, almshouses were the primary housing option in

---

Box 3.1 Major Programs of the 1935 Social Security Act

1. Old-age (OA) insurance, which evolved into the Old-Age, Survivors, and Disability Insurance (OASDI) program (These programs are what most Americans know as "Social Security.")
2. Unemployment insurance
3. Aid to Families with Dependent Children (AFDC).The Personal Responsibility and Work Opportunity Reconciliation Act of 1996 replaced AFDC with the Temporary Assistance for Needy Families block grant program
4. Federal support for state-run, means-tested, old-age assistance (OAA), which became the Supplemental Security Income (SSI) program and was later extended to children and adults with disability and low incomes

---

the early 20th century for many impoverished older people. Giving these individuals resources to afford their own housing helped spur the SSA's 1935 passage. In the majority opinion upholding the SSA's constitutionality, U.S. Supreme Court Justice Benjamin Cardozo wrote that the statute aimed "to save men and women from the rigors of the poorhouse as well as the haunting fear that such a lot awaits them when the journey's end is near."[12] In the short term, Social Security income contributed substantially to achieving this goal. Not only did more retirees own their own homes in 1982 than 40 years earlier, but also "new beneficiaries in 1982 were in better health and were more likely to retire because they wanted to than was true of their counterparts in the early 1940's."[13]

However, early provisions of the SSA perpetuated reliance on institutional rather than community-based supports for people with chronic disease or disability. Federal dollars available to states for the mean-tested Old Age Assistance program were prohibited from supporting people residing in public facilities, such as the many almshouses. This policy spawned a new industry, private nursing homes, and shifted institutional living from public to private facilities.[14] Further strengthening private nursing homes, 1950 SSA amendments required that payments for medical care go directly to nursing homes rather than to SSA beneficiaries. At their outset, the 1965 SSA amendments that enacted Medicare and Medicaid, Titles XVIII and XIX, respectively, further solidified support for institutional over home-based services for individuals needing PAS.

Medicare, Title XVIII of the Social Security Act

Medicare, federal health insurance for people ages 65 and older and qualified younger adults with disability, is "viewed as a government promise to its citizens" and a "'social contract' that must be honored."[15] The societal imperative of covering health care costs for older Americans who could not afford to pay out of pocket for hospital or doctor services drove Medicare's passage. In 1973 SSA amendments gave Medicare eligibility to qualified adults younger than 65 who receive Social Security Disability Insurance and meet other requirements.[16] Medicare accounts for 21% of total national health care spending, with expenditures of nearly $750 billion in 2018.[17] In calendar year 2019, Medicare covered 60.8 million beneficiaries, including about 52.2 million (86%) people eligible because of age (65 years of age and older) and 8.7 million (14%) younger adults eligible because of disability.[18]

Enacting federal health insurance—even for this subset of Americans—took three decades of concerted public and political pressure. When President Roosevelt's advisory Committee on Economic Security started drafting what became the 1935 SSA, it announced plans to study health insurance, prompting "so many telegrams to the members of Congress that the entire social security program seemed endangered."[19] Opposition from organized medicine and other groups forced Roosevelt to retreat from proposing government-run health insurance, afraid it would doom Social Security legislation entirely and imperil his upcoming reelection.

After several unsuccessful efforts to enact health insurance in ensuing decades, the 1965 political climate finally allowed passage of major national health care legislation, but carefully, to avoid aggravating deeply entrenched opponents. On July 30, 1965, in Independence, Missouri, former president Harry S. Truman's hometown, President Lyndon B. Johnson signed both Medicare and Medicaid into law with Truman, who had long championed expansion of health insurance, sitting to his left. In his signing comments, Johnson observed that Truman had "planted the seeds of compassion and duty which have today flowered into care for the sick, and serenity for the fearful."[20] Johnson then asserted that, with Medicare, "No longer will older Americans be denied the healing miracle of modern medicine. No longer will illness crush and destroy the savings that they have so carefully put away over a lifetime so that they might enjoy dignity in their later years."

In drafting Medicare, Congress established a two-part structure similar to the Blue Cross and Blue Shield private health insurance plans that organized medicine, including the American Medical Association, had endorsed since the late 1920s. Medicare Part A, in parallel with private Blue Cross insurance, covers acute hospital services and time-limited postdischarge stays at skilled nursing facilities or rehabilitation hospitals. Part B, modeled after Blue Shield plans, reimburses 80% of physicians' services in hospitals and outpatient settings. Importantly, Medicare focuses explicitly on covering medically necessary services: "No payment may be made under part A or part B for any expenses incurred for items or services which . . . are not reasonable and necessary for the diagnosis or treatment of illness or injury or to improve the functioning of a malformed body member."[21] Medicare's passage depended on these strict statutory limitations on covered services: There was a

> consensus in 1965 that Medicare should not directly address the growing burden of chronic disabling illness. . . . The secretary of health, education and welfare, for example, said in testimony to Congress that Medicare was not a program to pay the costs of managing chronic illness in short-stay hospitals. Other officials claimed to be horrified when Russell Long, chairman of the Senate Finance Committee, proposed amendments to Medicare to create a "catastrophic or long-term illness system." . . . Administration strategists feared that they would lose supporters in Congress . . . if the program appeared to be uncontrollably expensive.[22]

Since its early days, Medicare Parts A and B have covered in-home services but strictly limited to people who are homebound and need explicitly defined skilled services, including intermittent (not continual) skilled nursing care, speech-language pathology services, or physical or occupational therapy. Furthermore, these patients must be certified as confined to home, under a physician's care, and having a specified plan of care.[23] In very restricted circumstances, Medicare covers PAS (e.g., for beneficiaries receiving skilled nursing services for wound care, where the PA primarily assists the nurse).

Over the decades, Medicare has experimented with or implemented specific programs offering LTSS support, including PAS. For example, Medicare has funded LTSS through time-limited demonstration projects that authorized expanded benefits, including home-based supportive services and personal care; one of many examples was the social health maintenance organization demonstration in four regions around the country, which started in 1984.[24] Medicare provides LTSS through the Program of All-Inclusive Care for the Elderly (PACE), authorized by Section 4801 of the Balanced Budget Act of 1997. This provision added Section 1894 to Title XVIII of the SSA, making PACE a permanent component of Medicare. PACE covers in-home PAS to its participants, who must be Medicare and/or Medicaid beneficiaries at least 55 years of age and "nursing home certifiable" (i.e., severely disabled or requiring extensive supportive services; Chapter 14 describes Michael's [Dedication] PACE experiences).

The 1997 Balanced Budget Act also created Medicare + Choice (M+C) plans, later renamed Medicare Part C, with so-called Medicare Advantage (MA) plans offered by private health insurers. MA plans can cover services beyond those of original Medicare Parts A and B, generally at lower costs to Medicare beneficiaries. LTSS and home-based services are key components of certain MA plans—Special Needs Plans (SNPs)—introduced in the Medicare Prescription Drug, Improvement, and Modernization Act of 2003. SNPs explicitly enroll beneficiaries with complex health needs, which might require in-home supports; the availability of SNPs varies widely across states.[25] Finally, under the Bipartisan Budget Act of 2018 and new rules from the Centers for Medicare & Medicaid Services (CMS), which administers the program, some MA plans can now offer additional services, including in-home PAS.[26] However, these options are new (as of 2019, only 3.4% of MA plans offered in-home support services[27]), and plans may limit eligibility for them (only selected enrollees can receive them).

Medicaid, Title XIX of the Social Security Act

Unlike federal Medicare insurance, Congress designed Medicaid, a joint federal and state health initiative, as a welfare program.[28,29] Medicaid, in which the federal government provides matching funds to states, is voluntary for states. Some states initially rejected participation, but by 1982, all 50 states and the District of Columbia had joined Medicaid. (Medicaid also operates in the five U.S. territories: American Samoa, the Commonwealth of the Northern Mariana Islands, Guam, Puerto Rico, and the U.S. Virgin Islands.) The federal government pays the larger share of Medicaid costs, determined by the Federal Medical Assistance Percentage (FMAP) based on states' per capita incomes. The minimum FMAP is 50%, and the highest (75.65%) went to Mississippi in fiscal year 2018.[30]

Federal Medicaid statutes require that states make certain people eligible, largely based on having low incomes and limited financial assets (which today generally fall below $2,000 for individuals and $3,000 for couples).[31] However, states have discretion in setting certain Medicaid eligibility criteria. Medicaid enrollment surpasses that of Medicare, in 2019 totaling 75.8 million people.[32] Medicaid's annual expenditures are below Medicare's but totaled almost $597 billion in 2018, 16% of national health expenditures.[33]

Medicaid recipients are diverse, in 2019 including 29.0 million children, 16.0 million adults under age 65, 6.2 million adults at least 65 years of age, and 10.9 million people who qualify as blind or disabled. Another 12.4 million qualify from the 2010 Patient Protection and Affordable Care Act (ACA, also known as Obamacare) Medicaid expansion, which was central to ACA's efforts to increase insurance coverage nationwide.[34] In June 2012 the U.S. Supreme Court ruled the ACA's Medicaid expansion provisions unconstitutional, allowing states to choose whether to participate. As of November 2020, 39 states, including the District of Columbia, have implemented the ACA Medicaid expansion, but 12 states—primarily in the South—have not.[35]

Medicaid initially provided health insurance to people receiving cash assistance from federally funded income-support programs, primarily impoverished mothers and their dependent children, older individuals, and people who were very poor, blind, or disabled (ABD or aged, blind, and disabled categories). Some states used their optional authority to provide Medicaid to medically needy people in these categories. Although legislated in parallel, "Medicare and Medicaid reflected sharply different traditions. Medicare was buoyed by popular approval and acknowledged dignity of Social Security; Medicaid was burdened by the stigma of public assistance."[36] Medicare had uniform eligibility and benefit standards nationwide, but Medicaid left many decisions to individual states. Some states are more generous than others.[37]

In contrast to Medicare, Medicaid covers LTSS for people with disability. Medicaid's roots in welfare make it "program policy to (re)establish functional independence in individuals and families . . . [and] to blur distinctions between medical and social services, professional and practical care giving, so as to move a recipient toward disenrollment."[38] In recent years, however, Medicaid has become a

> locus of innovation in the health care system. Many states are designing and implementing new models of coordinated and integrated care for people with complex needs that may provide a model for health care delivery beyond the Medicaid context. Medicaid is also the fulcrum of ongoing expansion in access to community-based long-term services and supports that enable individuals with disabilities and older adults who would otherwise require institutional care to live independently in the community.[39]

Medicaid and Home and Community-Based Services

As noted above, early Social Security provisions—predating Medicare and Medicaid—sparked the growth of private nursing homes, institutionalizing people with ADL and other support needs. Decades later, when first enacted, Medicaid required all states to cover nursing home care for recipients 21 years old and older, perpetuating institutional bias. Medicaid also covered home health care, but as optional benefits, for states to choose. Over time, with public pressure, financial concerns and states' requests for greater flexibility, Medicaid laws and policies moved away from institutionalization toward home and community-based services (HCBS). By 1975, the newly enacted SSA Title XX aggregated federal social services assistance for states into block grants, explicitly aiming to reduce institutionalization and increase HCBS.

In 1970 home health care became a mandatory benefit for Medicaid recipients who were entitled to nursing facility care. In the mid-1970s, personal care became an optional Medicaid benefit under SSA Section 1905(a)(24). These early PAS provisions, however, stipulated strict medical oversight.[40] All personal care required physician authorization as "medically necessary," supervision by a nurse, and integration with formal care plans. Furthermore, regulations required these services to be provided only within a person's residence. Under this early authority, most states limited PAS to assisting people with basic ADLs. Although PAS workers could perform IADL tasks (e.g., meal preparation, laundry, light housekeeping), they must be limited and provided only incidentally to ADL support activities.

In 1981 Medicaid HCBS achieved a watershed. Among its many provisions, the Omnibus Budget Reconciliation Act of 1981 authorized SSA Section 1915(c) waivers for Medicaid to cover HCBS for individuals who otherwise required institutionalization. Under 1915(c) waiver authority, states can provide services not usually covered by Medicaid if these services prevent institutionalization of beneficiaries. Section 1915(c) waiver program services include personal care, homemakers, home health aides, case management, adult day health, habilitation, and respite care for family caregivers. Under this waiver authority in the 1980s, Medicaid LTSS funds began shifting away from institutions and toward HCBS.

In the late 1980s, some states wanted to broaden Medicaid's coverage of PAS, introducing supports for Medicaid beneficiaries outside their homes to enable participation in community life. In 1993 Congress added personal care to Medicaid's options, giving states the authority to provide these services outside beneficiaries' homes.[41] In 1994 Congress further relaxed PAS requirements, eliminating requirements for nurse supervision and physician prescriptions to authorize PAS. CMS issued a State Medicaid Manual Transmittal that "thoroughly revised and updated guidelines concerning coverage of personal care services."[42] Major provisions stipulated that:

- Personal care services could cover not only basic ADL supports but also assistance with IADLs, including medication management, grocery shopping, meal preparation, light housework, laundry, using the telephone, money management, and transportation.
- Medicaid could pay any relative other than "legally responsible relatives" (i.e., spouse, parents of dependent children) to provide personal care services to Medicaid recipients. Thus, relatives who

otherwise would forgo income by spending time caring for a family member could receive wages from Medicaid.

- Consumers could self-direct personal care services (i.e., consumer-directed PAS), including training and supervising their PAs. Self-direction is a core independent living principle (see Chapter 2), giving people with disability authority to control all aspects of their daily lives.

In succeeding years, new waiver authorities and other programs have expanded Medicaid's HCBS options. These new initiatives are complicated, constituting an alphabet soup of Medicaid waivers (Table 3.2). The Deficit Reduction Act (DRA) of 2005 mandated two Section 1915 waivers, (i) and (j). Section 1915(i) allows states to target HCBS plans to specific subpopulations requiring these supports, such as older people, technology-dependent children, people with intellectual disability, or individuals with certain diseases or health conditions.

The 1915(j) waiver provisions allow consumer self-direction. This authority gives Medicaid consumers the option to use their allocated budgets to purchase items consistent with their state-approved, person-centered care plan to enhance their independence or substitute for human assistance (e.g., home modifications, transportation, assistive technologies). Section 1915(j) also permits Medicaid payments to parents or spouses to provide PAS (previous measures prevented Medicaid from paying these "legally responsible relatives").

In 2010 the ACA (Obamacare) mandated the 1915(k) waiver called Community First Choice. It allows states to provide home-based PAS under their state plans to keep people in community-based settings appropriate to their needs. States can use either agency PAS (see Chapter 7) or permit consumer self-direction (see Chapter 8), which gives consumers both employer and budget authority (see below). Under the 1915(k) agency model, Medicaid can contract with agencies to provide PAS. An alternative is the hybrid "agency with choice" model, "whereby the participant is supported by an agency that functions as the common law employer of workers recruited by the participant. The participant directs the workers and is considered their co-employer. The agency performs financial management services and tasks, rather than the individual."[43]

These new plans and options have reoriented Medicaid LTSS from its initial institutional focus to facilitate community-based supports. In 1995 82% of Medicaid's LTSS expenditures went to institutions and only 18% to HCBS.[44] Since then, the proportion spent on institutions has fallen steadily and HCBS funding has risen. In fiscal year 2013, for the first time, the proportion of LTSS

TABLE 3.2 MEDICAID AUTHORITIES FOR HOME AND COMMUNITY-BASED SERVICES

Provision	Description	Mandatory/optional	Consumer self-direction[1]
	Authority: state plan		
Home health services	Part-time or intermittent nursing services; home health aides; medical supplies, equipment, and appliances for in-home use; and, *at state option*, physical therapy, occupational therapy, and speech pathology and audiology services	Mandatory	N/A
Personal care services: Section 1905(a)(24)	Assistance with ADLs and IADLs	Optional	Permitted
Community First Choice state plan option: Section 1915(k)	Home and community-based PAS supports for beneficiaries who would otherwise require institutional care; financial eligibility up to 150% of the federal poverty level	Optional	Required
Home health state plan option	Comprehensive care management, care coordination, health promotion, comprehensive transitional care and follow-up, patient and family support, referral to community and social support services	Optional	N/A
HCBS state plan option: Section 1915(i)	Case management, homemaker, home health aide, or PAS; adult day health; habilitation, respite, day treatment or partial hospitalization; psychosocial rehabilitation; chronic mental health clinic services; other services approved by HHS secretary (same as Section 1915(c) HCBS waivers)	Optional	Permitted

Authority: waivers

Section 1915(c)	Case management, homemaker or home health aide or PAS; adult day health; habilitation, respite, day treatment or partial hospitalization; psychosocial rehabilitation; chronic mental health clinic services; other services approved by HHS secretary (same as the Section 1915(i) state plan option)	Optional	Permitted
Section 1115	HHS secretary can waive certain Medicaid requirements and allow states to use Medicaid funds in ways not otherwise allowed under federal rules for experimental, pilot, or demonstration projects that in the secretary's view are likely to promote program objectives	Optional	Permitted

Authority: other HCBS programs

Money Follows the Person	HCBS for beneficiaries who transition from an institution to a community-based setting; includes supplemental services to facilitate transition; demonstration program, 2007–2019	Optional	Permitted
Balancing Incentive Program	New or expanded HCBS for beneficiaries with incomes up to 300% of SSI federal benefit rate	Optional	Permitted

Source: Adapted from Kaiser Commission on Medicaid and the Uninsured. Medicaid long-term services and supports: An overview of funding authorities. Henry J. Kaiser Family Foundation; 2013. https://www.kff.org/wp-content/uploads/2013/09/8483-medicaid-ltss-overview-of-services-and-funding-authorities.pdf
[1] Consumer self-direction of home-based care services.

payments going to HCBS exceeded expenditures for institutional care—51% for HCBS and 49% for institutions.[45] This trend continues today, although with substantial variations by state (see Chapter 14).

Medicaid and Self-Direction Employer and Budget Authority

As indicated in Table 3.2, consumer self-direction features prominently in Medicaid HCBS waivers. The concept traces back to core independent living principles. However, self-direction represents a significant paradigm shift away from professional authority. Historically, health care professionals or state employees have directed and overseen all decision making.[46]

Medicaid consumer self-direction provisions have expanded over the years. CMS recognizes two basic components of self-direction—employer authority and budget authority. Although CMS treats the two as distinct, states that offer the broader budget authority typically also offer employer authority. Under Medicaid employer authority, consumers (or their designated representatives) control recruitment of PAS job candidates, conduct candidate interviews, review references, make hiring decisions, set or negotiate PAs' schedules, train PAs, oversee and evaluate their job performance, and dismiss (at will) PAs who have not performed satisfactorily. All employer authority programs require consumers to participate in paying PAs, at a minimum by approving their timesheets.[47] In almost all employer authority programs, states determine the hourly wages PAs receive.

Budget authority offers more comprehensive, flexible self-direction, typically giving consumers a monthly budget that they can use to purchase goods and services they require to support their needs. Most Medicaid beneficiaries with budget authority use 80 to 90% of their allotted funds to pay PAs' wages.[48] Other goods and services that consumers purchase aim to substitute for human assistance, including not only assistive technologies and home modifications, but also "transportation services, laundry services, meal services, personal care supplies (e.g., incontinence pads), and uncovered prescription and nonprescription drugs."[49] Importantly, under budget authority, consumers negotiate wage levels with their PAs, although consumers must follow the applicable laws addressing minimum wages, overtime pay, disability insurance, and unemployment insurance (see Chapter 12). Consumers with complex needs who require skilled supports may offer higher wages to recruit and retain PAs. In some states, budget authority participants must comply with collective bargaining agreements negotiated by unions representing PAs. Union agreements can set minimum wages for PAs at higher levels than local state or federal minimum wages. In this situation, for budget authority to function, states must increase beneficiaries' allocations to account for higher PAs' wages.

States differ in how they provide funds to Medicaid participants using budget authority. Under the 1915(j) state plans, states can choose to deposit the monetary value of the designated benefit directly into the beneficiary's bank account. Another option involves having states designate a financial management service provider, which holds and dispenses funds as requested by the Medicaid beneficiary. Statutes governing these programs require participants to undergo periodic individual needs assessments to determine how much they will receive. Consumers (or their representatives) can ask for reassessments if their needs change. Beneficiaries—and often family members—can participate in these needs assessments and dispute decisions they view as inappropriate.

Through efforts of Charlie Carr and other advocates with disability, Massachusetts became the first state to build self-direction into its Medicaid PAS program. Massachusetts Medicaid started its personal assistance program in the mid-1970s with consumer direction, with administrative tasks channeled through the Boston Center for Independent Living (BCIL), founded in 1974. "Their efforts were opposed by the federal government, which did not want money for personal assistance services to go directly to disabled consumers, and by medical and rehabilitation professionals, who felt that people with severe disabilities would be unable to handle life in the community."[50] Later viewed as ground-breaking, programs like Massachusetts self-direction helped "pave the way for a state to broaden coverage of these services."[51] Today, BCIL remains the administrative go-between for Boston residents requiring in-home PAS and MassHealth, the current name for Massachusetts Medicaid. As needed, BCIL provides peer support to assist participants with self-directing their PAS.

Carr attended Boston University, obtaining a bachelor of science degree in journalism in 1982. He married Karen, whom he'd met at Wellington Hall, in 1977, and shortly afterward got his first job, as a vocational rehabilitation counselor at the Massachusetts Rehabilitation Commission, where he spent two years. Tapped by Governor Deval Patrick, Carr returned as commissioner from 2007 to 2015. When interviewed in 2001, about ten years after the ADA's passage, Carr was cautiously optimistic but recognized unfinished business:

> What we did get was our voices heard. We did get some political status. We are making gains that are measured gains. If you look back

ten years, . . . and you look at the number of people with all types of disabilities that have assumed mantles of power on local, statewide, national levels, to me, as someone who's been around as long as I have, I'm very happy. . . . What we've done is we've made gains in integrating people into the community. . . . But where's the rest of the dream? How many homeowners are there with disabilities? How many people are gainfully employed? How many people have families and have reached their full potential? Not very many. So we have a lot of work to do.

4

Paid Personal Assistance Services
Workforce and Labor Policies

E velyn Coke was born in Jamaica in 1934 and worked there providing home care.[1] She moved to the United States in 1970, living in Florida and Maryland and still doing home care, before settling in New York City. With long work hours and frugality—but without overtime pay—her home care earnings finally allowed her in 1973 to bring her children to the United States and in 1980 to buy a wood-frame house in Queens, where she lived until her death. According to her 2009 *New York Times* obituary,

> Year in and year out, Evelyn Coke left her Queens house early to go to the homes of elderly, sick, often dying people. She bathed them, cooked for them, helped them dress and monitored their medications. She sometimes worked three consecutive 24-hour shifts.
>
> She loved the work, but she earned only around $7 an hour and got no overtime pay. For years Ms. Coke, a single mother of five, quietly grumbled, and then, quite uncharacteristically, rebelled.[2]

In 2001 Coke was hit by a car, sustaining injuries that prevented her from resuming home care work, and she sought help from a lawyer. The lawyer reviewed her home care agency pay stubs and confirmed what Coke had claimed for years—she sometimes worked 70 hours per week without receiving overtime pay. In 2002 Coke sued, challenging federal labor regulations that exempted home care agencies from overtime pay requirements. Her case rose to the U.S. Supreme Court in 2007.

————

Chapter 4 reviews experiences of paid PAs since early in U.S. history and how evolving policies have affected this so-called domestic work and workers, like Evelyn Coke. Legacies of slavery and socioeconomic segregation underlie structural racism and sexism that still significantly affect the PAS workforce.[3] A disjuncture exists between HCBS policies and policies pertaining to workers providing these services. Although early policies favored institutionalization of consumers with disability and chronic health conditions, governmental actions (e.g., laws, legal decisions) from the 1960s onward have moved consistently toward community-based services, despite resistant regional differences (see Chapter 3). However, federal labor protections have only recently covered home-based PAS workers, most of whom are women of color.

Thus, while consumer-focused policies have steadily increased demand for home-based PAS, labor policies have not fully supported home-based PAS workers. In 2018, 831,800 people worked as home health aides (the occupational category closest to PAS).[4] In 2028 the projected home health aide workforce will be 1,136,600 workers, a nearly 37% increase—among the largest growth rates across U.S. occupational categories. However, at $24,200 in 2018, the median income for home health aides is among the lowest across occupations. Low wages and other labor policies pose significant barriers to hiring and retaining the PAS workforce Americans need in coming decades (see Chapter 14).

Early-20th-Century Labor Policies

The Great Depression brought social upheavals and labor unrest, with nationwide demonstrations of unemployed workers and industrial strikes. Unemployed White men were the public face of economic devastation. However, women who had subsisted through domestic labor also faced widespread unemployment.[5] Historically, society has seen paid PAS as "unskilled work that allegedly any woman could perform."[6] Poor White, Black, and immigrant women have long held these jobs, devaluing PAS work through gender and racial associations. New Deal programs targeting unemployed domestic workers linked paid home care with the legacies of "slavery and segregation that racialized the labor and defined it as low paid and unskilled."[7]

President Franklin D. Roosevelt's Works Progress Administration (WPA) administered the Visiting Housekeeper Program, which provided the major source of unemployment relief for domestic workers. The program aimed not only to benefit women doing domestic work by providing crucial income but also to give needy households free help with housework and childcare. Registered nurses and caseworkers supervised the visiting housekeepers, whose jobs combined heavy housekeeping with "ministering to the ill."[8] In total, the WPA supported 38,000 housekeeping jobs across 45 states and the District of Columbia,[9] as the major work relief program for Black women. Southern employers complained that WPA housekeeping jobs paid higher wages than agricultural and textile labor, causing workforce shortages in those sectors and "undermining the racial caste system."[10] However, WPA program policies preserved traditional gender and racial roles. For instance, across all programs, WPA supported only one worker per family, typically singling out male breadwinners. Workers performing domestic labor, like housekeeping, underwent mandatory syphilis testing, reflecting "official concern with protection of the white household."[11]

Among his New Deal policy reforms, President Roosevelt aimed to raise wages of low-paid workers and eliminate child labor, but he faced strong headwinds from industry and the U.S. Supreme Court. Throughout the 1910s and 1920s, the Supreme Court overturned laws protecting child workers and setting minimum wages for women. In 1933 Roosevelt included labor protections in the National Industrial Recovery Act, under which 2.3 million employers voluntarily agreed to 35- to 40-hour workweeks, paying minimum wages of $12 to $15 per week, and generally hiring only workers at least 16 years old.[12] In May 1935, however, the U.S. Supreme Court unanimously ruled various provisions of the act unconstitutional, including its progressive labor policies. In his 1936 presidential campaign, Roosevelt promised to enact labor protections that would withstand Supreme Court challenges.

With his 523-to-8 electoral college landslide in 1936, Roosevelt tried to pack the Supreme Court with justices more favorable to New Deal policies, a strategy that ultimately backfired. However, resistance to protecting labor rights began fading; for instance, in 1937 the Supreme Court upheld minimum wage laws in Washington state. Meanwhile, Frances Perkins, a sociologist and Roosevelt's long-serving secretary of labor, developed legislation supporting minimum wages, limiting work hours, and abolishing child labor, which would survive constitutional objections. Congress passed the Public Contracts Act of 1936, which applied only to government contractors and required 8-hour work days, 40-hour work weeks, payment of "prevailing minimum" wages, and permitted employment of boys and girls only 16 and 18 years of age or older, respectively.[13]

Over the next two years, Roosevelt, Perkins, and others negotiated intensively with diverse stakeholders to devise legislation protecting workers that could pass not only constitutional concerns but also staunch opposition from legislators from southern states, where employees often worked long hours at rock-bottom wages. Southern Democrats held leadership positions in Congress and wielded power aggressively to constrain New Deal initiatives. Some labor unions also opposed these efforts, worried that federal minimum wages and work-hour regulations would reduce unions' ability to attract members and negotiate with management. Representing a compromise, the Fair Labor Standards Act of 1938 (FLSA) set a 25-cents-per-hour minimum wage and a maximum workweek of 44 hours and prohibited child labor. However, the 1938 FLSA covered only one-fifth of workers nationwide, excluding domestic labor such as PAS.[14]

Domestic Workers and Federal Labor Standards Act Protections

To draft constitutionally sustainable labor protections, Roosevelt, Perkins, and their allies relied on federal authority to regulate interstate commerce. Initial FLSA labor protections therefore applied only to industries or manufacturers that shipped products or transacted business across state lines. Local industries or businesses that produced products for in-state consumption, service workplaces, and labor in private homes are not interstate commerce and thus fell beyond federal reach.[15]

Southern legislators vociferously opposed extending FLSA protections, seeking to keep wages low and work-hour restrictions lax. With agriculture and in-home domestic service depending on Black laborers, racism stiffened resistance to FLSA expansion. In Congress, powerful southern Democrats

> sought to leave out as many African Americans as they could. They achieved this not by inscribing race into law but by writing provisions that . . . were racially laden. The most important instances concerned categories of work in which blacks were heavily overrepresented, notably farmworkers and maids. These groups—constituting more than 60 percent of the black labor force in the 1930s and nearly 75 percent of those who were employed in the South—were excluded from the legislation that created modern unions, from laws that set minimum wages and regulated the hours of work, and from Social Security until the 1950s.[16]

A newspaper owned by a Black publisher criticized the 1938 FLSA for excluding from minimum wage protections the Black women who spent long hours earning only $4.50 per week in Warm Springs, Georgia, at the resort Roosevelt frequented to treat his polio.[17] By excluding agricultural and domestic workers, the 1938 FLSA covered about 20% of laborers nationwide, but only 14% of female workers, and almost no Black male or female workers.[18]

The phrase "domestic workers" encompasses heterogeneous occupations, which have evolved over time but generally include maids, housekeepers, cooks, babysitters, nannies, home health aides, personal care aides, companions, caretakers, handymen, gardeners, and family chauffeurs, who perform duties in or around private homes.[19] To delineate domestic workers, the U.S. Department of Labor considers private homes to include separate dwellings, apartments, condominiums, and hotels (including travel lodgings), but importantly not nursing homes or residential care facilities.[20]

The domestic workers who started mobilizing in the 1920s and 1930s, sometimes championed by Eleanor Roosevelt, were primarily servants working 60 to 80 hours per week and seeking better working conditions.[21] World War II brought new industrial job opportunities especially for White women, who happily left domestic service for more regular hours, greater independence, and higher wages. By 1970, only 5% of women workers performed domestic jobs; the vast majority of them were women of color.

In the 1960s and early 1970s, the civil rights and women's-rights movements coalesced around domestic labor. By 1971, the Household Technicians of America included dozens of local organizations made up largely of poor Black women, some immersed in the civil rights movement. They organized to protest conditions of domestic work, in which employers had overwhelming power, abuse was common, and mistreatment generally took place behind closed doors.[22] Before a 1972 national convention of domestic workers, Shirley Chisholm, the first Black woman in Congress and daughter of a domestic worker, urged action. "Organize and work together with the women's groups and labor and civil rights groups in your community," Chisholm exhorted. "Hold meetings and rallies. Talk to the local press. Let everyone know you are first-class citizens and that you will not settle for anything less than a fair and equal chance to share in the fruits of this country."[23]

Exempting Companionship Services

In 1974 Congress amended FLSA, increasing the minimum wage and expanding the categories of protected workers, finally including domestic workers with one exception—people providing so-called companionship services. The amended law stated that minimum wage requirements would not apply to workers who "provide companionship services for individuals who (because of age or infirmity) are unable to care for themselves."[24] The law viewed PAs as companions.

The legislative history of the companionship exemption exudes romanticized notions among some lawmakers about paid PAS. They envisioned low- and middle-income older people paying workers to provide social supports within their homes—workers they might need to fire if required to pay minimum wages. A congressional minority report decried the "sorry state of affairs when the Government forces such lifelong loyal employees and friends from households in their senior years."[25] Legislators also assumed that people providing these services to older individuals were casual workers and "not regular breadwinners or responsible for their families' support."[26] In their deliberations, legislators specified that the companionship exemption should not apply to workers who provide substantial personal care, medically related services, or housekeeping services. However, in 1975, when writing regulations to implement the 1974 FLSA amendments,

> Department of Labor . . . policymakers interpreted the companionship exemption broadly to include almost all workers who provided not only social support but also personal care and household services to the elderly and disabled. That is, they effectively excluded home health care and personal care aides, some of whom were paid by private individuals but many of whom were paid by government programs like Medicare and Medicaid. The Department of Labor also extended the exemption to include workers who were employed by third parties like homecare agencies, workers who had already been included in wage and hour protections before the passage of the 1974 amendment. . . . These regulatory interpretations thus led to the exclusion of hundreds of thousands of domestic workers from basic wage and hour protections.[27]

The companionship exemption catalyzed home care workers to organize and contest the restrictions. In the 1980s, the Service Employees International Union (SEIU) began recruiting home care workers, including many who were paid by Medicaid, reasoning they would have a strong collective bargaining position. Workers also formed Domestic Workers United in New York and other state-based organizations, striving to gain wage and work-hour protections, antidiscrimination provisions, employee benefit packages, and other worker rights at the state level. Publicity campaigns told individual workers' stories, highlighting the deep affection some workers had for their clients, the ways paid PAS empowered these clients, the moral value and societal worth of the work, and the practical benefit of supporting many thousands of workers participating productively in the U.S. workforce. These organizations achieved wins in New York, California, Hawaii, and other states.

Nevertheless, despite some state victories, the federal companionship exemption for PAS workers remained. In its next-to-last day in office in January 2001, the Bill Clinton administration proposed rules to give home care workers wage and work-hour protections. But the incoming George W. Bush administration jettisoned the proposal, arguing it would be too costly.

———————

In April 2002 Evelyn Coke sued her former employer, Long Island Care at Home, arguing that it had not paid her the minimum wage and overtime pay required by New York state law and FLSA.[28] Coke's lawsuit questioned whether Congress had truly intended to exempt home care agency workers and whether the U.S. Department of Labor had correctly interpreted the law in specifying the companionship exemption. The district court rejected her case, but the Second Circuit Court overturned its ruling, finding that the Department of Labor's home care agency regulations were unenforceable.

Coke's case (*Long Island Care at Home, Ltd. v. Coke*) rose to the U.S. Supreme Court, with oral arguments in April 2007. In court, Long Island Care at Home asserted that being required to pay overtime would impose "tremendous and unsustainable losses." In a friend-of-the-court brief, New York City estimated that paying overtime to home care workers could increase its Medicaid costs by $250 million annually, threatening that massive service cuts could follow.[29]

On June 11, 2007, the U.S. Supreme Court ruled unanimously against Coke. Addressing the narrow question of whether the Department of Labor had absolute authority to issue the 1974 FLSA regulations exempting home care workers, all nine justices found that it did. "I feel robbed," said Coke after the ruling. "People are supposed to get paid when they work."[30] Coke died in 2009, before the full consequences of her lawsuit were realized.

Ending the Companionship Services Exemption

The unanimous 2007 Supreme Court ruling against Coke galvanized home care worker advocates to pressure Congress to enact labor protections for this essential workforce. In August 2007, SEIU organized a home care visit for presidential candidate Barack Obama to show him firsthand what home care workers do.[31] Obama spent from 6:00 A.M. to 9:00 A.M. in Oakland, California, shadowing 61-year-old home health care worker Pauline Beck, as she assisted an 86-year-old man receiving round-the-clock home care. Beck instructed Obama in lifting, bathing, and dressing her client and helping with food preparation. During their encounter, Obama learned details about Beck's life: she worked two jobs to make ends meet, had no sick leave or vacation time, cared for several foster children, and relied on food banks. Obama announced that he would end the FLSA home care worker exemption if he became president.

In 2011 President Obama asked the U.S. Department of Labor to end the 1974 FLSA exclusion of home care workers from wage and work-hour protections, and the Department began a lengthy rulemaking process. During the public comment period, numerous individuals and groups weighed in. Comments largely supported the regulatory change, asserting that protecting wages and work hours would improve home care jobs, reduce staff turnover, and thus enhance home care quality. Some advocates invoked broad moral and social imperatives for home care, underscoring the interdependence of workers and consumers.

Important consumer groups supported the FLSA change, but others did not, raising thorny questions about access to services. Occasional heated exchanges erupted and even civil disobedience (e.g., people with disability blockaded Department of Labor offices). At a 2013 Department of Labor listening session, Bruce Darling from ADAPT (Americans Disabled for Attendant Programs Today), a prominent disability rights organization, argued that "Increasing the cost of home and community based services by requiring overtime pay, without increasing the Medicaid rates or raising the Medicaid caps for available funding, will result in a reduction in hours of personal assistance, forcing some people with disabilities into unwanted institutionalization."[32] Darling and some other disability rights advocates tied proposed FLSA regulatory changes directly to *Olmstead*, the 1999 landmark U.S. Supreme Court decision (see Chapter 2):

> [*Olmstead*] should be interpreted as prohibiting government agencies from setting policies that would increase institutionalization of people with disabilities, defining the undue institutionalization of people with disabilities to be a form of unlawful discrimination. That is, the Department of Labor was legally bound to consider the argument of disability advocates that including homecare workers in minimum wage and overtime protections may increase rates of institutionalization.[33]

Other disability advocacy organizations, however, supported the regulatory change—citing fairness, equality, and interdependence of workers and clients—and provided powerful counterpoints to ADAPT and like-minded groups. Data favored their arguments: people with disability did not have higher institutionalization rates in states that had already implemented wage and work-hour reforms for home care workers.

On October 1, 2013, the U.S. Department of Labor issued its final rule eliminating the home care worker companionship exemption. Acknowledging the complexities of implementing the change, the department set January 1, 2015, as the effective start date. Under the modified definition, "companionship" (i.e., services exempt from FLSA protections) "means the provision of fellowship and protection for an elderly person or a person with an illness, injury, or disability who requires assistance in caring for himself or herself." The phrase "companionship services" includes "the provision of care, when the care is provided attendant to and in conjunction with the provision of fellowship and protection, and does not exceed 20 percent of the total hours worked per consumer and per workweek."[34] The nature of home care workers' duties, who provide ADL and IADL supports, therefore falls outside this narrowed definition of companionship services.

The new rule faced legal challenges. An association of home care agencies filed suit in federal court in June 2014 to block the January 1, 2015, start date. U.S. district courts issued opinions in December 2014 and January 2015, respectively, vacating the new regulations. In *Home Care Association of America v. Weil,* the U.S. Department of Labor appealed the decisions to the U.S. Court of Appeals, District of Columbia Circuit. On August 21, 2015, the Court of Appeals unanimously ruled in support of the Department of Labor, reversing the district court judgments. The Home Care Association of America filed an appeal to the U.S. Supreme Court, which, on June 27, 2016, declined to hear the case. At last, the lengthy, convoluted labyrinth of court cases initiated by Evelyn Coke was over.

With this 2016 Supreme Court action, FLSA wage and work-hour protections for home care workers, including PAs, could finally take effect. Some states moved in that direction; for example, California, Massachusetts, and several other states strove to increase workers' wages to fair levels.[35] Other states, however, began capping the workweeks of home care workers to 35 or fewer hours, thus preventing them from getting time-and-a-half overtime pay and limiting their potential income. The work-hour restrictions raised concerns about reducing PAS quality for consumers.[36] Despite the Supreme Court victory, ensuring living wages and preferred work hours for PAs remains unfinished business.

Labor Unions and Personal Assistance Services

Labor unions played important advocacy roles for paid PAS workers trying to eliminate FLSA companionship exemptions. In recent years, however, some home care workers have resisted unions, especially requirements to pay union dues. Pamela J. Harris and eight other personal care assistants providing home care under the Illinois Department of Human Services program for people with disability filed suit against Governor Patrick J. Quinn. The PAs argued that being required to pay "fair share" payments to SEIU violated their rights under the First Amendment (freedom of speech) and Fourteenth Amendment (freedom of association). Their case rose to the U.S. Supreme Court. In the 5–4 *Harris v. Quinn* decision issued in June 2014, Justice Samuel A. Alito wrote for the conservative majority, declaring that requiring home care workers to pay SEIU dues violated their First Amendment rights.[37]

Another 5–4 decision, the 2018 ruling in *Janus v. American Federation of State, County, and Municipal Employees, Council 31*, extended First Amendment protections to all public-sector employees who decline to pay union dues. The unions had engaged in collective bargaining, for home care workers as well as others. How these two decisions might eventually affect the wages of PAS workers is still unclear. Anecdotal reports suggest that the *Harris v. Quinn* decision motivated greater grassroots efforts by unions to prove their value to home care workers.

Implications of Nurse Practice Acts
for Personal Assistance Services

States regulate nursing services through nurse practice acts (NPAs), which vary across states. NPAs delineate services that must be provided either by or under the direct supervision of licensed nurses. Some consumers require services, such as tube feeding (as for Michael; see Dedication) or urinary catheterization, which state NPA regulations stipulate must be done or supervised by licensed nurses. Agency PAs, who are not licensed nurses, cannot perform these tasks. NPAs thus threaten the ability of some consumers to live in the community. In states with restrictive NPA provisions, people "with skilled nursing needs are often admitted to nursing homes because it is impractical and prohibitively expensive to send licensed nurses to their homes to administer medications and perform other tasks that must be done daily or multiple times daily."[38] Under a self-directed PAS (see Chapter 8), which falls outside NPA jurisdiction, consumers can instruct PAs to perform these tasks.

Nurse delegation requirements vary across states:

> Generally speaking, a skilled task that can be delegated needs to be highly routinized and its outcome must be highly predictable, especially insofar as the task can be safely performed without life threatening consequences. NPAs typically require the nurse to document the teaching provided, to observe the satisfactory performance by the [unlicensed worker] of the tasks taught, and to provide written instructions for the [worker].[39]

States also vary in what constitutes subsequent nurse supervision. Some states require periodic, onsite supervision by nurses, other states allow monitoring by telephone, and a few states require only that nurses be available for follow-up as needed. Different tasks require different oversight. Throughout supervision, nurses are accountable for the nursing care under their oversight. If the supervisory nurse becomes unavailable, that nurse must formally transfer oversight responsibility to another licensed nurse.

Even when NPAs give nurses broad authority to delegate a skilled task, concerns about civil or professional liability erect substantial barriers to nurse delegation. Nurses can fear legal consequences if complications occur involving an unlicensed worker they trained and supervised. Oregon and Washington state mitigate this fear by explicitly absolving nurses from professional liability (e.g., loss of their nursing license) if they comply with clearly defined delegation procedures.[40]

NPAs generally exempt family caregivers—and domestic employees in the home—who routinely perform skilled nursing tasks. Under these exemptions, the family member who performs the tasks can also train other family members or workers to do those tasks. In these situations, licensed nurses do not need to provide ongoing supervision—nor would nurses who initially trained a family member be responsible for subsequent mistakes in performing the task. Some states have used NPA exemptions to support self-direction of paid, home-based PAS. However, narrowly crafted exemption provisions can be confusing. For example, New York state exempted its consumer self-directed program but not its PCA program.[41]

A 2001 review of NPAs in all 50 states examined delegation and exemption provisions, particularly measures that affect consumer self-directed care. At that time, nine states—Connecticut, Florida, Kansas, Nebraska, New York, New Mexico, South Dakota, Texas, and Vermont—had specific consumer self-direction exemptions, although each took a different approach. The 50-state review concluded that

> most states have broad enough language to support delegation, if not exemption. However, even in those states like Oregon that have a decade of experience in permitting delegation, nurses continue to be confused about what can and cannot be delegated. As one board of nursing executive director described the situation, nurses continually call her office to ask the proverbial question, "Mother, may I?" . . . In addition, the acute care focus of most board members, and pressure from nurse unions who generally represent the concerns of nurses practicing in hospitals, reinforce the drive for detailed lists of what can and cannot be delegated, rather than broad guidelines that offer

the kind of flexibility needed for home and community-based care, particularly consumer direction.[42]

State nursing boards are established to protect public health rather than to further goals of consumer self-direction. Efforts to support consumer self-direction should ideally bring together relevant stakeholders "to discuss . . . policy options to balance consumer protection and independence, internal consistency in state practice regulations, [and] consistency across state departments."[43]

Significant changes have occurred in recent years, although variations by state remain. A 2017 report found that 16 states allow registered nurses (RNs) to delegate 16 tasks, from a sample set of tasks, to aides.[44] However, failure to expand delegation has wide-ranging consequences. "When states restrict RNs from delegating tasks to aides, it can result in more expensive care and increased family caregiver stress, especially for employed family caregivers, who may have to leave work to perform these routine tasks."[45] As efforts grow to include PAS workers in health-related tasks—or as members of interprofessional care teams—addressing the issues raised by NPAs is critical (see Chapter 14).

Immigration Laws and Personal Assistance Services

Documented and undocumented immigrants provide substantial in-home paid PAS, filling critical gaps in the PAS workforce. In 2017 immigrants accounted for approximately 16% of the U.S. population: naturalized citizens comprised 7% of the U.S. population; legal, noncitizen immigrants, 5%; and unauthorized immigrants, 4%.[46] Comprehensively reviewing U.S. immigration policy, which is complex and evolving, is beyond this book's scope. Briefly, immigrant direct care workers typically enter the United States through family reunification policies, refugee status, a green-card lottery, or without authorization.[47] Changes in these policies or immigration channels could affect availability of immigrant workers for home-based PAS jobs. Political debates about immigration have chilling effects not only on future but also current nonnative LTSS workers. This uncertain environment is likely to become a significant barrier to recruitment just at the time when many organizations are experiencing serious worker shortages.[48]

Immigrants contribute disproportionately to the home-based care workforce. In 2017 8% of native-born Americans worked for home care agencies, and 5% worked in the "nonformal sector" (i.e., in households under consumer self-direction or in non-medical residential settings).[49] In contrast, 13% and 7% of all immigrants worked, respectively, for home health agencies or in the nonformal sector. Among unauthorized immigrants, 15% worked for home health agencies, and 8% worked in the nonformal sector. While naturalized citizens accounted for 7% of the U.S. population, they comprised 16% of home health agency workers. More than 214,000 immigrants provided care in nonformal settings, accounting for 26% of that workforce.[50] Policies "curtailing immigration will almost certainly move us in the wrong direction, worsening the shortage and the availability of high-quality care for elderly and disabled Americans."[51]

PHI studied immigrant experiences among direct care workers, which includes not only PAs but also home health aides and nursing assistants. They found that, in 2015, roughly 1 million immigrants worked in direct care in the United States, and one in four direct care workers was an immigrant.[52] Immigrants were especially prominent in the direct care workforces of California (48%), Florida (40%), Hawaii (45%), New Jersey (47%), and New York (56%)—states with large immigrant populations. Mexico, the Philippines, and Jamaica were the most common countries of origin; Spanish was the most common primary language. Immigrant direct care workers were older, with an average age of 48 years, and they were more likely than native-born workers to have higher educational degrees.[53] U.S. licensure and qualifying professional boards typically do not recognize academic degrees obtained abroad (even medical and nursing degrees), resulting in highly educated immigrants sometimes taking low-wage PAS jobs.[54]

PHI also compared the socioeconomic status of immigrant with that of native-born direct care workers in 2015.[55] Immigrants generally did marginally better than native-born direct care workers, but all fell within the confines of low-wage work, as follows:

- 44% of immigrant direct care workers earned at or below 200% of the federal poverty level (FPL), as compared with 49% of native-born workers
- 26% of immigrant direct care workers earned at or below 138% of the FPL (the income level at which individuals qualify for Medicaid in states that have expanded Medicaid coverage under the Affordable Care Act; see Chapter 3), as compared with 31% of native-born workers
- 15% of immigrant direct care workers earned at or below 100% of the FPL, as compared with 20% of native-born workers
- 40% of immigrant direct care workers used public benefits, with 22% obtaining nutrition assistance and 24% receiving Medicaid; in comparison, 44% of native-born workers accessed public benefits

Depending on prevailing policy, using public benefits could pose downstream problems for immigrants. In January 2018, the Donald J. Trump administration proposed rules intended to erect barriers to immigrants seeking public assistance, including for benefits to which they are legally entitled. Under the Immigration and Nationalization Act, the Trump administration policy required immigrants (except for refugees, asylum seekers, people granted asylum, and certain other classes with specific protections) who sought a visa to enter the United States to demonstrate that they were unlikely to become a "public charge" (i.e., depend on public benefits).[56] Once living in the United States, most immigrants would again have needed to prove they are not public charges when they tried to change their status, such as seeking a green card. If immigrants avoid nutrition assistance, Medicaid, and the Children's Health Insurance Program for their children "for fear of becoming a public charge, they are likely to be uninsured, and unable to receive necessary care. That is likely to affect their ability to stay healthy and be productive workers."[57] In March 2021, the Joseph R. Biden administration announced it would not support this policy, stating that the "public charge rule was not in keeping with our nation's values."[58] However, immigration policy in general remains a highly fraught political issue.

Hiring PAS workers from abroad to reduce the widening workforce gap has important attractions. Nevertheless, such a strategy also merits caution in light of the risks to immigrant workers:

> Perhaps [the] most important [challenge] is the potential for financial, emotional, and even physical exploitation of workers; because most foreign-born workers are not hired through managed migration schemes, they are paid very low wages, often receive little to no benefits, and have no social protections. For those hired privately, typically there are no job guarantees and little job stability. Given the lack of any formal agreements, there is no oversight infrastructure ensuring the workers are not financially, physically, or emotionally exploited by consumers and family members.[59]

Other considerations include potential communication barriers from language differences between immigrant workers and PAS consumers. In paid PAS, communication failures can pose significant risks both to consumers and PAs (see Part IV). Lack of cultural concordance between paid PAs and consumers could affect views on performing certain tasks, including ADLs (e.g., feeding). Cultural differences in perceptions of disability and aging could also complicate relationships between consumers and immigrant PAs. Nevertheless, immigrants like Evelyn Coke are the backbone of the PAS workforce in many U.S. communities.

II

Introduction to PAS Consumers and PAS

Part II introduces the consumers receiving paid PAS, the home-based supports that they need, and the PAs providing these services. Chapter 5 describes consumers' underlying disabling conditions and the types of ADL and other supports they need to live in their homes and communities. Some tasks go beyond standard ADL supports and cross into health-related activities, which fall under the jurisdiction of skilled nurses in some states. Chapter 6 describes the people providing paid PAS and what motivates them to perform these low-wage, often demanding jobs. These chapters raise an undercurrent that winds throughout the rest of the book—questions about whether and how much the incentives and perspectives of paid PAS consumers and PAs align or diverge.

5

Consumers of Personal Assistance Services

I n his early forties, Michael was diagnosed with primary progressive multiple sclerosis—a relatively uncommon form of multiple sclerosis in which impairments continually worsen, without remission. Within seven years, he needed a power wheelchair. Michael adapted his home, striving to continue doing his ADLs by himself. He moved his bedroom from the second to the first floor and made the nearby bathroom fully accessible. In his bedroom and bathroom, he installed battery-powered, ceiling-mounted lifts to transfer between his wheelchair and his bed, toilet, or shower chair. Initially, Michael could operate the lifts himself. But his functional impairments kept worsening and, finally, Michael faced a tipping point—he needed human assistance:

> I had increasing difficulty doing very basic stuff, like washing and toileting by myself. The tipping point was that it was both taking so much energy from me that it was no longer really possible to do, and also it was clear that it could be dangerous. So, it wasn't a specific event, for instance, like having a fall. But it was pretty clear I was getting too close to that point for comfort.

Michael was married at the time with two young daughters, but his family could not provide his ADL supports. A physicist, he still led scientific projects and needed to get to work each morning. He therefore hired his first PA—a woman recommended by a neighbor with disability who also used PAS. The PA spent two hours with Michael every morning, assisting with toileting, showering, and dressing. Each evening, by operating his lift, Michael could put himself to bed independently over the next year, until another tipping point occurred. With worsening functioning, Michael needed increasing PAS support, not only in the morning but also at night—and then, several years later, throughout most of the day.

———

No one chooses to have a disability. Nonetheless, disability is "a continuum, relevant to the lives of all people to different degrees and at different times in their lives," a virtually universal and an "(indeed natural) feature of the human condition."[1] In the United States, "disability affects today or will affect tomorrow the lives of most Americans."[2] Anyone can become disabled in a flash, with a grievous injury or a catastrophic health event. Disability has many formal definitions that depend on the context. For example, the Americans with Disabilities Act defines persons who qualify for federal civil rights protections (Box 2.4). The World Health Organization's *International Classification of Functioning, Disability and Health*[3] uses a broad, multidimensional definition (Box 5.1). Various factors—ranging from underlying health conditions to their social and physical environments—have important implications for determining consumers' PAS needs. To describe ADL support needs, Chapter 5 relies on the perspectives of consumer interviewees, especially the four people listed in Box 5.2.

Box 5.1 Definition of Disability

World Health Organization

Disability is an "umbrella term for impairments, activity limitations or participation restrictions,"[1] conceiving "a person's functioning and disability . . . as a dynamic interaction between health conditions . . . and contextual factors,"[2] including the physical, social, and larger societal environments and individuals' personal attributes.

[1] World Health Organization. *International Classification of Functioning, Disability and Health.* World Health Organization; 2001:3.
[2] Ibid., 8.

Box 5.2 Consumers Quoted Frequently in Chapter 5

- **Ernie**, early fifties, White, quadriplegia from spinal muscular atrophy
- **Matt**, mid-fifties, White, quadriplegia, spinal cord injury 30 years earlier
- **Michael**, early sixties, White, quadriplegia from primary progressive multiple sclerosis
- **Natalie**, early fifties, White, quadriplegia from spinal muscular atrophy

Patterns of Disability, Underlying Conditions, and ADL Support Needs

Disabilities are diverse. Some disabling conditions are congenital and are life-long. Others occur suddenly with injury or illness and may resolve over time or become permanent. Yet other functional impairments progress gradually, sometimes with sporadic exacerbations, over years. Some conditions have constant functional limitations across time, such as congenital blindness or deafness, and may not require medical intervention or ADL support. In contrast, other congenital conditions, such as some developmental disabilities, require extensive ADL supports with functional difficulties that can progress over time. Yet other disabilities result from chronic health conditions, such as arthritis—the most common disabling condition among U.S. adults, affecting approximately 24 million Americans[4]—as well as diabetes, heart failure, serious mental illness, dementia, and numerous other diseases. ADL support needs for people with chronic conditions may fluctuate over time, with periodic disease flare-ups, or may increase over time with progressive functional declines. Sometimes certain treatments, such as knee and hip replacements for people with debilitating arthritis, can largely restore functional abilities—at least for some time.

People with disability risk developing other conditions related to their disability—so-called secondary disabilities. They include urinary tract, bladder, and bowel problems, injuries (e.g., from falls), pressure injuries (i.e., pressure ulcers or sores), mental health concerns, fatigue, substantial weight gain, and pain. Rates of obesity and extreme obesity are much higher among U.S. adults with disability (42% and 9%, respectively) than among people without disability (29% and 4%, respectively).[5] Obesity itself can cause significant mobility disability.[6] Furthermore, U.S. adults with disability have higher rates of diabetes, hypertension, high cholesterol, cardiovascular disease, and asthma than people without disability.[7] People with disability also have higher rates of health risk factors, including tobacco use and lack of exercise.[8] Among U.S. adults without disability, 30% report excellent health, in comparison with 6% of people with physical disability; also, only 0.5% of adults without disability report poor health, as compared with 15% among individuals with physical disability.[9]

Focusing on physical disability, ADL support needs over time fall into four common patterns that relate to the cause:

- **Congenital conditions** that can require ADL supports from birth, which include cerebral palsy, spina bifida, some muscular dystrophies, spinal muscular atrophy, osteogenesis imperfecta, and genetic neurodegenerative conditions; functional impairments can range from mild to severe and worsen over time

- **Sudden, catastrophic conditions** that cause long-term impairment and require immediate ADL support, including spinal cord injury, other major trauma, transverse myelitis, and severe stroke; the extent and nature of functional impairments from these causes vary widely
- **Progressive chronic conditions** that at some point may require people to need ADL support; these conditions include arthritis, spinal or back problems, other musculoskeletal disorders, obesity, diabetes, heart failure, chronic obstructive pulmonary disease and emphysema, neurodegenerative diseases (e.g., Parkinson's disease, amyotrophic lateral sclerosis or Lou Gehrig's disease)
- **Fluctuating or relapsing-remitting functional limitations** that can necessitate periodic ADL support over time, such as relapsing-remitting multiple sclerosis, rheumatoid arthritis, and systemic lupus erythematosus; these conditions may become progressive, without periods of recovery

Different patterns and causes of disability have important practical implications for ADL support needs across the lifespan. For instance, for people with congenital or early onset disability, their most likely informal caregivers are parents, who may themselves become disabled in later life.[10] With aging parents or family caregivers, organizing PAS support for now-adult children with congenital conditions can pose significant challenges.

People with progressive chronic health conditions who have relied on informal caregivers might find that, at some point, these family members or friends can no longer fully support their ADL needs. Many people do not have adequate financial resources to afford additional paid PAS. People with fluctuating functional impairments might have problems obtaining ADL supports during exacerbations. Family members employed outside the home can seek time off to help under the federal Family and Medical Leave Act of 1993,[11] but without pay.

Sociodemographic Characteristics of People with Disability

In 2018 26% of noninstitutionalized Americans 18 years old and older had some type of disability.[12] Among adult Americans, almost 4%—or about 9.5 million people—had a self-care disability[13] and thus might require support from either informal caregivers or paid PAS. Table 5.1 shows rates of

TABLE 5.1 DISABILITY STATUS BY AGE, GENDER, RACE, AND ETHNICITY: NONINSTITUTIONALIZED U.S. RESIDENTS AGES 18 YEARS AND OLDER

Characteristic	No disability	Any disability	Mobility disability	Vision disability	Hearing disability	Cognitive disability	Self-care disability
			Disability type[a]				
		Age-adjusted percentage (%)					
All	74.0	26.0	12.4	5.0	5.9	11.5	3.5
Age							
18–44 years	81.5	18.5	4.6	3.3	2.3	11.8	1.8
45–64 years	70.8	29.2	17.8	6.4	6.6	11.9	5.5
65+ years	56.2	43.8	27.3	7.9	16.2	10.2	5.6
Gender							
Male	75.3	24.7	10.8	4.6	7.5	10.3	3.5
Female	72.8	27.2	13.9	5.4	4.5	12.7	3.6
Race and ethnicity							
White, non-Hispanic	75.6	24.4	11.2	3.8	6.0	11.1	2.9
Black, non-Hispanic	69.8	30.2	17.3	7.0	4.8	13.6	5.7
Asian	83.6	16.4	6.6	3.6	3.9	6.2	1.6
Native Hawaiian or other Pacific Islander	74.6	25.4	12.4	5.5	6.5	11.2	—
American Indian or Alaskan Native	60.1	39.9	21.9	10.0	11.4	19.4	7.6
Other/multiracial	64.2	35.8	17.3	7.8	8.5	17.4	5.4
Hispanic	68.7	31.3	15.5	8.6	6.0	13.3	5.1

Source: National Center on Birth Defects and Developmental Disabilities, Division of Human Development and Disability, Centers for Disease Control and Prevention. 2018 behavioral risk factor surveillance system survey, Disability and Health Data System (DHDS) Data. Accessed August 19, 2020. https://dhds.cdc.gov
[a] Some persons have more than one specific type of disability.

various types of disability in 2018 by age, gender, race, and ethnicity. Disability rates generally rose as age increased; however, self-care disability remained just below 6% for people 45 to 64 years old and those 65 years old and older. Women and men had similar self-care disability rates, but rates of this disability varied across racial and ethnic groups. Self-care disability prevalence was highest among American Indian or Alaskan Native populations (8%) and Black Americans (6%) and lowest among White (3%) and Asian (2%) Americans. The reported rates came from surveys in which participants reported their disability status. Cultural or personal factors could affect participants' willingness to report disability on these surveys.

No good statistics exist about the characteristics of relatives or friends who might be available to provide PAS to people with self-care disability. Table 3.1 shows the disability status of U.S. adults by marital status. Among adults without disability, 58% have a spouse or partner, as compared with 40% of people with self-care disability. Having a spouse or partner, however, does not guarantee informal ADL support. For example, one interviewee had progressive disability that worsened, and he needed ADL support. "My then-wife absolutely did not want to do any of my personal care, simple as that," he recalled. "Basically, she didn't want the burden." He sought paid PAS, and the marriage ended shortly afterward.

For people with congenital or early-life disabling conditions, parents generally provide PAS supports. This can affect the decisions usually made when transitioning from child to young adult, such as whether and when to leave the parental home for college, a job, or other pursuits. Family and friends provided ADL supports to Ernie, who has spinal muscular atrophy (SMA), until the day he left for college. Ernie's parents supported his desire to attend college wherever he wanted, even if that meant finding new ADL supports. "I had one way of living for 18 years and 3 days," said Ernie. Once in college, he transitioned to the new way, with paid PAS.

Not all parents provide loving support to their children with congenital disability. Unlike Erie, Natalie, who also has SMA, received little notice from her largely "absentee father" and mother, who had serious mental illness. Natalie described being "very neglected at home. I didn't get to pee when I needed to. I didn't get bathed very often." In her mid-teens, after being hospitalized for pneumonia, she went into a nursing home, where "everybody was waiting for me to die." Natalie spent more than a year there and then engineered her escape. Through a complicated chain of events, she landed in an apartment with a disabled friend. From that point onward, Natalie hired her own PAs, even though she was only in her teens. Natalie remembers being "terrified. I had no idea what I was doing. I was a terrible attendant manager."

Today, Natalie believes that her mother's neglect "taught me and my siblings how to be fiercely independent. It's like a blessing and curse."

Tasks Performed by PAs

Consumer interviewees described PAs assisting them with basic activities, such as:

- Getting in and out of bed, sometimes using an assistive transfer device, such as a Hoyer or other lift device
- Bladder and bowel management, including using urinary catheters and rectal suppositories, emptying leg bags or drainage bags from a suprapubic tube that drains the urinary bladder, and handling urinary and fecal incontinence
- Showering, always using a shower chair and sometimes a lift device (e.g., for his morning shower, Michael needs two PAs to safely transfer him using his ceiling-mounted lift); or, if shower facilities are unavailable or inaccessible, sponge or bed baths
- After showering, thoroughly drying and inspecting skin (e.g., for redness, scrapes, or areas suggesting injury or infection)
- Dressing, following consumers' preferences but sometime negotiated with PAs (e.g., some people use disposable paper underwear or other absorbent products because of urinary incontinence)
- Feeding, primarily orally but sometimes via a tube implanted directly into the stomach (e.g., in the Dedication photograph, Nelita is giving Michael his evening tube feed)
- Positioning in wheelchairs, sometimes using a Hoyer or other lifting device
- Other mobility assistance (e.g., pushing a manual wheelchair)

Interviewees also generally required support with IADLs, including cooking, laundry, light housework, and grocery shopping.

Interviewees typically described routine assistance with only one or two ADLs. Natalie, however, has more complex needs. In her early fifties, she lives with her long-time partner, Gary, in their own house, working from home in disability rights advocacy. Natalie and Gary never married because their joint income would exceed Medicaid's income threshold, making Natalie ineligible for Medicaid and its PAS program. Gary does not routinely assist Natalie with her ADLs because it would take too much time, and he could risk losing his job. They need Gary's income to supplement the Medicaid

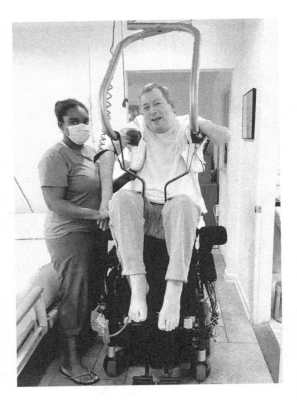

After his shower, Michael in his automated lift device outside his bathroom, assisted by one of two morning PAs on October 21, 2020. She and the other PA are about to finish dressing him and settling him into his power wheelchair for the day. (Photo credit: Pat Gilleo)

wages of Natalie's PAs with extra payments that allow Natalie to attract qualified PAs and cover more PAS hours than Medicaid allows.

Natalie's only remaining limb function is limited use of one hand. She can cook a little—if someone serves as sous-chef—and generally feeds herself. But performing even these tasks is arduous, and she needs support with all other ADLs. Natalie currently has eight PAs working 14 hours per day under her direction. Weighing only 60 pounds, she has severe osteoporosis and has broken bones during transfers. She therefore prefers having a PA lift her rather than using an assistive lift device. "I'm very fragile," Natalie admits. "It's been challenging to find workers, because not everybody's comfortable lifting a person. Sixty pounds is small, but it's still a lot." Natalie's typical day starts as follows:

> The alarm goes off at 7:25. The PA usually shows up at 7:30. . . . They make me tea. They do my stretches. They help me with bathing, dressing. The bathroom is not accessible, and I don't use it. . . . I do the bed pan every morning. I can do my own bowel care. I have a suprapubic

tube with a leg bag the PA empties once or twice each day. . . . I do bed baths. I haven't been able to get into a bathtub or shower since I was 21. I used to be carried into the bathtub, but that's just too dangerous. And I can't sit in a shower chair because of my scoliosis. . . . I have to lean over sideways and wash my hair in a bucket, with a plastic drape. I've been doing the bucket thing for so long, we have it down. It takes about five minutes to set up. My hair takes about 10 minutes to wash and condition; then it takes another 15 minutes to dry. I have long hair.

Because of her scoliosis and upper-body weakness, Natalie wears a body jacket when out of bed. After her morning bathing, Natalie's PA puts this body jacket on her—an orthotic brace with a rigid plastic outer shell, molded to her body, and interior padding. The body jacket covers her thoracic, lumbar, and sacral spine, providing external support; however, it exerts considerable pressure, making it hard for Natalie to breathe. At night while sleeping, Natalie breathes using a ventilator through a mask. But, during the day, when she is up in her wheelchair and wearing the body jacket, she breathes air through a mouthpiece attached to the ventilator. Her PA must periodically suction Natalie's secretions.

During the day, Natalie works from home. But she likes going out around her neighborhood, which is generally accessible to wheelchair users. Nowadays, however, previously minor barriers seem life-threatening.

I used to be able to go all around town. But now I'm fragile enough that, if I hit a bump on the sidewalk, my head falls over, or my respirator tube drops out of my mouth. I need to have someone there to help in those situations. Before if it happened, I was often able to just grab a person on the street—"Hey, would you help me pick this up?" But now it happens too often, and I feel too horrible. I used to ride public transit by myself, but I can't push the buttons on the elevators. I used to be fine asking strangers to do that. But now I know if I was stuck in the elevator, and I drop my respirator hose, and I have to wait for the next person to push the button, I might be in trouble.

Natalie no longer goes out alone.

Natalie's situation is complex, but she has been supported by other people her entire life. She knows what she is doing. "I feel like if something happened to me, unless one of my workers did something deliberately egregious, they're not responsible. I'm the one responsible for my care." She lives a full life, with Gary, many friends, and her disability advocacy work. Natalie would prefer more privacy—not having PAs around her small home 14 hours each day—but that's how it must be.

At night, Natalie and Gary make compromises. "It's very interesting to schedule your sex life around attendant schedules," Natalie laughed. "It's like having three-year-old kids around all the time." Although Gary can do PA tasks, "it doesn't feel right if he does the personal care for me to be ready for sex. . . . Most of it's pretty tedious—'Oh shit, the leg bag just spilled!'" Noting trade-offs, Natalie conceded, "It's nice to have attendants help, but my partner has to be patient and accepting." PAs eventually go home, leaving Natalie and Gary alone.

Support Tasks Beyond ADLs

Beyond basic ADL supports, some consumers reported needing assistance with more health-related needs, such as providing wound care, stoma care (e.g., for tracheostomies), ventilator management and suctioning secretions, medication administration, flushing urinary catheters, monitoring skin for signs of cellulitis and treating it accordingly, performing range-of-motion exercises, feeding through a percutaneous endoscopic gastrostomy (PEG) tube or G-tube, and monitoring vital signs. Agency PAs rarely perform these tasks because of states' NPA limitations on what they are allowed to do (see Chapter 4). Under self-directed PAS, consumers can instruct their PAs in performing these tasks and oversee their performance. The following sections describe several tasks beyond standard ADLs.

Medications

Consumers reported their PAs routinely organizing and administering prescription medications—although these activities varied by type of PAS, agency, and consumer self-direction. Requiring medications more often than once daily can pose problems. For example, Michael's state had changed its NPA regulations to allow trained PAs to give medications under nurse delegation. Although the change happened a year previously, Michael's managed care health plan, a Program of All-Inclusive Care for the Elderly (PACE; see Chapters 3 and 14), had not yet trained its PAs to provide medications; instead, PACE sent a home care nurse to Michael's house once daily to administer his prescription drugs. When Michael developed excruciating, all-consuming, neurogenic pain, his neurologist prescribed an oral antiseizure medication, which rapidly dissipated the pain for about 12 hours. He therefore needed this medication twice daily, but PACE would send the home care nurse only once daily, and they threatened to place him in a nursing home if he needed more frequent medication. Michael, a physicist, engineered a work-around.[14]

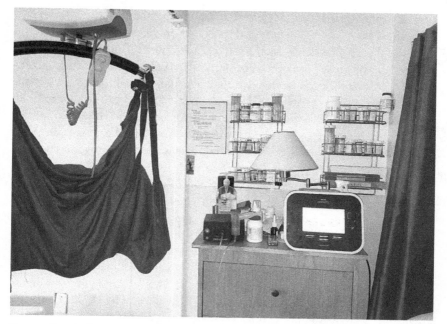

Two wall racks hold medications of a consumer who is quadriplegic from a spinal cord injury and later developed unrelated and complex medical problems, requiring many prescription drugs. His automated Hoyer lift hangs from the ceiling and framed, to the left of the medications, is a detailed list of emergency instructions, names of people to call, and telephone numbers. A device that noninvasively clears lung secretions—by gradually inflating the lungs with air and then rapidly reversing, drawing both air and secretions out of the airways—sits on the bedside table. (Photo credit: Unknown personal assistant)

He had a gooseneck tube clamped to his kitchen countertop; had a plastic straw affixed to its end; and the home care nurse fitted the second daily pain pill into the straw, peeking out enough that Michael could snare it with his teeth. Michael self-administered his evening pain medication from this countertop-gooseneck-straw device, and PACE permitted his PA to give him water after he snagged the pill.

Wound Care

People with severe mobility impairments risk developing pressure injuries, also known as pressure ulcers, decubitus ulcers, or bed sores. Some consumers described PAs checking their skin for early signs of pressure injuries during daily bathing or dressing routines. Once injuries occur, PAs can provide wound care, applying lotions, ointments, or dressings typically under direction of a home care nurse. Ernie and Michael reported pressure injuries failing to heal for more than a year and their PAs providing wound care.

Several years previously, Matt, who has quadriplegia from a spinal cord injury, had major surgery for a pressure injury in his ischial area. His surgeon estimated Matt's postoperative recovery would take many months, during which his managed care plan intended to place him in a nursing home. But Matt refused, arguing that nursing homes frequently experience rampant infectious outbreaks, such as with norovirus or *Clostridium difficile* (*C. diff.*, a bacterial infection). Norovirus and *C. diff.* cause severe diarrhea, which would be dangerous because of the location of Matt's wound, as well as physically miserable. Matt had had *C. diff.* once in a hospital and wanted to avoid repeating that calamity. "They're not going to know how to turn me," he argued further, raising the frequent repositioning required to offload pressure, allow wound healing, and prevent additional injury. "And they're not going to turn me enough."

The novel coronavirus pandemic underscored the dangers of nursing homes, as COVID-19 infections raged within many facilities, claiming both residents and staff. By November 6, 2020, long-term care facility residents and staff accounted for 6% of total U.S. COVID-19 cases but 39% of deaths.[15] Especially early in the pandemic, these facilities lacked adequate personal protective equipment and virus-testing capacity. Matt tells me that, during this time, he is more terrified of nursing homes than ever.

Matt took charge of his postoperative care. The acute care hospital discharged him directly to his apartment, and with training from his nurse practitioner, Matt's team of PAs performed all his postoperative care, including managing surgical drains, frequent repositioning, and physical therapy. During six months of recovery, Matt's PAs "were doing everything." Sometimes—but not always—he organized 24/7 PA coverage. In the best of circumstances, recovering fully from such surgery is uncertain. With intensive support from dedicated PAs, Matt finally returned to his power wheelchair and resumed active disability advocacy in person—rather than via videoconference.

Tube Feeding

Ernie and Michael received feedings through a G-tube or PEG tube—narrow, flexible tubes, generally made of silicone or polyurethane (durable materials resistant to damage from acidic gastric secretions), inserted through the upper abdominal wall directly into the stomach. PEG and G-tubes are placed using different procedural techniques, but both tubes function the same way. Specially prepared bags of nutrients, suited to the user's needs, are hung on a pole, and the feed flows by gravity or is propelled by a small, electronic pump clamped to the pole (see the photo in the Dedication). Feeds are not puréed standard food. Michael also receives his medications, dissolved in water, through his PEG tube. With a PEG or G-tube, people can still consume food or drink by mouth (e.g., Michael needs his morning coffee).

Providing tube feedings requires excellent hygiene, the ability to measure quantities of feed, and attention to detail. Willing family members can be trained to give tube feeds to relatives who can no longer safely eat or swallow. For people receiving paid PAS, NPA regulations generally require skilled nurses to perform tube feeds; agency PAs therefore cannot provide tube feeds. Under consumer self-directed PAS, PAs can generally provide tube feeds, although rules vary somewhat by state.

For complex personal reasons, Ernie got a G-tube several years ago, at the same time surgeons inserted the tracheostomy for his ventilator. Ernie self-directs his PAs and oversaw their introduction to his G-tube. "I had my personal assistants trained in how to use the G-tube and pump," Ernie said. "My PAs are not required to have any certification and, therefore, are not prohibited from performing many tasks. It's not complicated." Without incident, his PAs fed Ernie through his G-tube for two years.

During the last year, Ernie changed his mind, deciding that with food prepared to a proper consistency, he could move away from G-tube feeds and resume eating by mouth. Ernie now consumes "puréed food full-time, for my nutrition but mostly for my enjoyment. There are lots of videos on YouTube about puréeing, and my life is a party again." Ernie no longer instills bags of nutrients into his stomach, and he "discovered something about the nature of living. There is something primal about the desire to taste, enjoy, chew, and swallow." Ernie acknowledged that "science says all the nutrition one needs is in the formula, so that's enough. No, it's not. The mind-body experience of the action technically may not be necessary for living, but it sure does feel better psychologically."

Ernie's feeding story has additional implications, notably about consumer choice—Ernie first wanted the G-tube and then, later, able to do so, he resumed eating specially prepared foods by mouth. As Ernie's preferences changed, his self-directed PAs carried out his wishes, finally learning to purée the foods he chooses. Michael's situation differs from Ernie's. Increasing difficulty swallowing because of his primary progressive multiple sclerosis forced Michael to switch—likely indefinitely—to the PEG tube. Chapter 8 describes the implications for Michael's PAS support.

Bladder and Bowel Management

Toileting is a basic ADL. Bladder management is generally straightforward, with today's availability of superabsorbent pads and other disposable prod-

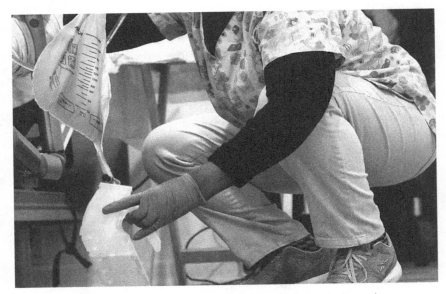

Nelita at Michael's bedside emptying his suprapubic tube drainage bag on December 29, 2019. The drainage bag must be positioned below the level of Michael's bladder, so that gravity will drain the urine into the bag. The bottom of the bag has a valve, which Nelita opens to drain the urine into the urinal. Opening the valve with one hand while holding the urinal in the other, all in the squatting position, can be physically difficult—some valves are poorly designed for one-handed opening. (Photo credit: Hanniel Dossous)

ucts for handling urinary incontinence. Multiple consumers use suprapubic, Foley, condom, straight, or other types of urinary catheters, which drain urine into a leg bag or directly into a urinal or toilet. Condom (external) catheters involve a condom-like sleeve that fits over the penis, allowing urine to drain into a bag. A straight catheter is a long, thin tube inserted through the urethra and into the bladder; it is disposable—thrown away after a single use. Some consumers can "straight cath" themselves without assistance.

In contrast, Matt needs a PA to empty his suprapubic catheter leg bag midday, but he is rarely home during most weekdays. "I'll meet my PCA downtown to empty the leg bag," Matt said, "and get something fast to eat. It's like a 20-minute deal." Matt has trained his PAs to change his suprapubic catheter about once a month—no complications have ever occurred. Typically, for most consumers, nurses perform the periodic suprapubic and other indwelling catheter changes. (Some nursing homes and even hospitals require urologists to change suprapubic and other indwelling catheters.)

Bowel management can be complicated. Consumers have distinct personal preferences. For instance, one woman prefers cleaning herself after bowel movements. She designed "a contraption that I've been using for years to wipe myself. But there are days when it's way beyond what my contraption can take care of." Her long-time PA cleans her in those situations. Another woman worried that her recurrent urinary tract infections likely occurred because her anal and perineal areas were cleaned poorly after bowel movements. When her PAs protest that they have cleaned her adequately, she politely but firmly asks them to clean her again using wet wipes.

Insertion of a rectal suppository to stimulate bowel movements is another flashpoint. People with spinal cord injury, multiple sclerosis, or other conditions decreasing bowel motility frequently depend on rectal suppositories to avoid severe constipation, intense discomfort, and potentially life-threatening bowel rupture or other complications. Agencies often prohibit PAs from manually inserting rectal suppositories. Consumers who self-direct their PAs and need suppositories generally mention the task in describing their job and seek PAs willing to perform it.

Jerry is in his early fifties and paraplegic from a spinal cord injury over 30 years ago. Bowel management is his only ADL support need—he can do all other tasks himself. Performing his bowel regimen takes two hours; he does it every third day and therefore requires only six hours of PAS each week. Jerry estimates that inserting the suppository takes about 15 seconds. Jerry hires his own PAs, whom he pays privately, and when recruiting PAs, "I make it clear to them up front that that's the hardest part of the job for someone, and it's certainly the hardest part for me to have to allow someone to do." He's had the same PA for many years. "I'm very blessed that my attendant Condi is super dependable, super easy to get along with, and very understanding." They work together efficiently. When Condi arrives in the morning, "I'm up. I've made coffee. I've got the lights on. I'm already in the bathroom and waiting."

In contrast, bowel management has become a battleground for Nicky, mid-forties, who had a spinal cord abscess that left him paraplegic. Nicky, who had a college degree and a professional job before his illness, is now unemployed and frequently despondent. Bowel wars with PAs feel like one further insult.

> I have PCAs from 9:00 A.M. to 9:00 P.M. Generally, they get me up between 9:00 and 10:00, and we then do the bowel program, which I have to do daily. With my bowel program, I've got about a two-hour leeway, or I can develop problems, either constipation or diarrhea. Constipation can lead to dysreflexia [see below]. . . . I need the PCA to insert the suppository. I have a tool for the PCA to use to do that. . . . It's something that I'm still not comfortable with, but I don't have a choice, right?

Nicky's concerns about constipation causing dysreflexia are understandable. Dysreflexia, also known as autonomic dysreflexia or hyperreflexia, affects people with spinal cord injuries at the high thoracic or cervical levels of their spinal column. It occurs with stretching of the smooth muscles of the viscera, such as in a constipated bowel, distended urinary bladder, or vaginal walls stretched during Pap tests or gynecological exams. In autonomic dysreflexia, people develop urgent symptoms, such as pounding headaches, sweating, and dangerously elevated blood pressures; it can be fatal if not treated immediately. If a rectal suppository does not work, another option is inserting a gloved, lubricated finger through the anus into the rectum and doing digital stimulation ("digi-stim")—moving the finger gently in a circular pattern for 20 to 30 seconds, repeating as needed to stimulate peristalsis and bowel movement (typically within 5 to 10 minutes).

Nicky's agency prohibits PAs from manually inserting a suppository or performing digital stimulation. Nicky therefore created two tools, a small device to insert the suppository and another to perform digital stimulation. One day, Nicky's agency sent a substitute, rather than his usual PA.

> We were both like we're just going to make it work, and it'll be fine. She got me up, she inserted the suppository. It fell out. She had to do it again. And then I asked her for a digi-stim using my tool I'd created. But she didn't want to do that. She said, "We're not allowed to do that." I said, "You can't do it with your finger, but I have a tool that you can use." And she said, "Well, I don't want to do that" . . . and she got short. I picked up my phone to call the agency. . . . She took my phone from me, called the agency, wouldn't give my phone back. There was this altercation. She's screaming at me. I'm yelling back. I'm saying, "Just get me in the shower and get me back to bed and go home."

Nicky did not have a bowel movement that day, which was not only emotionally exhausting but also put his health at risk.

Bowel management can have significant long-term consequences. One man with a neurodegenerative disorder, who is largely bedbound, has alternating periods of constipation lasting up to a week, followed by intensive laxative use, and then one- to two-day episodes of bowel incontinence in his bed. His PAs clean away the feces, which is challenging (e.g., requiring turning him on his side, sometimes while stool continues flowing). The man's physiatrist initially believed that, by following consistent daily practices, he could train his bowels over time to become more regular. Inserting a rectal suppository would be essential to train his bowels, but the man's morning PA was erratic, sporadically absent, straining interpersonal relationships.

Although he uses self-directed PAS, he felt awkward about requesting the suppository and feared his PA's unreliability would impede a regular bowel routine. Eighteen months have now passed with recurrent episodes of fecal incontinence, exacerbating the fragility of the skin on his buttocks. The physiatrist was beginning to contemplate a drastic step: surgery to create a colostomy, so his feces could be emptied through a bag secured to his abdomen.

Nail Trimming

One seemingly trivial but important concern among consumers involves trimming fingernails and toenails. With untrimmed nails, tough, knife-sharp, alpha-keratin lengthening nail plates can be dangerous and uncomfortable for both consumers and PAs. For example, Michael has severe spasticity and contractures in both arms and hands. When his nails are long, his tightly clenched fingers dig painfully into his palms, leaving deep, crescent-shaped indentations.

Agency rules typically forbid PAs from cutting consumers' fingernails or toenails, largely because of liability concerns (e.g., risks of injuries to consumers and PAs). After admitting that her agency PA trims her fingernails and toenails, one consumer laughingly warned not to tell anyone. She then acknowledged that

> if I were diabetic, I could see the concern, but I'm not. I can see where things can happen. Like you can get nipped, or you can get an infection, or get an ingrown toenail. All those things can happen. But how else am I supposed to do it, unless I go to the doctor? And that's a whole ordeal. . . . [Going for a manicure or pedicure wouldn't work for me.] I wear braces. I can just see me going! I'll be at the mani-pedi, and I'd have to take my pants off. I'd have to take my braces off. And I couldn't get on those chairs anyway. So, the whole thing would be impossible.

It is unclear whether her PA, who is breaking agency rules, feels comfortable or fears being injured or losing her job. Presumably, despite her agency's prohibition, the PA cuts the consumer's nails because she genuinely wants to help with a vexing problem.

6

People Providing Personal Assistance Services

After high school, Sarah started vocational school, took babysitting and restaurant jobs, and traveled around the country. At the age of 20, she returned home and saw an advertisement at the local university on providing PAS to students with disability. "The ad said no experience necessary," Sarah laughed. "I thought, 'I guess I qualify. I'll try that.'" She applied for the job, planning to simultaneously complete her vocational training in graphic arts.

In the university's program, students with disability interviewed PA candidates, made hiring decisions, and self-directed their services. "My first referral was to a man who drooled and didn't speak clearly," Sarah said. "I was mortified, and I said, 'Oh my God, no. This work is not for me. I can't do this.'" The man hired her, however, and she did a good job. But PAS work didn't initially excite Sarah.

> The real reason that I stuck with it—what really drew me in—was the disability community, the people. I had created a poster for the disabled students' program. I brought it to their office and talked to [a woman with disability], who said she had heard about me, because you start hearing about good attendants. So, she offered me a job. I told her I wasn't planning on taking any more attendant work, and she said, "Well, I pay $5 an hour," which was 50 cents more than I was making at the time. I said, "Okay." It was just going to be temporary. But she really helped me. She encouraged me. She gave me a sense of worth that I had never felt before in my life.

Sarah assisted the woman for nearly 10 years.

For almost 40 years—except when a job-related back injury kept her from working for many months—Sarah has provided home-based PAS. Nowadays, she doesn't take jobs requiring heavy lifting and, because of low wages, she always has a second job (currently administrative work). Sarah advises people considering PAS work to have outside interests: "I don't think this job is going to be completely fulfilling all by itself in your life." Sarah also has clear views about PAS and her role:

> Most of the work itself is things we're doing for ourselves. It's commonsense work: bathing, dressing. If you can follow directions, and if you can relate to the person that you're working for, you can do the job. . . . I don't consider myself a caregiver. I work for people; I provide a service; I'm their employee; I'm their attendant. They need a service, not care. They need to get up and out of bed in the morning. They need assistance going to the bathroom, and they need assistance getting dressed, and showering, and all that. But that's service, not really the same as caring for somebody.

Over her PAS career, Sarah has had about 15 long-term consumers. "Now my favorite client is the man who drooled and doesn't speak clearly," Sarah remarked, laughing (her first university PAS program referral). "He's got a great sense of humor and, physically, he's fairly easy to work for, doing the transfer and just assisting him with dressing and everything. There's no struggle there." Sarah has recently had personal demands that affect her reliability, but her longest-lasting consumer has not complained. "It's a really crazy time for me," Sarah admitted, "and I've been late every single day. I don't get any grief from my client, and I really appreciate that."

As described in Chapter 4, the U.S. Department of Labor reports that 831,800 people worked as home health aides in 2018, the occupational category that includes PAS.[1] To meet increasing demand from population trends, by 2028 the projected home health aide workforce must grow to 1,136,600 workers, a 37% increase.[2] However, many structural barriers impede recruitment and retention of PAS workers, notably the low wages Sarah mentioned. In 2018 the median hourly wage for home-based PAS workers was $11.40;[3] the median annual income was $16,200.[4] High job turnover, primarily because of poor job satisfaction, causes about three-quarters of the need for new PAS workers.[5] At home care agencies, PAS worker turnover reached 82% in 2018, up 15% from the 2017 rate.[6] Furthermore, occupational

---

Box 6.1 Personal Assistants Quoted Frequently in Chapter 6

- **Chandra**, mid-fifties, East Indian, immigrant, has provided PAS for 30 years
- **Isaiah**, mid-fifties, Black, has provided PAS for 40 years; usually has a second job
- **Lakisha**, late forties, Black, has provided PAS for slightly more than a year; has a second job
- **Michelle**, late thirties, Black, has provided PAS for 20 years; now being paid to support her fiancé, who was disabled by a spinal cord injury
- **Sarah**, late fifties, White, has provided PAS for almost 40 years; has a second job
- **Shauna**, early thirties, Black, has provided PAS for two years; has a second job

---

injuries, complex interpersonal dynamics, and other factors hinder efforts to grow and retain the PAS workforce.

Chapter 6 describes PAS work, people's motivations for becoming PAs, job requirements, logistical challenges, and career paths. To give voice to PAS workers, this chapter quotes PA interviewees, primarily the six listed in Box 6.1.

Nature of PAS Jobs

As noted throughout this book, PAS confronts an ineluctable irony. On the one hand, PAS is low-wage, physically demanding work, with few job requirements or opportunities for career growth. For some observers, in "cleaning bodies . . . home care workers engage in intimate labor, a kind of toil that is at once essential and highly stigmatized, as if the mere touching of dirt or bodily fluids degrades the handler."[7] On the other hand, PAS consumers such as Ernie, Matt, Michael, and Natalie (Chapter 5) cannot live in their homes without paid ADL supports. PAS is essential to their day-to-day survival. The discordance between how consumers value PAS and the worth society ascribes to this work—as measured by income, public recognition, and prestige—is vast.

Women and girls have performed PAS-type work within their families and broader communities for millennia, without expectation of recognition or reward. Although she performs identical work, Sarah argues that she is not a caregiver but instead provides a service. Several decades ago, this frame switch was essential for PAS workers, who were mostly women and often women of color, to seek higher wages and other labor protections:

The nonwage labors of the wife or mother, performed out of love, obligation, and duty, morph into the low-wage tasks of the housekeeper, personal attendant, health aide, and child or elder minder. Before caregivers were even able to bargain for higher wages, benefits, and better working conditions, they had to see themselves as workers and fight for such recognition from the public, the state, and the very users of their services. They had to gain visibility and dignity, two key phrases in both self and the media representation of home care providers.[8]

During decades of striving for higher wages and labor protections (see Chapter 4), paid PAs confronted barriers related to the nature of their job that other workers did not experience. Starting in the New Deal, labor organizers assumed that industries employ workers who share a common worksite. The National Labor Relations Board model presumes "an unambiguous employer-employee relationship."[9] Neither assumption applies to home-based paid PAs. Their workplace is the consumer's home, where generally they are the only employee present during their shifts. In addition, the employer-employee relationship is not unambiguous: in paid PAS, complicated interpersonal dynamics inevitably affect consumer-PA relationships (see Part IV). The nature of PAS—supporting routine daily tasks relevant to everyone—reinforces assumptions that the work requires little skill, justifying low wages and prestige.

For people with physical disability, in-home PAS generally encompasses three broad types of activities (Box 6.2).[10] As previously described, state regulations (e.g., NPAs) or home care agency rules often limit paramedical tasks that PAs can perform. The lack of national PA job training or certification standards perpetuates presumptions that PAS work requires little skill or training. A 2014 report about Medicaid home-based PAS programs

---

Box 6.2 Services Provided by In-Home PAs

1. **Assistance** with basic self-care tasks (activities of daily living [ADLs]: bathing, toileting, dressing, feeding, transfers and in-home mobility) and more complex routine tasks (instrumental ADLs [IADLs], such as light housework, preparing meals, shopping)
2. **Paramedical tasks,** such as medication administration, wound care, and catheter care
3. **Social supports,** to reduce social isolation and enable full participation in community activities

found that few states had rigorous certification or training standards, and more than one-fifth of states had no training requirements for PAS workers.[11] Furthermore, "training standards for PCAs, where they exist at all, vary by state and also by program and population served within a given state."[12] In addition, 70% of home care workers providing consumer-directed care are family members or friends, making them generally exempt from training requirements, nurse delegation rules, and other regulations. Skill levels and worker preparedness therefore differ significantly across states and employment models.[13]

Characteristics of PAS Workers

PAS and home care workers, in general, are 45 years of age or older and disproportionately female, of racial or ethnic minorities, and have low incomes, education levels, and other socioeconomic disadvantages (Table 6.1).[14] Beyond their jobs, many PAs also have informal caregiving obligations within their own families, further complicating their lives. The 2007 National Home Health Aide Survey found that 30% simultaneously care for children or a sick family member.[15] About 10% have missed work because of childcare problems, and 17% have absences due to caring for a family member or friend.[16] Of the 38% of home care workers who work part-time, one-third do so because of family caregiving or other personal obligations.[17] With frequent school closings during the 2020–2021 COVID-19 pandemic, PAs who had small children found themselves deciding between staying home with their kids and going to work.

With often bleak socioeconomic prospects, 50% of direct care workers—including home-based PAS workers—leave their jobs within a year.[18] The COVID-19 pandemic exacerbated that flight.[19] The 2007 home health aide survey found that 20% of workers were currently looking for another job, and 35% were likely to leave their job in the next year.[20] Low wages were the primary reason for departing these jobs. Other reported causes included meager job benefits, poor supervision, difficult travel demands, heavy workloads, part-time rather than full-time work, work-related disability, and few opportunities for advancement or upward mobility in the job.

Longer time in the job does not assure substantially higher wages. In the 2007 survey, home health aides who had worked less than a year earned median wages of $10.15 per hour, and those who had worked more than ten years had median hourly wages of only $12.00.[21] Furthermore, as elsewhere in the U.S. economy, wage disparities exist from race, ethnicity, gender, and other personal characteristics. Women and people of color earn less than White male direct care workers. In 2017, among home care workers, median

TABLE 6.1 CHARACTERISTICS OF DIRECT CARE WORKERS PROVIDING HOME CARE: 2017	
Age	(%)
16–24	11
25–34	18
35–44	19
45–54	22
55–64	21
65+	9
Gender	(%)
Female	87
Male	13
Race and ethnicity	(%)
White	38
Black or African American	28
Asian or Pacific Islander	8
Other	4
Hispanic or Latino (any race)	23
Citizenship	(%)
U.S. citizen by birth	69
U.S. citizen by naturalization	16
Not a U.S. citizen	14
Educational attainment	(%)
Less than high school	19
High school graduate	35
Some college, no degree	26
Associate's degree or higher	20
Median annual personal earnings	$16,200
Median hourly wages adjusted for inflation	$11.30
Employment status	(%)
Full-time	62
Part-time, noneconomic reasons	31
Part-time, economic reasons in local area (e.g., aspects of local labor market, business conditions of employer)	7
Income compared with federal poverty level (FPL)	(%)
<100% of FPL	18
<138% of FPL	29
<200% of FPL	48

(continued)

TABLE 6.1 CHARACTERISTICS OF DIRECT CARE WORKERS PROVIDING HOME CARE: 2017 *(continued)*	
Receives public assistance, by type of assistance	(%)
Any public assistance	53
Food and nutrition assistance	30
Medicaid	33
Cash assistance	3
Health insurance status	(%)
Any health insurance	84
Health insurance through employer or union	38
Medicaid, Medicare, or other public coverage	42
Health insurance purchased directly	13

Source: PHI. Workforce data center. Last modified August 30, 2019. https://phinational.org/policy-research/workforce-data-center/; 2017 1-Year Public Use Microdata Sample (PUMS) from the American Community Survey.

wages for women of color were $11.13, as compared to $11.50 for White women, $12.00 for men of color, and $12.38 for White men.[22]

Motivations for Doing PAS Work

The primary motivation for becoming a home health aide is wanting to help people, reported by 58% of people answering the 2007 survey. Other reasons included having time to interact with clients (16%) and aspiring to become a nurse (6%).[23] About two-thirds of home health aides learn about the jobs while working in another health care setting, and 40% get recommendations from family members or friends.[24]

Among PA interviewees, several common reasons drew them to PAS. One frequent route is growing up among generally female family members (mothers, grandmothers, aunts, cousins) who have been PAs. For example, Michelle's grandmother and two older cousins worked as PAs. Michelle became a paid PA right after graduating from high school and has had no other jobs.

Another frequent pathway is having provided PAS to family members, generally parents or grandparents. After serving as informal caregivers to relatives, some people decide to become paid PAs. One woman started caring for her mother during childhood, and she never finished high school, diverted by the time demands of caregiving. After her mother died, she tried different jobs, but for the last six years, she has worked full-time in PAS. She never received her GED.

Michelle worked for an agency providing PAS when her fiancé had a car crash and suffered a spinal cord injury. His health insurer contracted with her agency to provide PAS, with Michelle assigned as the paid PA to her fiancé. They want to marry. However, her fiancé has recently obtained Medicaid coverage, but their state's Medicaid program does not permit spouses to be paid PAs, as some states do (see Chapter 3). Michelle and her fiancé are contesting this Medicaid restriction, as she continues providing 24/7 support.

The passion to help others motivates many PAs. Interviewees emphasized that PAS work "has to come from the heart," with many describing themselves as "people persons." Shauna, who is in her early thirties, worked in retail for eight years and "knew it was not something I wanted to continue to do for the rest of my life. I enjoyed taking care of people. I love older people. I feel like this is my passion." Shauna acknowledges wages are low, and she has a second job. "So, I'm not doing it just for the money. I do it because I build relationships with these people." Similarly, another PA in her early forties said about her PAS job, "For me, as a human being, as a person, I think when somebody need me, it makes me feel good. So, I want to give them the best of me." Mona (see Chapter 1) described her deeply held desire to alleviate suffering wherever she sees it. "We need compassionate, loving, caring people to provide that service for people who needs it," said Mona, "and it's always been in me. For some of us, we always have that caregiving ability in us."

Religious faith plays powerful roles, moving some people toward PAS to assist others. "God would want me to help this person," said Isaiah, "and that's what I do." Another woman wondered, "What if this is my mother or my grandmother that need help, and I turned my back on them? That's not right. God won't forgive me for that." Michelle expressed similar views: "It's God that puts them in their situation and puts us there to take care of them." For Michelle, her fiancé's injury and 24/7 support needs brought this conviction even closer: "God is with us daily. He's always with me because I have to constantly ask for strength and to keep going, because it's my fiancé there, and I'm taking care of him."

Lakisha's experiences exemplify the desire to have more time to assist consumers, rather than being rushed in performing ADL tasks. Many years previously, Lakisha earned her certification as a licensed practical nurse (LPN), and she says, "I've been very blessed with having different types of nursing jobs." Her last position was at a rehabilitation hospital, but when new management took over, her workload increased significantly. "We were having at least 11 to 14 patients. We had all their ADLs that we had to do, as well as their vital signs, and then also your nursing care. So, it was getting to be way too much. I just could not physically do it anymore." A friend told

Lakisha about home-based PAS, and she took an agency job, supporting one consumer 36 hours per week. Her consumer was a young man with quadriplegia, who despite being married, used paid PAs for all his ADL supports. Lakisha assisted with his morning routine and accompanied him to his workplace; another PA supported him at night. "It's very laid-back," said Lakisha, describing her relationship with her consumer. "It's very professional, so it's cool."

Seeking work flexibility is another frequent reason for taking PAS jobs. Chandra, now in her mid-fifties, immigrated from South America to the United States almost 30 years ago and immediately took home-based agency PAS work. "That's the only job that could keep me flexible," Chandra said. "You wake up in the morning, and one of your children is sick. You can't go to work. I'm going to call out sick today. I can't be calling out sick all the time on another job. But in this job, you can ask to be flexible." Before work-hour protections with overtime pay were enacted (see Chapter 4), Chandra could work as much as she wanted. "When there was no limit, I work 70 hours. But that time, I had no kids!" Chandra has worked for the same agency for 25 years, reducing her hours to 40 per week as she got older and the job became too physically demanding. If she needs more hours to make ends meet, Chandra gets additional work at another agency.

Finally, despite the low wages, people often take PAS jobs because they need money, and getting this work is relatively easy. People frequently start by providing PAS as a second or third job. One woman who worked at a large retail store noticed that most of her coworkers had second jobs, and she sought PAS work following one coworker's example. She eventually left her retail job and worked only in home-based PAS, averaging 60 to 70 hours per week—between two different agencies—to earn enough to make ends meet. Isaiah, in his fifties, would like to leave PAS work for various reasons, but he has to provide for himself and his family. He has children and grandchildren to feed.

Practical Concerns

The nature of home-based PAS raises important practical concerns.

Multiple Jobs

As discussed earlier, to make ends meet, many home-based PAs take two or more jobs. Some PAs obtain jobs at two agencies to get past overtime restrictions and work more than 35 to 40 hours weekly. Other PAs take jobs in retail or other service industries. One PA in her mid-forties worked three jobs—PAS, part-time bus driver, and answering telephones at her union's call center—while studying to obtain her GED.

Long hours raise risks of job burnout. "During the week, I have two jobs," said Shauna. "I don't know how I do it, but through the grace of God, everything falls into place." Shauna described having job burnout early in her PAS career:

> Honestly, my first two years with the agency, I was working Monday through Sunday, no days off. Yes, I was draining myself. But I cut back. "You know what?" I tell the agency, "I have to take time for me, because ain't nobody going to take care of me. [If I leave,] then who's going to take care of your clients?"

Shauna reduced her PAS hours to 25 per week and keeps a second job that goes late into the evening but is very different—bartending, which offers interactions with the regulars. The balance suits her well.

Transportation and Other Logistics

According to the 2007 survey of home health aides, 96% drove themselves to consumers' homes or their agency, and only 4% used public transportation.[25] About 5% had missed work in the last month because of transportation problems.[26] PA interviewees raised several transportation concerns, starting with costs. Some agencies compensate PAs who drive to clients' homes for their gas, pay by mileage, or both (see Chapter 7). Agencies do not pay transportation costs for PAs taking public transportation, although these costs are often high. "It would be nice to get reimbursed for my bus pass," said one woman who spends more than $20 per week on bus passes. "It's not fair that the girls that have cars, they get mileage and gas reimbursed." PAs with cars who work under consumer self-direction reported that consumers ask to be driven places but do not compensate the PA for mileage costs. "She wanted me to drive her to the outskirts of everywhere," said one PA about her consumer, "but she never paid me for gas."

Because of the critical support needs of some consumers, PAs must show up on time, as scheduled. However, severe weather upends even the best intentions. In locales with effective public transportation systems, PAs generally reported that reaching their clients even in the winter is not too burdensome. However, with unreliable public transportation, winter commutes can be brutal. One woman in the Northeast described getting up extra early on bitter winter mornings to check train and bus schedules while also making sure her children were bundled up to get safely to school. Another woman feared getting frostbite while traveling between consumers' houses. In 2015 Boston had record-breaking snowfalls, halting the city's subway system—which admittedly dates to the 1890s. Without operating subways, some PAs had no transportation and decided to stay overnight with consumers rather than risk their clients lacking essential support. Some PAs scrambled to arrange child-care and made other personal sacrifices. Stories about extraordinary devotion and heroic efforts of PAs circulated within Boston's disability community during that memorable snowbound winter.

Transportation into or through neighborhoods with widespread crime or gun violence raises serious safety concerns. For instance, Isaiah lives in a large city with alarming rates of drive-by shootings and gang violence. He has several clients who live in high-crime neighborhoods, and he considers carefully the safest way to get there by bus—his primary mode of transporta-tion. "You don't want to go on the bus when it gets late in the evening," said Isaiah. "I don't trust the area. I try to make my hours early in the day." But sometimes choice isn't possible, and "you just have to prepare yourself to go." Isaiah would like to take taxis, but he can't afford it. He has refused clients living in certain neighborhoods, and now his agency makes sure to minimize his transportation fears. For Isaiah to take on a new client, "it would have to be where I can get there comfortably and get home comfortably."

Rural Concerns

Accessing home-based PAS in sparsely populated rural regions is complex, starting with an inadequate workforce. Providing skilled home-based ser-vices, such as nursing and rehabilitation therapies, is difficult in most rural areas, which have few health care providers of any sort, lack home care agen-cies, and span great distances and rugged terrain. Recognizing these difficul-ties, Medicare and Medicaid increased reimbursement for rural home care, albeit generally temporarily, aiming to increase the availability and quality of rural services.[27] Nevertheless, recruiting PAs in rural areas is hard, impeded by very low wage levels. For skilled services, rural providers increasingly turn to telehealth and remote monitoring technologies, despite concerns about inadequate broadband internet access, high costs, and other barriers in rural America. However, telehealth cannot substitute for hands-on ADL supports.

Extreme rural poverty often differs from urban poverty. In some impov-erished rural enclaves, homes lack running water and electricity, essential to PAS tasks.[28] Rural home care workers face special transportation barri-ers: "workers often are deterred by the long drive times ('windshield time') required to visit many rural clients, which in poor weather conditions or on poorly maintained roads can be very difficult. Some rural areas require the use of ferries to get to patients, which further extends drive times."[29] In addition, unreliable or absent cell phone coverage in rural areas poses safety risks for PAs traveling to and from consumers' homes.

The Role of PAS Worker Unions

Unionization aims to improve PAS workers' wages and labor protections (see Chapter 4). Early efforts to unionize PAS workers were uphill battles, as paid PAs themselves failed to recognize that they constituted a definable workforce. In the mid-1990s, the lead organizer for Service Employees International Union (SEIU) Local 250 recalled that at "the first meeting, many people were amazed at how many others were there who were doing the same work. . . . They had absolutely no identity as workers."[30] An initial goal of SEIU Local 250 organizers was to instill a shared identity among PAS providers, as a large workforce performing jobs that merited respect and labor protections.

In addition to advocacy, unions serve convening and training functions. This is especially important for in-home PAS, where PAs are often the only employee at their worksite—the consumer's home. While agency employees get together for in-service training and share stories during other agency meetings, PAs working in consumer self-directed jobs can feel isolated and alone. Union membership can alleviate those feelings.

Unions also offer training for PAS workers, such as programs on medication safety, dementia, nutrition, diabetes, and body mechanics. These union training sessions are available to both agency and consumer self-directed PAs and thus provide excellent opportunities for workers from various backgrounds to share their work experiences. One PA working directly for consumers learned the "do's and don'ts" of PAS through 1199 SEIU courses— her clients never required her to complete formal training. Once she enrolled in 1199 SEIU, she realized that she would have benefited from training much earlier in her PAS career, teaching her how to perform some tasks more effectively. "Once I did that training," she said, "it really made me see like, 'Oh, wow. All this time I was picking my client up, I was doing it wrong. I should've had my legs like this.' I believe I have a lot of wear and tear on my body from how I cared for my clients in the past."

1199 SEIU also offers longer courses and training programs to become a certified nursing assistant (CNA). To pursue 1199 SEIU CNA training, PAs might need to meet certain requirements (e.g., length of PAS employment) and pay a fee (e.g., $99) upfront to enroll. In this program, the union returned the fee to participants who completed the CNA program. According to one PA, getting back the $99 fee is an incentive to finish training: despite its attractions, the CNA training program has low completion rates.

Career Advancement

PAS jobs generally offer few opportunities for career advancement—another reason for low worker retention. Although unions have proactively tried to bolster PAS workers, such as by offering CNA training, the educational programs and workforce development initiatives are often too expensive and time-consuming for low-wage workers.[31] Developing skills training targets for PAS workers has been difficult. "One challenge to establishing training standards for personal care aides is that little is known about the effectiveness of training on worker satisfaction, retention, and injury rates, or on consumer outcomes or satisfaction with worker training."[32]

Another complexity in developing career advancement strategies is that PAs begin providing PAS at different stages in their work lives. Among the PA interviewees, some had started their careers in retail and customer-service occupations, others started in health care jobs, some used home-based PAS as a steppingstone to various jobs, and some had worked only as PAs. One PA in her early thirties recalled that

> I've been working since I was 15, and I've done a whole gamut of different types of jobs: retail, warehouse, sales, food service. Everything that you can find in a city center. I did office work. . . . I had trouble staying happy at those jobs because they felt not worth it to me. I really liked that with home care I was able to help people. When I was working at, let's say, an art supply store, obviously the nice thing is I get the discount. But if I didn't show up, what's the worst that could happen? Somebody doesn't get their paintbrush.

This PA subsequently received a college degree. Nonetheless, she still provided home-based PAS, viewing herself as "an artist with a day job." She anticipated cutting back her PAS hours slowly as her art career evolves, but she could also envision providing PAS for 10 to 20 more years because she values helping people with their basic needs.

Other PAs use home-based PAS as a springboard to different careers. One PA in her early fifties is a military veteran with multiple two-year certificates in various skill sets. After nine years in active duty and another 20 years in the National Guard, she struggled to decide what to do next. While working for a package delivery service, she began considering health care: "Everything was pointing to home care. Every time I looked in the paper or online, those jobs came up. I said, 'It's got to be my calling.' And I've been doing it ever since." She started supporting private-pay PAS consumers. She later pursued more schooling, becoming credentialed as a surgical technician, which is now her primary job. But she keeps a second job providing PAS to one long-term, private-pay client.

Despite the challenges of theirs jobs, 50% of home care aides surveyed in 2007 had worked in the field for 11 or more years.[33] In addition, 47% reported their jobs were extremely satisfying, and 41% said they were somewhat satisfied—only 2% described being extremely dissatisfied with their jobs.[34] Older home health aides (age 45 and above) were more likely to describe their work as extremely satisfying (51%) than younger workers (age 30 and younger, 38%).[35] The top reason for staying in their home health aide jobs was caring for others (49%), followed by feeling good about their work (11%) and job flexibility (8%).[36] Most (92%) home health aides felt respected by their consumers, and 94% said they would definitely or probably take this job again.[37]

———————

When asked how to improve PAS jobs, Sarah offered clear advice: "The absolutely number one thing is pay. It just has to pay better. There's no doubt that we could keep people in the field that way." Nonetheless, she also succinctly summarized her overall feelings about providing PAS: "For me, it's being of service." Sarah sees dignity and purpose in PAS work that her earlier jobs lacked.

> What drew me to the work and kept me in the work early on is that it's nonexploitative. I knew from working in a restaurant, you work behind that counter, you're making those sandwiches—fast, faster, faster. I literally had a job where the boss sat at a table that was on a level above and looked down at his workers. I thought that was really demeaning. I don't need to be exploited like that.

During nearly 40 years providing PAS, Sarah developed long-term working relationships with many consumers and feels she functions as their equal, a partner in supporting the consumer to live life as they wish. "If I can enhance somebody's life," said Sarah, "what better thing is there to do on this earth than to help other people live a good life?"

III

Approaches to
Providing Paid PAS

ART III describes the two major approaches to organizing and providing paid home-based PAS—agency and consumer self-directed services. Each approach or model has advantages and disadvantages, with
fundamentally different ways of hiring, training, supervising, and evaluating
PAS workers, as well as the range of support tasks that PAs are allowed to do.
These PAS models also vary by how and how much PAs are paid. PAS models
differ regionally, in accordance with the state's Medicaid program and home
care marketplace. States' NPA provisions also have different implications for
the two PAS models. Chapter 7 introduces agency-model PAS, and Chapter
8 describes consumer self-directed PAS. The distinct employment and oversight approaches of these two models significantly affect the dynamics of
consumer-PA relationships, with important consequences for the experiences
and perceptions of both consumers and PAs. Neither model is clearly superior
to the other. Different consumers have their own practical realities, needs,
preferences, and values for how they want to receive their paid home-based
PAS, just as different PAs have their personal preferences, expectations, and
values for who organizes their job and who's their boss.

Personal Assistance Services from Agencies

Penny is now in her late sixties. In her twenties, she started having episodes of sciatica—shooting pains in her lower back and legs from pressure on her sciatic nerve. Penny kept working her managerial job in a warehouse, but "as the years progressed, the bouts got more frequent and more intense. It really just about crippled me."

In addition, Penny said, "I'll be very honest with you. I'm what is considered morbidly obese, and I have a really bad stomach hang on my left side"—flesh folds, making it hard to keep skin underneath clean and dry. Several years previously, Penny had emergency surgery for an acute intestinal problem, and postoperatively she had repeated complications, including multiple bouts of cellulitis (bacterial skin infections) under her skin folds. With one setback after another, Penny moved among several hospitals and rehabilitation facilities for more than a year before finally going home. Concerned about recurrent cellulitis, her doctor approved one hour per day of PAS to assist Penny with bathing and skin care, ensuring her skin was clean, dry, and infection free.

Her health insurer contracted this daily PAS through an agency, which worked well for Penny. She lives in a mountainous rural region, where distances are great and workers scarce. Agency PAS spares her the hassle of finding PAs. Penny's agency continually searches for new employees so they can reliably serve their current consumers and add new clients. Sometimes PAs "travel 20 miles between patients," Penny said. "There's lots of time on the road that takes them away from working." Heavy winter snows exacerbate travel demands. Nonetheless, Penny praises her PAs' efforts to reach her despite inclement weather. She only missed one PA visit "because of snow.

My motto to them is, 'You don't risk life or limb.' I can go a day without my shower if I have to."

Penny also praises her agency for assigning the same three women as her PAs over several years. She knows these PAs well and feels comfortable with them. However, Penny is worried. "One just turned 70, another's in her early to mid-sixties, and the other's probably close to 50. So, they're not going to be there for 20 or 30 more years." Penny wonders what will happen if her agency can't find staff to cover their clients. "I'm not agonizing over it," Penny said, "but I know I'm one step away from losing my services because I only have the three people." Penny nevertheless trusts her agency to maintain adequate staffing, sparing her—at least for now—from being without PAS.

———

A gency PAS offers important advantages to consumers needing ADL supports. Like Penny, who lives in a sparsely populated rural area, many people do not want the burden of recruiting, managing, and paying PAs. They prefer having agencies perform these tasks.

Agencies offer traditional client-provider relationships. Consumers presume that agency PAs meet minimal standards, such as passing background checks and receiving basic training. Agencies often supply back-up workers if PAs are out sick and can sometimes organize replacements when PAs don't show up. When consumers have concerns about PAs, they can speak to an agency supervisor—communication channels about PAs' performance are generally clearly specified. Supervisors can reassign unsuitable PAs, making staffing changes until the consumer feels comfortable with the PA. More PAS consumers nationwide use agency supports than consumer self-directed services (see Chapter 8). In 2017 an estimated 1.4 million people worked as agency home-based personal care aides, and another 325,000 worked as independent providers, hired directly by consumers.[1]

Consumers may have no choice about using agency PAS. For example, Penny's health insurer contracted with an agency to provide her PAs. Medicaid programs funding home-based PAS specify whether consumers must receive agency services, must self-direct their PAS, or have a choice. A 2016 survey of selected Medicaid PAS programs found that 28 states allowed people to choose between agency and self-directed PAs, 12 states required self-direction, and seven required agency PAs.[2]

With increasing demand from aging baby boomers and other demographic shifts, agencies providing home-based PAS are constantly juggling swiftly rising needs with chronic workforce shortages. The marketplace is changing rapidly. Traditional home health agencies, established to provide

---

**Box 7.1 PAS Consumers and Personal Assistants
Quoted Frequently in Chapter 7**

Consumers
- **Joe**, mid-fifties, Black, stroke seven years ago
- **Michael**, early sixties, White, quadriplegia from primary progressive multiple sclerosis
- **Penny**, late sixties, White, sciatica, "morbidly obese"

Personal Assistants
- **Chandra**, mid-fifties, East Indian, immigrant, has provided PAS for 30 years
- **Lakisha**, late forties, Black, has provided PAS for slightly more than a year
- **Michelle**, late thirties, Black, has provided PAS for 20 years; paid to support fiancé

---

in-home skilled services, such as nursing, are expanding into PAS. New organizations are springing up nationwide that exclusively provide in-home PAS. Unlike Medicare-certified home health agencies, many agencies providing in-home PAS are not licensed by states.[3] This chapter introduces agency PAS, drawing on observations from three PAS consumers and three PAs (Box 7.1).

Agencies Providing Home-Based PAS

Today, numerous forces are upending agency provision of home-based PAS, including new for-profit companies entering the marketplace, traditional nonprofit providers reconfiguring their service offerings, and the transformative influx of money. The largest newcomer is Medicare, which since its inception had covered only limited PAS. Under the Bipartisan Budget Act of 2018, some MA plans can now offer in-home PAS (see Chapter 3).[4] Medicare thus opened the spigots for large expenditures on home-based PAS. It is too soon to assess the results of the change.

Traditional Home Health Care Agencies

Standard home health care agencies historically have provided skilled services from nurses, rehabilitation therapists, and other licensed professionals. These agencies originated in efforts of religious charities and other benevolent organizations to support families caring for sick relatives in their homes in early 19th-century America (see Chapter 2).[5] Home health care agencies, as they exist today, emerged after passage of Medicare, Medicaid, and the Older Americans Act in the mid-1960s (see Chapter 3). In 1967 Medicare-certified home health care agencies numbered 1,753, and by 1997, the sector had grown to 10,444 agencies.[6] Medicaid initially included home care as an optional benefit; Medicaid made home care mandatory in 1971, stoking further agency growth. In 1980 the Omnibus Budget Reconciliation Act opened Medicare participation to for-profit home care agencies, along with other changes that drove agency growth (e.g., eliminating limits on the number of home care visits allowed).

> By the end of the 1980s, one-third of all Medicare-certified home care agencies were for profit, and by 2003, nearly half were proprietary. . . . While the hope was that competition would lower costs, traditional nonprofit home care providers argued that the profit motive was antithetical to the altruistic mission of home care. Given the financial incentives for home care, proprietary agencies predictably tended to provide more visits compared with those by nonprofit or governmental agencies. In 1993, for example, proprietary agencies provided beneficiaries with an average of seventy-eight visits per year, whereas voluntary and governmental agencies provided an average of forty-six visits.[7]

Medicare's home care expenditures rose 350% from 1990 to 1996, and in 1997 the 3.6 million Medicare beneficiaries receiving home care averaged 73 visits, primarily from licensed health care professionals.[8] Viewing home care costs as out of control, the 1997 Balanced Budget Act (BBA) radically changed Medicare's home care benefit, limiting allowable expenditures per beneficiary and per visit costs. "The outcomes of the BBA were swift and dramatic. By 1999, more than three thousand home care agencies (14 percent) had closed; the proportion of beneficiaries using home care had fallen by 20 percent; the number of visits per patient had decreased by 40 percent; and the public spending per enrollee had declined by 52 percent."[9]

In 2000 Medicare made other changes to home care payments, moving from cost-based reimbursements to episode-based payment: agencies receive a fixed amount for each 60-day episode, regardless of number of home visits, with reimbursement levels adjusted by complexity of patients' needs. This program started in 2002, intending to create financial incentives for efficient care. After 2002, the number of Medicare home visits fell, and the mix of services changed, including fewer visits from home health aides.[10] In 2010 about 62% of Medicare-certified home care agencies were for-profit, with substantial regional variation—roughly 92% for-profit in the South, 84% in the West, 81% in the Midwest, and 55% in the Northeast.[11]

Unlike Medicare, which covers almost exclusively skilled services, Medicaid home care programs—which vary widely by states—can provide long-term PAS (see Chapter 3). Home care spending by Medicaid began growing significantly in the late 1990s, spurred by the 1999 U.S. Supreme Court *Olmstead* decision (see Chapter 2). Medicaid's home care resources especially targeted younger populations, including children and young adults with significant disability: "home care was once again deemed a more suitable and less expensive alternative to institutional care."[12] To provide community-based supports, agencies sought workers beyond skilled, licensed professionals—they needed PAs. Thus, to compete for Medicaid business, traditional home care agencies had to fundamentally transform their workforce and rethink their missions.

New Home Care Chains and Franchises

During the last decade, private-pay consumers catalyzed a new industry to meet growing demand for in-home PAS. Often operated as for-profit franchises or chains, these agencies—sometimes called nonmedical private-duty home care[13]—typically bear names that convey warmth, reassurance, and appreciation of consumers' wishes to remain in their homes. Powerful investors have entered the PAS market in some regions, including private equity firms, large health care provider organizations, and health insurance companies. With challenges recruiting workers and high staff turnover, companies in some areas compete aggressively for staff, angling to lure PAs away from other firms. New PAs must sometimes sign noncompete clauses or other employment provisions in their hiring contracts.

Most new companies focus primarily on basic ADL and IADL supports and are not generally licensed by states or certified as providers by Medicare or Medicaid. These agencies typically perform employee background checks and provide minimal training to their PAS employees. They also strictly limit what these unlicensed employees can do, as defined by NPA regulations and company-specific policies. Some franchisees hire registered nurses (RNs), who perform initial evaluations of new clients, establish care plans, and conduct periodic monitoring—paralleling traditional home health care agency practices. For much higher hourly fees than for PAs, some franchise agencies can arrange for company RNs or LPNs to perform tasks that NPAs consider skilled (e.g., medication administration, tube feeding). Some franchise agencies offer private duty nursing, for a price.

The home care agency marketplace varies across geographic regions. In rural areas, home care agencies are often associated with hospitals or other institutional providers. In 2012–2013, 31% of rural hospitals provided home care services, as compared with 19% of urban hospitals.[14] Hospital-based rural home care services rarely turn a profit and generally must rely on community support for their survival. Furthermore, hospital-affiliated agencies typically provide skilled services, not home-based PAS. In some rural areas, the number of consumers seeking PAS support is too small to sustain an agency. Certain rural areas have diverse ethnic minority populations who speak only Spanish, Farsi, Chinese, Vietnamese, Tagalog, or other languages.[15] Recruiting local PAS workers who communicate effectively in these languages is particularly challenging.

———

Urgent need drove Michael roughly 15 years ago to seek PAS from a commercial franchise agency. As Michael's disability progressed, he needed human help to perform morning ADLs (see Chapter 5). He had hired a PA whom he paid privately. At some point, a work colleague met a woman who was starting a franchise PAS agency—with a company name connoting warmth and reassurance. The woman proffered her business card, which his colleague turned over to Michael. "I gave her a phone call to introduce myself," Michael recalled.

Michael's private-pay PA had worked well for about a year. "Then things broke down badly," Michael recalled, "and she left in a huff." The dispute involved Michael paying time and a half for holiday coverage, which he willingly did for major holidays. "It hadn't occurred to me," said Michael, who was born in England, "that President's Day is considered a major holiday!" The PA disagreed and quit on the spot. Michael was stuck, unsure what to do. Then he remembered the woman starting the PAS agency and telephoned her. The franchise owner

> came by a day later with the person who was, if not her only home aide, one of the few. It really was a small operation at that point. It was just getting started, and they agreed to take me on. To be honest, clearly because they were starting, they needed and wanted the business. But things seemed to fit together very well. . . . [The aide] was able to start almost right away. I think I was only out of home service for 48 hours, at the most.

The agency PA who started working for Michael was Nelita (see book Dedication). Nelita was the second PA hired by the new franchise.

Experiences Working for Home Care Agencies

According to a 2007 survey of home health aides, 63% work for for-profit agencies like the franchise serving Michael, and 37% work for nonprofit or private employers or in other arrangements (e.g., consumer self-direction; see Chapter 8).[16] Private-pay clients pay commercial agencies an hourly fee, of which a fairly large fraction supports agency overhead costs or contributes to profits, leaving PAs with low hourly wages. Anecdotal reports—this information is sensitive and therefore hard to obtain—suggest that franchise PAs receive perhaps 60% of hourly fees paid to commercial franchises. The fraction likely varies regionally, in response to local unemployment rates, the marketplace for PAS providers, and other factors affecting labor costs. Nonprofit and other private agencies that contract with insurers have similar payment arrangements, where PAs receive considerably less than agencies are reimbursed. In 2016 Medicaid paid agencies an average of $19.01 per hour for personal care services,[17] but workers received much lower hourly wages.

Some agencies offer certain benefits to their home health aide employees. According to the 2007 survey, 75% of agency employees were offered health insurance, 55% a retirement plan, 53% paid sick leave, 53% paid holidays, 38% bonuses, and 35% tuition subsidies or reimbursement.[18] However, among home health aides offered agency-supported health insurance, only 52% took such coverage—28% said they could not afford their employer's health plan.[19] At for-profit agencies, only 33% of home health aides took their employer's health insurance.[20]

Travel and transportation costs are major concerns for PAs (see Chapter 6). In the 2007 home health aide survey, three-quarters of agency workers said they drove to various locations throughout the day for their job assignments, and two-thirds were reimbursed for travel expenses.[21] Agencies reimbursed only 21% of workers for travel expenses between their home and their first consumer each day—or between their last consumer and home. Just 10% received travel payments from agencies for running errands for consumers, such as picking up or delivering supplies. Home health aides were also rarely reimbursed for travel costs to agencies for meetings (9%) or in-service training sessions (6%).[22] Aspects of home care agency work that lowered employees' job satisfaction included problems with benefits (29%), agency management (19%), wages (19%), consumers (18%), travel (16%), communication (15%), consumer's families (13%), and scheduling (11%).[23]

Assessments of PAs' job performance by agency supervisors also raise concerns. "They have reduced the job to household maintenance and bodily care, in contrast to intangibles, such as keeping someone company or chatting together about family and friends, which aides constantly remark as being essential to work well done."[24] Building trust and negotiating relationships are not part of formal job evaluations, although many PAs report these are the most critical aspects of their work.

Employment Qualifications

The State Medicaid Manual requires states to develop employment qualifications for PAs supporting Medicaid beneficiaries but does not specify required standards. Instead, the manual offers brief examples of what states could do when employing PAs, such as:

- **Perform criminal background checks**, to screen PAS job candidates
- **Train** workers
- **Monitor workers' competency**, for example, by case managers
- **Set minimum employment requirements**, such as relating to age, health requirements (e.g., test negative for tuberculosis, have no communicable diseases, and be physically able to perform required tasks), and education[25]

A federal agency studied PAS employment requirements set by Medicaid programs and found widespread confusion. Across 43 state Medicaid programs, the oversight agency identified 301 different sets of requirements for PAS workers.[26] "For example, in one State, a 16-year-old with 8 hours of training could provide services through the consumer-directed model, but could not provide services through the agency model until he or she turned 18, received 24 hours of training, and passed a background check."[27] Only seven states had uniform employment standards for Medicaid-covered PAS workers.[28] However, agency-model Medicaid programs were more likely than consumer self-directed models to include training in employment qualifications.

Competencies and Training

Federal regulations mandate minimal requirements for training and evaluation of Medicare-certified home health aides, in addition to requiring that they meet state-specified standards. For home health aides, some states offer different levels of certification and specify training requirements for each level. However, national training requirements do not exist for paid PAs, nor are there national standards about the competencies PAs must demonstrate to perform their jobs. States vary widely in their standards for training of agency-employed PAs. Seven states have no standards, and only 14 states have consistent training standards for these workers.[29]

Iowa is one of many states with inconsistent standards for training PAs, and its experiences suggest the complexities of implementing uniform training requirements.[30] In 2006 Iowa long-term care leaders voiced concern that, although their state had training requirements for PCAs, they were minimal compared with standards for home health aides. Over the next half-dozen years, Iowa policy makers tried to reach consensus about more intensive training standards for PCAs, but various factors stymied their efforts, including the difficulties of establishing a state board to oversee these standards and certifications; potential restrictions on the ability of consumers with self-directed PAS to train their own PAs; the possibility of hampering efforts to recruit new PAs; and the burden on employers, who must track certification of their PAS employees. Nonetheless, Iowa requires agency PCAs to complete 13 hours of training, which covers the role of aides (4 hours), communication (2 hours), understanding basic human needs (2 hours), maintaining a healthy environment (2 hours), infection control (2 hours), and emergency procedures (1 hour).[31]

Minimum Core Competencies for Personal Care Aides

The absence of minimum core competencies for personal care aides prompted CMS to convene a group of national stakeholders to develop basic standards for this field.[32] The resulting list of 12 core competencies (Box 7.2) aims to be comprehensive and encompass the needs of various populations requiring PAS support, including older individuals and younger people with physical, developmental, intellectual, or mental health disability living in community-based settings. They also are intended to apply not only to agency PAS workers but also to PAs employed directly by consumers (see Chapter 8), who might find the competencies to be helpful guidance for training their PAs. The competencies cover wide-ranging skills, and meeting each involves specific approaches or activities. Nevertheless, a recent review of training curricula in six states found that they primarily emphasize technical skills.[33]

Training

No evidence exists about where or how PAs are trained nationwide. In any case, even for home health aides, where training standards do exist, "little is known about the effectiveness of training on worker satisfaction, retention, and injury rates, or on consumer outcomes or satisfaction with worker training."[34] Training programs rarely undergo rigorous evaluation.

Box 7.2 Direct Service Workforce Core Competencies

Centers for Medicare & Medicaid Services

1. **Communication:** Direct service workers (DSWs) build trust and productive relationships with the people they support, coworkers, and others through respectful and clear verbal and written communication.
   - Use positive and respectful verbal, nonverbal, and written communication in a way that can be understood by the individual and actively listen and respond to him or her in a respectful, caring manner
   - Explain services and service terms to the individual being supported and his or her family members
   - Communicate with the individual and his or her family in a respectful and culturally appropriate way
2. **Person-centered practices:** DSWs use person-centered practices, assisting individuals to make choices and plan goals and provide services to help individuals achieve their goals.
   - Help design services or support plans based on the choices and goals of the individual supported and involve the individual in the process
   - Build collaborative professional relationships with the individual and others on the support team
   - Provide supports and services that help the individual achieve his or her goals
   - Participate as an active member of service or support team
   - Work in partnership with the individual to track progress toward goals and adjust services as needed and desired by individual
   - Gather and review information about an individual to provide quality services
   - Complete and submit documentation of services on time
3. **Evaluation and observation:** DSWs closely monitor an individual's physical and emotional health, gather information about the individual, and communicate observations to guide services.
   - Help with the assessment process by gathering information from many sources
   - Use the results of assessments to discuss options with the individual and with team members to guide support work
   - Collect data about individual goals and satisfaction with services
   - Observe the health and behavior of the individual within his or her cultural context
4. **Crisis prevention and intervention:** DSWs identify risk and behaviors that can lead to a crisis and use effective strategies to prevent or intervene in the crisis in collaboration with others.
   - Recognize risk and work to prevent an individual's crisis in a way that meets the individual's need
   - Use positive behavior supports to prevent a crisis and promote health and safety
   - Use appropriate and approved intervention approaches to resolve a crisis

- Seek help from other staff or services when needed during a crisis
- Monitor situations and communicate with the individual and his or her family and support team to reduce risk
- Report incidents according to rules
- See own potential role within a conflict or crisis and change behavior to minimize conflict

5. **Safety:** DSWs are attentive to signs of abuse, neglect, or exploitation and follow procedures to protect an individual from such harm; they help people to avoid unsafe situations and use appropriate procedures to assure safety during emergency situations:

Abuse and neglect
- Demonstrate the ability to identify, prevent, and report situations of abuse, exploitation, and neglect according to laws and agency rules
- Recognize signs of abuse and neglect, including the inappropriate use of restraints, and work to prevent them

Emergency preparedness
- Maintain the safety of an individual in the case of an emergency
- Help individuals to be safe and learn to be safe in the community
- Use universal precautions and give first aid as needed in an emergency

6. **Professionalism and ethics:** DSWs work in a professional and ethical manner, maintaining confidentiality and respecting individual and family rights.
- Follow relevant laws and regulations and are guided by ethical standards when doing work tasks
- Support individual in a collaborative manner and maintain professional boundaries
- Show professionalism by being on time, dressing appropriately for the job, and being responsible in all work tasks
- Seek to reduce personal stress and increase wellness
- Respect the individual and his or her family's right to privacy, respect, and dignity
- Maintain confidentiality in all spoken and written communication and follow rules in the Health Insurance Portability and Accountability Act of 1996 (HIPAA)

7. **Empowerment and advocacy:** DSWs provide advocacy and empower and assist individuals to advocate for what they need.
- Help the individual set goals, make informed choices, and follow through on responsibilities
- Support the individual to advocate for himself or herself by encouraging the individual to speak for himself or herself
- Support the individual to get needed services, support, and resources
- Assist the individual get past barriers to get needed services
- Tell the individual and his or her family their rights and how they are protected

8. **Health and wellness:** DSWs play a vital role in helping individuals to achieve and maintain good physical and emotional health essential to their well-being.

(**Box 7.2** *continued on next page*)

Box 7.2 Direct Service Workforce Core Competencies *(continued)*

- Support the spiritual, emotional, and social well-being of the individual
- Give medications or assist the individual to take medication while following all laws and safety rules
- Assist the individual to learn disease prevention and maintain good health
- Assist the individual to use infection control procedures and prevent illness
- Help the individual make and keep regular health and dental care appointments
- Help the individual follow health care plans and use medical equipment as needed
- Help the individual to learn the signs of common health problems and take actions to improve health

9. **Community living skills and supports:** DSWs help individuals to manage the personal, financial, and household tasks that are necessary from day to day to pursue an independent, community-based lifestyle.
   - Assist the individual to meet his or her physical and personal care needs (e.g., toileting, bathing, grooming) and provide training in these areas when needed
   - Teach and assist the individual with household tasks such as laundry and cleaning
   - Assist the individual to learn about meal planning and shopping and safe food preparation
   - Provide person-centered support and help the individual to build on his or her strengths in life activities

10. **Community inclusion and networking:** DSWs help individuals to be a part of the community through valued roles and relationships and assist individuals with major transitions that occur in community life.
    - Encourage and assist individuals in connecting with others and developing social and valuable social and work roles according to his or her choices
    - Support the individual in connecting with friends and in living and being included in the community of his or her choice
    - Help the individual transition between services and adapt to life changes, including moving into home and community-based settings
    - Respect the role of family members in planning and providing services

11. **Cultural competency:** DSWs respect cultural differences and provide services and supports that fit with an individual's preferences.
    - Provide or access services that fit the individuals' culture or preferences
    - Seek to learn about different cultures to provide better support and services
    - Recognize own biases and don't let them interfere in work relationships
    - Respect the cultural needs and preferences of each individual
    - Help the individual to find social, learning, and recreational opportunities valued in his or her culture

12. **Education, training, and self-development:** DSWs obtain and maintain necessary certifications and seek opportunities to improve their skills and work practices through further education and training.
    - Complete training and continue to develop skills and seek certification
    - Seek feedback from many sources and use them to improve work performance and skills
    - Learn and stay current with technology used for documentation, communication, and other work activities

Adapted from National Direct Service Workforce Resource Center. Final competency set. Centers for Medicare & Medicaid Services; December 2014. Accessed June 4, 2021. https://www.medicaid.gov/sites/default/files/2019-12/dsw-core-competencies-final-set-2014.pdf

Each agency—or commercial franchise—generally has its own PAS employee training requirements. Typically, applicants for agency PAS jobs must receive the agency's training regardless of the candidates' educational backgrounds or employment histories. While these training activities are redundant for some employees, such requirements ensure that all agency staff meet some minimum standards. For example, Lakisha worked previously for her agency as an LPN (see Chapter 6 and Box 7.1). To become an LPN, she had undergone clinical training, and in her LPN work, she assisted patients with ADL needs. Nevertheless, Lakisha's agency required her to complete their home-based PAS training program. Lakisha valued this training, feeling it deepened her understanding of her new home-based job responsibilities:

> It's different [from serving in an institution as an LPN] because you're on your own—the autonomy that you have. You have to make decisions yourself. The things I would normally ask a coworker like, "This patient doesn't look right. Come look at them with me." You can get that second eye [in institutions], but you can't do that in home care. You just kind of go on what you know.

Lakisha, along with several other agency PAs, said their agency training included reading material from books and pamphlets on specific topics, viewing lectures or videos, and completing written tests. Frequent topics include hygiene, common chronic diseases, fire safety, Alzheimer's care, preventing pressure injuries, and assessing whether consumers are feeling unwell. Initial training generally lasts between two and four weeks. Some agencies offer periodic in-service training, from monthly to yearly, to reinforce knowledge about important topics. Refresher courses can cover material from the initial training program and require workers to demonstrate that they perform tasks correctly. Certain agencies give workers opportunities to talk about their workplace experiences during in-service meetings, so that staff can learn from each other. Agencies also sometimes give short quizzes as periodic refreshers. PA interviewees suggested that agency training concentrates on technical skills and knowledge rather than broader concerns, like communication or interpersonal dynamics.

Nurse Practice Act and Other Agency Rules

In most states, agencies must first send a licensed nurse to assess potential PAS clients and, from the assessment, develop a formal care plan.

> The care plan specifies what services will be provided by personal care aides and what services will be provided by other workers. In some states the tasks that can be delegated to a personal care aide are wide-ranging, including medication administration, assisting with insulin pumps, and other nursing-related tasks. However, in other states personal care aides are prohibited from performing tasks such as placing pills in a client's mouth or administering over-the-counter eyedrops.[35]

A 2020 survey of nurse delegation provisions assessed whether states allowed personal care aides to perform 16 tasks typically covered by NPA regulations (Box 7.3).[36] Eighteen states permitted RNs to delegate all 16 sample tasks (up from 16 in 2017), and half of states (26) allowed delegation of at least 14 tasks to home care workers.[37] Florida, Indiana, Pennsylvania, and Rhode Island permitted delegation of none of the 16 tasks.[38] Nurse delegation does not apply to PAs hired directly by consumers (see Chapter 8).

Box 7.3 Selected Tasks Addressed by Nurse Practice Acts

- Administer oral medications
- Administer medication on an as-needed basis
- Administer medication via prefilled insulin or insulin pen
- Draw up insulin for dosage measurement
- Administer intramuscular injection medications
- Administer glucometer test
- Administer medication through tubes
- Insert suppository
- Administer eye or ear drops

- Feed via gastrostomy tube
- Administer enema
- Perform intermittent catheterization
- Perform ostomy care, including skin care and changing appliance
- Perform nebulizer treatment
- Administer oxygen therapy
- Perform ventilator respiratory care

Adapted from AARP Foundation, The Commonwealth Fund, The SCAN Foundation. Long-Term Services and Supports State Scorecard 2020 Edition. Appendices. AARP; 2020. Accessed August 11, 2021. http://www.longtermscorecard.org/~/media/Microsite/Files/2020/Full%20Appendices.pdf

Little research has assessed how nurse delegation regulations affect quality of care or whether consumers can continue living in communities rather than being institutionalized. "Some evidence indicates that the expansion of personal care aide scope of practice, particularly in the administration of medications and other treatments, would allow them to provide more well-rounded care while reducing the workload of licensed nurses. No research demonstrates that restrictive regulations improve client safety or outcomes."[39]

Responsiveness of Agencies to PAs' Concerns

Little research has explored how PAs feel about working for agencies and what factors affect their job satisfaction. Eleven of the 20 PA interviewees worked exclusively for agencies, and two worked both for an agency and directly for consumers. Among agency PAs, whether their agency responded to PAs' concerns primarily drove their job satisfaction. This finding parallels results from the 2007 home health aide survey, which found that supportive agencies and supervisors significantly improved job satisfaction.[40]

Most PA interviewees described agency supervisors as approachable, supportive, and responsive when they sought help. Providing in-home PAS can be isolating, and some PAs valued their agency supervisor calling regularly to see how things were going. PAs especially appreciated in-service sessions where they shared stories about their work experiences with other agency PAs, saying these interactions were not only educational but also provided emotional support. Some agencies required PAs to prepare reports at the end of each visit about their consumer's needs and services provided. However, PAs felt that agency supervisors generally disregarded these reports. When supervisors did review the reports—giving helpful rather than intrusive feedback—PAs valued that acknowledgment and support.

PAs rely on agency rules to protect them from demands from consumers that they view as outside their job descriptions, and they know their agencies will back them up. Agency rules typically prohibit consumers from asking PAs to perform tasks for their relatives, such as preparing and serving meals or doing laundry for consumers' family members. These rules also typically ban PAs from caring for consumers' pets or children or driving consumers in the PA's car. Although some consumers and PAs privately negotiate arrangements that break these rules (mostly around pet care), many PAs prefer not to use their own cars to drive consumers.

A top priority for PAs is whether agencies respond supportively to their safety concerns. For example, Chandra, who has worked 25 years for the same agency, was filling in for a consumer she didn't know and became uneasy:

> He was a male in his late sixties. Kind of crazy. I was very alert looking at him. Halfway into the day, he was starting to argue . . . like he was having a tantrum with himself. He said, "Oh, I was in the world war, and I killed a lot of people, and you're nothing for me to kill." I took my pocketbook, and I ran out the door right away, and I called the agency.

Chandra recounted what had happened, and the agency supervisor told her to leave immediately. She felt reassured that the agency was concerned about her safety, but she also trusted that agency staff would check in on the consumer to assess his well-being.

PAs also prioritize having flexibility in their work hours and schedules—flexibility is a major attraction to PAS jobs for some PAs (see Chapter 6). Responsiveness to requested schedule changes therefore significantly affects how PAs feel about their agencies. One satisfied PA described how her agency readily switched her hours when her young son was sick and she needed to be home. The agency gave her extra hours later, and so she did not lose wages for that week.

Other PAs describe agencies trying to match PAs' preferences with clients' needs, striving for a good fit. One common example is not placing PAs afraid of dogs with dog-owning consumers or PAs allergic to cats with cat owners. Many PAs value being assigned to the same client over time—with familiarity, training needs ebb and PAs know what to expect. Michelle's story exemplifies a PAS agency making concerted efforts to accommodate its employee (see Chapter 6). Michelle had been supporting an agency consumer with cerebral palsy when her boyfriend (now fiancé) was paralyzed with a spinal cord injury. Michelle tried to assist both her agency client and her boyfriend—who now had 24/7 needs—but she was overwhelmed. Michelle's agency and her boyfriend's health insurer worked out a solution, with the insurer contracting with the agency and thus Michelle to provide his support. "When the accident happened, I took it very hard," Michelle recalled. "The agency was there for me. Everybody was just welcoming." Over time, agency staff grew fond of her fiancé: "They love him to death. They're very supportive."

Agencies Not Responding to PAs' Concerns

PA interviewees also described agencies dismissing or ignoring their requests or concerns. Common complaints involved agencies failing to address problems with payments, employment benefits, schedule changes, additional training, and career advancement. These concerns can also affect consumers. "If I call out that I'm not coming in today," said one PA, the agency "finds it very difficult to find someone to send in. Sometimes the patient is left without anyone for the day."

One complexity involves lack of job security for PAs whose primary consumer is hospitalized or dies and thus no longer needs PAS. In these circumstances, agencies call PAs—sometimes at the last minute—and tell them not to show up for work. If no other clients are available through that agency, the PA may be out of a job. This situation strikes PAs as unfair, since they lose their agency employment through no fault of their own.

Lack of agency responsiveness to safety concerns is a major complaint for some PAs (see Chapter 11). Several interviewees reported difficult clients or dangerous workplaces to their agency supervisor, who failed to respond. Examples include the following:

- **Hazards in home.** One PA repeatedly complained about dangerous conditions in her client's home—a man in his eighties with dementia who lived alone. "The situation was absolutely horrific. Every time, I called the agency and said, 'I need help here,' I was told, 'Don't worry about it. Everything will be okay.'" The PA described being unable "to sleep at night because I was worried about what was going to happen to him during the night." After the PA complained for several weeks, the agency's nurse came by with the client's nephew. The visitors falsely claimed that no one had alerted them about the dangerous conditions. The man was sent to a nursing home. The hazards in the consumer's home threatened not only the client but also the PA.
- **Bedbug infestation.** Another PA reported that her agency knew a consumer's home was infested with bedbugs but sent her anyway, without warning her. When she arrived, the PA found the consum-

er incessantly scratching himself. "The guy finally showed me his bed. It was bad, very bad." The PA called her agency and, "When I told them, I felt like they didn't really care. Somebody told me this wasn't the first time somebody said to them that this person had bedbugs." Given how bedbugs spread, the PA worried that she—or her belongings—could easily have become contaminated and subsequently infected her own home.

- **Dangerous location.** One PA asked her agency not to send her to the projects—massive, high-rise, public housing complexes—because she was afraid. Nevertheless, the PA took a job in the projects that her agency offered. When she arrived, "One of the elevators is broken. The next elevator was working but had no lights. I'm like, 'Oh, my gosh. What am I going to do?'" She went to the stairwell, and "it was full of urine and all types of drug paraphernalia." The PA called her agency and told them, "Listen, the elevator's not working. I don't want to be here." The agency told her that the building's manager needed to fix the elevator. Despite her fears, the PA climbed the stairs: "I let money control me. I stayed because I needed the money."

In each of these cases, consumers needed PAS support. The question is how agencies should balance consumers' needs against the safety or well-being of their employees. Beyond physical safety threats, agencies also must recognize the toll of anxiety, stress, and fear on their employees. PAs who report that their agencies downplay their safety concerns generally quit those agencies and find other employers. While changing agencies might appear easy in tight employment markets, PAs can still lose income—difficult for workers living paycheck to paycheck.

Consumers' Experiences with Agency PAS

Penny is happy with agency PAS—comfortable with her team of PAs and pleased not to have to recruit workers in her remote rural region. Penny is reassured that her agency PAs communicate directly with her health care team. Her PAs carry tablet computers, and at the end of their visit, they record their observations of Penny and upload the notes into her electronic health records. With her history of recurrent cellulitis, Penny is pleased that her PAs' daily visit notes become part of her permanent health record and thus are easily accessible to her doctors.

In contrast to Penny, Joe lives in a densely populated inner-city neighborhood. He is similarly happy with his agency's PAS—fortunately so, since

Medicaid, his health insurer, assigned him to that agency and tightly controls the services he receives. Joe is in his mid-fifties and disabled by a stroke. He needs help with showering and various IADLs, including taking his medications. Medicaid covers agency PAS five hours per day on weekdays but not on weekends; therefore, Joe's sisters assist him on Saturdays and Sundays. Before starting, an agency nurse visited his home and evaluated Joe, delineating his PA's duties. Since then, the agency will "come and check on me once a year," Joe said. The agency has sent the same PA, Jasmine, for the last two years. "There's a little list of things that she's supposed to do," said Joe about Jasmine, "and then there's what I would like her to do. I'll talk to her, and if she's comfortable with it, she'll do it." For example, Joe would like Jasmine to drive him to doctor appointments, but that violates agency rules. Joe takes a taxi, and Jasmine drives separately, meeting him at his doctor's office. If Jasmine is sick or needs a day off,

> She'll call and let me know, and then she'll tell the agency that she won't be able to make it, and then the agency will call me and tell me they're sending somebody new. . . . Sometimes I'll say I'm doing fine; I'll just wait till she comes back. I can let her go for one day, and I'll be fine. I just either don't do nothing or just stay in the house.

Joe has Jasmine's supervisor's telephone number if he has any concerns. But he has been pleased with her performance and has never called. "Now that I've known her for a couple of years," said Joe, "it's kind of second nature. I think that I've been blessed with my caregivers."

For more than five years, Michael was also largely pleased with his commercial franchise agency PAS, which he paid for out of pocket. He had frustrations, such as scheduling mishaps; frequent staff changes, necessitating training new PAs about every task, down to the tiniest details—an exhausting process; and occasional PAs who were unreliable, chronically late, incompetent, lazy, unhygienic, or who had difficult personalities. Michael felt he could judge within 15 seconds whether that person was going to be competent, and—albeit rarely—he asked the agency to stop assigning him certain PAs. He felt he would wear out his welcome by complaining too much and therefore had to accept imperfections in his PAs. Nonetheless, the agency generally worked well for Michael, reassuring him that PAS support would be there. The agency had an emergency call number with an answering service during off-hours, which was generally responsive (e.g., when a PA did not show up). They gave him a small discount on his hourly fee, since he was among their first customers and was well liked by agency management. However, at some point, Michael needed more ADL support than he could afford out of pocket through the franchise agency. He enrolled in PACE, a Medicare and/or Medicaid program (see Chapter 3), which has its own PAS staff.

Control

For some consumers, concerns about PAS distill down to control—who makes decisions—in this most intimate and private workplace, the consumer's home. "The agency model is really one about dependency," asserted one consumer. "I'm the dependent one; I'm the client; I'm there to have done for me what is believed to be in my interest." Agencies follow the medical model of care (see Chapter 2), in which professionals—such as the nurse who did Joe's initial assessment—decide what PAs should do for consumers, who thus assume a position of dependency. Furthermore, agency workers are trained to provide ADL supports following agency or professional practices, rather than the preferences of consumers. According to Ernie (see Chapter 5),

> Agencies turn my home into a hospital and treat me like a houseplant. The agencies are strictly regulated in the medical model and are highly restrictive in what is allowed. They barge into people's homes as if they have a right to do so, based on the phony premise that we are incompetent and incapable of making our own informed decisions. So as soon as I was able to quit them I did.

For Ernie, the most important qualities in a PA are "trustworthiness, punctuality, reliability, honesty" and the "ability to follow directions"—Ernie's directions.

8

Self-Directed Personal
Assistance Services

If you are a consumer, you have the right to hire and fire. The PAs work for you—they are not the boss. They are an extension of your life. They are there to assist you with the issues that you need assistance with. They are not there to tell you what to eat, what to wear, where to go, who to talk to. . . . It's our civil rights to be able to live where we want and to have who we want to work for us.

— GEORGE

George was born with cerebral palsy and in his late teens had a spinal cord injury, leaving him severely disabled. Now in his early sixties and single, George has lived in and out of eight nursing homes over many years. He has had difficulties managing on his own in the community, and his health sometimes suffers, forcing him back into nursing homes. Recently, with support from his local CIL, George prepared intensively for transitioning into his own accessible apartment. "This time, before I got out of the nursing home," George said, "I made sure that I was ready physically, as well as mentally, to put all my services together and really be able to manage my PAs." Taking charge of his PAS—and thus of his daily life—would be central to success.

George belongs to a state program that pays for his PAs, determines how many PAS hours he receives, and authorizes equipment purchases (e.g., Hoyer lift for his bedroom). George manages everything else, with backup from his CIL when needed. He receives eight hours of PAS daily, across four PAs—two are CNAs George met in his last nursing home (these CNAs kept their nursing home jobs, working for George during their off-hours). This transition is going well. George feels his health is improving, he's eating well, taking his medications, and getting enough sleep. He also works full-time as a peer counselor, helping other people with disability learn from his experiences to manage their PAS and remain in their homes.

Consumer Self-Direction and Principles
of Independent Living

Consumer control is a core tenet of independent living (see Chapter 2). Self-direction has special importance for PAS, because of its physical intimacy and role in supporting consumers to live as they wish. Ed Roberts and his fellow students in Berkeley, California, founded the independent living movement on principles of self-determination and consumer direction of their essential support services. The 1978 amendments to the 1973 Rehabilitation Act codified these independent living principles, including consumer control and self-determination (Box 2.3). In the mid-1970s, after moving from an institution into his first apartment, Charlie Carr and other disability rights advocates helped make Massachusetts the first state to implement self-directed, Medicaid-funded PAS (see Chapter 3).

In self-directed PAS, also known as consumer-directed or participant-directed PAS, consumers control the major decisions:

- **What:** consumers determine which ADL and other support services they need
- **Who:** consumers recruit, hire, and fire their PAs
- **When:** consumers set work hours and schedules for their PAS
- **Where:** consumers determine where PAS is provided, locations inside and outside the home
- **How:** consumers train and supervise their PAs[1]

Publicly funded, self-directed PAS programs sometimes have restrictions. For example, George's state-financed program does not pay for PAS outside consumers' homes. Self-directed PAS programs funded by Medicaid fall into two basic types: employer authority and budget authority (see Chapter 3). Employer authority empowers consumers to hire, fire, train, schedule, and perform other human resources–type activities for their PAs. Budget authority—which typically comes along with employer authority—gives consumers added flexibility by providing monthly budgets that consumers control to purchase items and services to support their independent living needs.[2]

This chapter reviews self-directed PAS, focusing primarily on Medicaid programs. Most of the 21 consumer interviewees used self-directed PAS. This chapter draws heavily on the comments of George and six other consumers (Box 8.1).

Paying for Self-Directed PAS

In 2016 slightly more than 1 million Americans used self-directed LTSS, including PAS, funded by Medicaid and the Veterans Health Administra-

> ## Box 8.1 Consumers Quoted Frequently in Chapter 8
> - **George**, early sixties, Black, cerebral palsy and spinal cord injury
> - **Matt**, early fifties, White, quadriplegia, spinal cord injury 30 years earlier
> - **Natalie**, early fifties, White, spinal muscular atrophy
> - **Sam**, early fifties, White, muscular dystrophy
> - **Suzanne**, early seventies, White, postpolio syndrome
> - **Tom**, early sixties, White, spinal muscular atrophy

tion (VHA).[3] Medicaid- and VHA-funded self-directed HCBS programs increased 43% from 2011 to 2016, with 253 self-directed programs nationally in 2016 across all states and the District of Columbia.[4] However, many of these programs operate only in certain regions, with fewer than half extending statewide. Some also serve only specific subpopulations, such as people with designated health conditions.

In addition to Medicaid and the VHA, several other public programs fund home-based PAS. The Older Americans Act (OAA), enacted in 1965, finances Aging Services Networks, dedicated to helping older adults remain in their homes and communities. Spurred by OAA's National Family Caregiver Support Program, OAA networks are increasingly moving toward consumer self-direction.[5] Only 7 to 8 million Americans have private long-term care insurance,[6] which sometimes covers home-based, self-directed PAS. The amount that people spend out of pocket on self-directed PAS is unknown.

Medicaid

Medicaid—the joint federal and state health insurance program for poor and disabled individuals—had a historical bias toward institutional care but increasingly is supporting HCBS, despite substantial variations across states (see Chapter 3). Which Medicaid waivers they implement determine whether states can offer beneficiaries agency PAS, self-directed PAS, or combinations of both. Several factors drive states' decisions about their Medicaid PAS programs. States choosing agency PAS typically view that approach as providing higher quality and greater protections for consumers, whom they consider highly vulnerable to abuse or neglect.[7] Some state policy makers believe that agencies lessen their legal liability if problems arise. In contrast, states offering self-directed PAS generally see it as more cost-effective than agencies, thus freeing up dollars to spend elsewhere.

Medicaid state options and certain waiver authorities support self-directed PAS (see Table 3.2). A 2016 survey found that 49 out of the 50 states plus the District of Columbia offered self-directed plans under Medicaid HCBS programs.[8] Although each Medicaid funding authority has specific features, self-directed programs share several requirements stipulated by CMS. All Medicaid recipients with a self-directed PAS must have a service plan: a "written document that specifies the services and supports that are to be furnished to meet the preferences, choices, abilities and needs of the individual, and that assist the individual to direct those services and supports and remain in the community."[9] Consumers must direct development of these person-centered plans, although they can choose to involve a family member, friend, or other representative in specifying their plan. The planning process aims "to identify the strengths, capacities, preferences, needs, and desired measurable outcomes of the individual."[10] The plan must address contingencies, such as handling worker absences (e.g., because of sickness), with explicit backup plans, and it must assess risks to the consumer, specifying how identified risks will be handled. Budget authority gives consumers an individualized budget that the consumer controls and that provides resources for PAS.

CMS also requires states to assist Medicaid consumers with PAS financial management and to train consumers to perform various employer roles. Consumers can choose whether to use these financial management services, which aim to inform consumers about billing and documentation responsibilities; payroll taxes and other federal, state, and local taxes; purchasing workers' compensation and other insurance; processing workers' timesheets; issuing payroll checks; monitoring expenses; and identifying budget shortfalls.[11] Finally, CMS stipulates that states have systems for continuous quality monitoring and improvement of self-directed PAS programs. Specific quality requirements vary across Medicaid's funding authorities, but they "must include activities of discovery, remediation, and quality improvement so that the state learns of critical incidents or events that affect individuals, corrects shortcomings and pursues opportunities for system improvement."[12]

Consumers Paying Out of Pocket for Self-Directed PAS

For consumers who pay out-of-pocket for PAS, personal circumstances and preferences determine whether they seek agency services or obtain self-directed PAs in the gray market—privately hiring people without official employment records or tax documentation. Because these hires happen behind closed doors, no good estimates exist for gray market PAS use or expenditures. Consumers often pay gray market PAs less than agencies charge, perhaps rationalizing that workers only receive a fraction of hourly rates paid to agencies. Thus, a consumer hiring privately could pay higher wages directly to the worker, benefiting both the consumer and employee. Agency rules about allowable tasks do not apply, which offers important advantages to some consumers; however, workers risk the potential for abuse, especially if the PA is undocumented (see Chapter 10). Gray market employment provides few job protections to PAs.

Private arrangements can work well. Suzanne, in her early seventies, is a lifelong advocate for independent living principles and has never considered using agency PAS. With a professional career, Suzanne earns too much for Medicaid eligibility and has therefore always paid out of pocket for PAS. Some PAs have worked for her for many years. Hiring her own PAs gives Suzanne flexibility in where and how she uses them, from walking her dog to having PAs accompany her on business trips and vacations. She needs 35 to 40 hours of PAS weekly and pays approximately $3,000 total to PAs each month. Suzanne admits she continues working largely to afford her PAs.

Determining PAS Needs and Hours of Supports

People who pay out of pocket for self-directed PAS decide what supports they need, how many hours they require, and their PAS schedules. To determine PAS hours, self-pay consumers often balance their needs against what they can afford. In contrast, third-party payors typically decide how many PAS hours consumers will receive, although budget authority gives Medicaid beneficiaries control of PAS hours within the constraints of their monthly allotments. States vary in how they approach needs assessments, which typically involve having consumers answer questionnaires, in-home assessments by nurses or case managers, and evaluations of the following:[13]

- Medical or health conditions
- Functional status and impairments, including ability to perform ADLs and IADLs
- Living situation
- Availability of unpaid individuals to provide supports
- Social environment
- Geographic isolation
- Behavioral factors that might complicate meeting consumers' needs

Medicaid requires all self-directed service plans to describe how identified needs will be met, including the amount, frequency, and duration of services authorized for coverage.

Tom's experiences suggest how payors typically determine eligible PAS hours. He works full-time in a professional job, and his wife's employer-based health insurance covers his medical care costs. Fortunately, his state has a program that covers PAS using general revenue funds rather than Medicaid, which allows Tom to continue working although his income is insufficient to cover his extensive PAS needs. For Tom to receive PAS under this program,

> A social worker from the state Department of Health and Human Services comes in once a year . . . and does the whole reevaluation thing with you. Then you get authorized for a certain number of hours a month. You can use them however you wish, just so it doesn't go over. I get 300 hours a month, which in theory is 10 hours a day. But it doesn't mean that I have to use 10 hours every day. It could be 8 one day and 12 another day.

Tom figures out schedules and staffing that work best for him, totaling 300 hours per month. He has five or six PAs covering regular shifts and 11 PAs on his PAS payroll to ensure backup. Over the decades, Tom estimates he has had approximately 100 PAs.

Determining allowable PAS hours is complicated in certain states and some PAS programs. For instance, one state program gives Natalie the maximum allowance, which supports less than 10 hours per day and is insufficient for her needs. She receives additional hours through another Medicaid HCBS waiver program. Natalie uses 14 hours of PAS daily, staffed by eight PAs. George also had problems getting adequate PAS hours from his state's non-Medicaid, public PAS program:

> The managed care company kept telling me, "No, we can't give you more hours." So I had to go to my rehabilitation physician and have him write a very detailed letter of medical necessity to state specifically why I needed more hours to stay in the community. And then I had to get various people on the health care team to back that up. . . . I did get the hours that I requested. But it doesn't always happen that way. Consumers have to be persistent. It's a very daunting process.

Identifying PA Candidates

Finding PAs is the most difficult part of self-directed PAS. Consumers' interest in using self-directed PAS therefore often depends on whether they have family members, friends, or other trusted individuals they can employ.[14] As in any human relationship, complex factors govern the interpersonal dynamics between consumers and PAs (see Part IV). Finding committed employees who are the right fit is therefore essential. Sometimes, family or other household members disagree with consumers about who to hire, complicating staffing decisions. Identifying PA candidates, vetting them, and hiring is time-consuming and stressful; anxiety and pressures escalate when consumers urgently need PAs to support immediate needs. Consumers may feel compelled to hire someone, anyone, to provide essential supports. External and demographic forces further complicate this process (see Chapter 14).

Hiring PAs is a multistep process, which takes time, can be expensive (e.g., fees to post jobs on websites, to perform desired background checks), and can feel overwhelming. As one consumer said, finding PAs is "a crap shoot. Either it works out or it doesn't." Suzanne, who pays out of pocket for PAS, lives in a high-cost area, where few local residents have low-wage jobs. To attract candidates, she therefore offers the highest hourly wage she can afford but is nevertheless resigned to spending weeks or months searching for a new PA. Suzanne has hired PAs for many years and honed her recruitment strategy, starting by asking everyone she knows for recommendations and next posting her position on Craigslist. "And then many, many responses come in," Suzanne observed. "You can eliminate 95% of them pretty quickly. They'll be responses like, 'Yo, what's the pay?'" When an interesting reply arrives, Suzanne asks the candidate to email, describing why the job would be a good fit. Suzanne invites applicants with intriguing rationales to meet face-to-face in her home.

People using self-directed PAS pursue multiple channels to seek workers, including the following:

- **Hiring family members, friends, or acquaintances.** Many Medicaid programs permit most family members or friends to serve as paid PAs. In 2016 29 states allowed consumers to hire family members, albeit some exclude legally responsible relatives (i.e., spouse, parents of dependent children).[15] Hiring someone consumers already know reduces concerns about strangers coming into the home; however, having relatives or friends as PAs can exacerbate long-standing dysfunctional relationships. Ethnicity and cultural factors, including immigration and acculturation status, also affect willingness to hire relatives.[16] Family members who already provide considerable informal supports may prefer having paid nonrelatives take over much or all of this effort.
- **Word of mouth.** Asking current PAs for potential candidates can be fruitful, as is reaching out to friends, acquaintances, and contacting social networks. One consumer found his PA at his yoga class, where she was assisting another yogi. Another consumer belongs to the local trans and gender-neutral community, which is tight-knit, and word-of-mouth requests spread rapidly.
- **Online PAS worker registries.** Some programs offer online registries of local people seeking PAS jobs. Worker registries typically

perform criminal background checks before posting candidates' names. One consumer reported, however, that funding cuts and inadequate maintenance reduced her local registry's usefulness for finding PAs.

- **Websites.** Like Suzanne, more than half of consumer interviewees post their positions online, including on Craigslist, Facebook, Care.com, Rewardingwork.org (Massachusetts, Connecticut, Rhode Island, and Vermont; the New Jersey chapter no longer operates), Nextdoor.com (California), MySupport (California, New York, Virginia), and other online job boards and social networks. Some websites are regional and require updating to function well. Certain websites charge fees prorated by the number of words or length of time an ad is posted; à la carte options (e.g., background checks) increase costs.
- **Local schools, colleges, and universities.** Community colleges, technical schools, and universities are often fruitful sources of PAS workers. Many students are eager for part-time positions that help people, although they are generally transitory workers. Recruiting from nursing schools or programs training rehabilitation therapists can be particularly productive, as students seek relevant work experiences. Some educational institutions require consumers to get permission before posting their job.
- **Centers for Independent Living.** Several interviewees mentioned CILs as helpful resources for training about PA recruitment and hiring. Some CILs also have lists of potential PA candidates.
- **Other approaches.** Additional approaches include posting flyers at churches, community centers, and coffeehouses and placing ads in local newspapers and newsletters, such as those popular with local artists (who might appreciate ways to make extra money). Hiring people who are already working but want a second job, perhaps during nonbusiness hours, can be productive.

Interviewing and Screening Candidates

As described further in Chapter 13, after identifying potential PA candidates, people using self-direction generally screen and interview applicants, although sometimes payors stipulate certain vetting requirements (e.g., criminal background checks). For many consumers, the bottom line is finding the right fit. Tom acknowledged that the process is complex, but he urges taking time to do it right:

Think about what you need and keep standards high even though it may be frustrating at times: "I'm not getting the kind of applicants I want, so I'll take this one here, even though I'm very reluctant to hire them." . . . There's some stuff that's hard to learn, and I don't always obey those rules myself. But I've compromised on hiring staff, and most of the time I regret it. . . . It's hard to explain, but it's someone who's comfortable with intimacy, is reliable and respectful, and seems to want to be there with you. There's a certain attitude that I can see in a person, and that's what matters the most.

Optimally, consumers must feel comfortable with their PAs. Having applicants show up on time for job interviews is a first test: no-shows are common. Some consumers prefer first meeting job applicants outside their home, at a coffee shop, public library, or park, cautious about giving their address to strangers. Consumers ask questions to elucidate the applicant's personality, interests, attitudes, personal preferences, and other traits. Box 13.4 suggests questions that consumers might ask potential PAs. However, as for Tom, consumers often develop an almost sixth sense about PA candidates. For example, Sam is Buddhist and seeks PAs who would respect his belief system and desire for a quiet, peaceful ambience in his home, which he views as his safe zone. A long-term PAS consumer, Sam felt he "can teach the job to anyone, but I can't teach the morals. Are you loyal? Are you hardworking? Are you on time? Are you honest?" One consumer with a severe speech impediment views in-person interviews as critical to see how PA candidates respond to communication difficulties. He describes being patient and willing to repeat himself, but he knows that makes some people uncomfortable. He believes he can generally tell within 10 seconds of meeting whether a PA candidate will work out.

Some people must seek self-directed PAS because their needs cross the boundaries of NPAs (see Chapter 4)—agency PAs cannot perform certain tasks without nurse delegation (Box 7.3). PAs working under consumer direction are not limited by NPAs—they can perform whatever tasks the consumer and they negotiate. In this context, consumers must recruit PAs whom they view as capable of performing these tasks with care and competence.

For example, in 2018, Michael's primary progressive multiple sclerosis left him unable to eat safely or swallow medications (see Chapter 5).[17] Michael now receives all nutrition and medications through his PEG tube. The transition upended the fragile PAS balance he had achieved at the time, relying on a mix of agency PAs. His franchise agency could send a nurse to perform tube feeds at $75 an hour, but with three tube feedings daily, two hours per feed, costs would have been $450 per day. Michael needed to switch to self-direction. He advertised online for PAs, mentioning at the outset his need for tube feeding—thus ensuring applicants would know what to expect. Although tube feeding is straightforward (see Chapter 5), Michael needed PAs comfortable with small electronic devices (pump that propels the feed), with good manual dexterity, facile with simple mathematics (e.g., to measure out individual meals within preprepared bags), and excellent understanding of basic hygiene. Over the last two years, some PAs have performed these tasks easily, and others have been less proficient.

Preferences for PA Gender

Most PAs are women. Under self-direction, consumers can seek workers with whatever attributes they prefer, limited only by their local pool of PA candidates. Most consumer interviewees expressed preferences for women PAs, largely on the assumption that women are more nurturing, caring, and easier to get along with than men. Feeling physically and emotionally safer is the strongest argument favoring women over men. "You're having a conversation about something while you're naked in the shower," Suzanne said. She has considered having male PAs and decided against it. "I don't know if I can articulate it very clearly, but my comfort level with women is much greater in general. . . . I'm just not that comfortable with that level of intimacy with a man."

Men consumers express similar views but emphasizing different rationales. Matt had his spinal cord injury (SCI) in his early twenties, more than 30 years ago. For the first few years, Matt preferred women PAs: "I just didn't want a guy helping me out." He recalled worrying that male PAs would threaten his masculinity, that he would appear "weak." Decades later, Matt began hiring PAs regardless of gender, sometimes valuing the physical strength of male PAs. Another man with SCI had diametrically opposite views from Matt's. After his injury, he "struggled with a lot of issues with body image and what I could and couldn't do and how others perceived me." He felt that women providing supports would see him as unattractive, sexually inadequate. During the first few years after the SCI, he only hired male PAs.

People's gender, gender identity, and sexual orientation vary, potentially affecting decisions about hiring PAs. Natalie describes herself as bisexual and having no gender preference for her PAs. She has hired male, female, transgender, and gender-neutral PAs without discomfort, safety worries, or other concerns. One male consumer always hires women because he likes women. He also likes visiting adult entertainment venues but realizes doing so can distress some women. "Being a male, I'm a sexual person," he said. "In the interview, I ask if they feel comfortable going with me to an adult establishment." He does not hire candidates who express discomfort. This consumer does have a clear rule about his PAs: "Number one, don't fall in love with them."

PAs with Complex Personal Histories

Difficulties finding PAs and other factors can lead consumers to hire individuals with complex personal histories that often make it hard for them to get jobs, such as those with criminal records or histories of serious mental illness or substance use, undocumented immigrants, and sex workers. Some states' PAS programs require candidates for self-directed positions to pass criminal background checks before they can go on the payroll, with some exceptions for family members.[18] States differ in how they treat histories of misdemeanors versus felonies and recent versus distant offenses.

Although Tom urges consumers to keep standards high when hiring PAs, he does not immediately reject candidates with criminal or drug-use histories:

> I don't necessarily consider a record along those lines to be a liability. I'd want some assurances, and I would want to check it out. But I've had both good and bad people with records and good and bad people without records. . . . It says what you were; it doesn't say what you are. If I determine that you are not that anymore, then I'll go with you.

Matt observed that "a very high percentage of my PCAs, my best PCAs, would fail any criminal background check. Some have violent offenses. They were young. They grew up in environments where they are survivors. Do I justify it? No." Matt feels that people can change, and he gives them the benefit of the doubt—albeit after conducting online searches about them. Matt admits that hiring people with criminal histories is not for everyone.

Some consumers hire PAs with histories of drug use, potentially viewing PAS as an opportunity for redemption or a pathway to self-worth. These situations do work out, but not always. For instance, Sam believes that hiring workers with complex histories represents a special type of reciprocity: he receives PAS that he needs, while his PAs gain feelings of empowerment. Sam is proud of having hired PAs who had been "former drug addicts, homeless, people who were down and out." Sam noted that

> a lot of my employees come from those kinds of backgrounds. . . . They appealed to me because (A) they were people who want to work; (B) they want to better their lives, and they usually aren't given the shot to do it. I can take this small amount of money and use it to

empower people. . . . That appeals to me as a liberal, and it appeals to me as a human being. It was the right thing to do, but that comes with danger.

Sam hired, as a live-in PA, a woman with a history of substance abuse and bipolar disorder, who said she was in recovery. However, after she resumed taking drugs, her severe bipolar disorder returned. Almost overnight, the PA became unable to perform her job. "Holy shit," Sam recalled thinking, "I'm in trouble." He contacted a former PA who had been a reliable stand-by and immediately took over. Sam's PA with bipolar disorder required inpatient psychiatric care, and he fired her.

When having trouble finding PAs, consumers might consider atypical options. Natalie lives in a high-cost area with a tight labor market, making it nearly impossible to find PAs. She has hired sex workers and believes this helps both her and the workers. Natalie describes sex workers as nonplussed by intimacy and the intensely personal nature of PAS. These workers "are grateful to have an employer who's not judgmental," said Natalie. "They don't have to hide it. And sex workers are not shy about body stuff. They're comfortable with bodies, and they're not judgmental either." Natalie benefits from the ease and dexterity of sex workers in performing ADL tasks, and she feels these PAs value having stable work in a nonthreatening environment.

Suzanne's views mirror feelings of many consumers willing to hire PAs with complicated histories. She requires applicants to be "open with me and straight with me about it." After surmounting that threshold, Suzanne's decisions come down to interpersonal connections. "It has to do with the chemistry and sense of feeling safe," said Suzanne, "whether I think they're going to be able to show up." She acknowledged that histories of crime or drug use suggest unreliability, but she believes that perception is "a stereotype. So, yeah, I would certainly consider those folks if all other things look like they might work."

Training Self-Directed PAs

All consumers, regardless of agency- versus self-directed model of PAS, must train their PAs on their preferences for how they want specific things done (e.g., sequence of getting dressed, whether shirts or tops must be tucked into waistbands). In self-directed PAS, consumers—perhaps with family support—control training, starting with designating the support tasks PAs must perform. Some states require that self-directed PAs receive minimal training, like attending sessions about basic topics like hygiene, safety, how to detect and respond to abuse, neglect, and exploitation.[19] Some community organizations (e.g., local Red Cross chapters) offer this training. State programs supporting self-directed

PAS sometimes require PAs performing skilled tasks to undergo a professional evaluation, assessing PAs' abilities to provide such tasks.[20]

Consumers use different approaches to train their PAs. Some provide instruction as PAs perform the tasks, talking them through every step and underscoring the consumer's preferences. Others have new PAs shadow current PAs or ask current PAs to train the new PAs. Tasks that can be witnessed and replicated are relatively straightforward to teach. Suzanne found that, to effectively train new PAs, she needs to fully understand her assistive technology herself. She started using a Hoyer lift several years ago and took time to find the best sling for her needs. Now, when Suzanne trains new PAs, she asks them to lift themselves with the Hoyer device. Suzanne believes that firsthand experience allows PA trainees to learn the geometry and body mechanics more quickly and stop fearing the Hoyer lift.

Training about interpersonal interactions and communication preferences is more complicated. "At some point, you're going to see me naked," said one male consumer, describing training new PAs. "If you don't realize that then that's gonna be strange. And you're going to have to touch me at some point, to get the Hoyer underneath me. . . . Can the person jump in and show some confidence? What's the expression on the person's face? Are they comfortable?" Often, trainees require time to learn and feel at ease in the job. Sometimes new PAs find the work is not for them: "they'll get the first paycheck, and they're gone." Other times, trainees never adequately learn the tasks or remember the routine, and consumers fire them. Under self-direction, consumers have the right to fire PAs at will, which can complicate already complex interpersonal dynamics (see Part IV).

Tom avoids hiring PAs who have worked for agencies or in institutional settings because he needs to unteach them ingrained approaches that he dislikes. "I feel that they've been told there's a certain way of doing things," said Tom, "and they've been trained they are in charge. I have to break them of that habit and tell them, 'No, you're not in charge. I'm in charge. And I do things a certain way for a reason.'" While they know standard approaches toward supporting ADLs, Tom said, "No one can teach them how to help me except me."

Benefits of Self-Directed PAS

In self-directed PAS, consumers most value having control. They also benefit from:

- **Flexibility**—the ability to set goals and standards for their PAS
- **Reciprocity**—the opportunity for consumers and PAs both to benefit from their interactions and relationship, beyond standard employer-employee expectations

- **Building a team**—for consumers with more than one PA, the ability to foster collaboration among their PAs

Flexibility

Consumer interviewees offered many examples of self-direction enhancing flexibility:

- **Work hours.** Consumers often willingly adjust PAs' work hours at the PA's request, as long as PAs give advance notice and are flexible themselves with their work hours to meet consumers' needs. It's a give and take.
- **Types of tasks.** With self-direction, consumers set job expectations. Unlike agency PAS, which circumscribes allowable tasks, self-direction has no specific rules or boundaries, beyond obvious legal constraints (e.g., prohibitions against abuse). States' NPA regulations do not constrain self-directed PAS. Therefore, consumers can have PAs perform wide-ranging activities, from pet care to wound care. As did Michael for tube feeding, consumers can specify, in advertising their job, special skills and needs required, so applicants can tell, up front, whether the position is right for them.
- **Location and order of tasks.** Self-direction generally allows consumers to specify where various support tasks can occur, specifically inside versus outside the home. Some state self-directed programs, such as George's, cover only PAS performed within the home. In programs without this constraint, consumers might ask their PAs, for example, to start their shift by stopping at the grocery store before coming to the home.
- **Special requests.** Consumers might periodically make special requests of PAs. In these situations, their interpersonal dynamics affect whether the requests seem more like demands than options. For example, both Suzanne and Matt travel frequently for business, accompanied by their PAs. Each trip requires several days, and PAs who have home responsibilities or dislike travel would likely not want to accompany them. Consumers should not expect willingness to travel or perform other nonstandard tasks without negotiating these job expectations up front with PAs.

Reciprocity

Some consumers feel that, with self-direction, consumers and PAs both benefit from a "win-win situation. I'm helping you. You're helping me." Consumers provide jobs, while PAs support consumers to live on their own terms. Many consumers invoke notions of reciprocity when offering jobs to people from disadvantaged groups, subject to discrimination or stigmatization. Consumer interviewees offered many examples of reciprocity, including the following:

- One consumer has a master's degree in rehabilitation counseling; he serves as the disability services coordinator at a prestigious college. He likes recruiting students from technical schools (e.g., medical assistant programs) as his PAs. He enjoys teaching them and feels he provides good learning experiences, which hospitals and other institutional settings often deny them. He offers to write strong recommendation letters for PAs seeking more education.
- Matt recruits students from a nearby university that trains rehabilitation therapists. He commits himself to teaching these PAs not only technical skills but also critical aspects of life with a disability. Matt's student PAs have told me that his life lessons are as valuable to them for their future careers as the technical skills they learn at their university.
- Sam hired an immigrant from Tibet as his PA despite misgivings about transportation logistics: the PA needed to walk a mile to catch the train that would bring him to Sam's home daily by 6:30 A.M. Nevertheless, the PA was reliable, true to his word, and Sam described the relationship as the "beginning of my Tibetan family." Two years later, Sam cosigned immigration papers so the PA could bring 10 relatives from Tibet to the United States.
- Suzanne has numerous connections throughout her community, fostered over decades in her professional career. She is strongly committed to supporting her PAs however she can, serving as their "reliable fix-it person if they need something fixed." PAs come to her with personal troubles that she tries to help resolve. In turn, Suzanne's PAs make accommodations to meet her needs, such as changing their work hours to ensure she attends medical appointments.
- One consumer in her early sixties hired a woman, also in her early sixties, as a live-in PA. The PA needed a home, and the consumer valued having someone with her 24/7, not for round-the-clock supports but more for her presence. The consumer ensures that her younger PAs perform ADL tasks requiring physical strength. "It's a two-sided relationship," said the consumer. "They're not only taking care of you, but you're taking care of them too, not putting them in any harm."

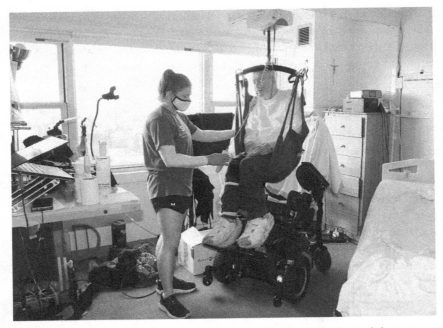

On December 13, 2020, Matt being transferred by his PA, a physical therapy student, with Matt's automated Hoyer lift. Matt spent much of his day participating in videoconference meetings on his laptop, located on the stand on the table to the left—during the pandemic almost all meetings became virtual. Matt can operate most of his computer and communication technologies using a mouth stick or voice commands, but occasionally he needs assistance from his PAs. His student PA witnesses Matt living an active life, interacting with disability advocates nationwide, and advising state and national government policy makers about disability issues. (Photo credit: Unknown personal assistant)

Team Building

The team notion fits into self-directed PAS in several ways—consumer-PA teams, teams of PAs serving the same consumer, and sometimes teams of PAs across colocated consumers. The primary team goal is to ensure consumers reliably receive the PAS coverage they need. For example, Mona manages multiple PAs around the clock to support brothers Bob and Dan and their ailing mother (see Chapter 1). Mona attributes "making their days happen" to mission-driven teamwork. Other examples of teamwork include the following:

- One consumer who needs 24/7 support has several PAs with clearly defined hours and roles. He expects his PAs to interact among themselves to make sure all hours and tasks are covered, with PAs contacting each other by telephone, text, or Facebook. When PAs are sick, he wants them to arrange their own coverage from other team members. Some PAs have worked for the consumers for many years, one for 16 and another for 14 years.

- Natalie also expects her multiple PAs to function as a team to ensure her full coverage. PAs who want time off must negotiate a trade or substitute with another PA. Natalie learned 20 years ago that arbitrating coverage schedules among her workers was complicated and time-consuming. Shifting responsibility to her PAs improved the process. "On the team, there's sort of a buddy and favor system," said Natalie. "'Hey, I'll cover you when you're out of town in October. Will you do my shift on Christmas?'"

Finally, Matt also gives his PAs scheduling responsibility: "I tell them, 'Don't call me if you're not coming in. You guys should work as a team.'" Matt organizes dinners for his PAs and is pointedly absent from the events, giving his PAs freedom to "share Matt stories." Matt believes that these gatherings foster team building, enhance feelings of shared responsibility, and release stress.

Matt lives in a high-rise building inhabited by many people with disability. Some PAs work for multiple consumers in his building, going from apartment to apartment. Work hours and thus total earnings add up, and PAs avoid the hassle of traveling outdoors between clients. "I think it's really positive, neighbors' PCAs helping each other," said Matt. A close friend who lived several floors below Matt's apartment died recently. As her health worsened, their PCAs frequently helped each other and, in her final year, Matt's PAs sometimes spent half their hours allotted to Matt assisting his friend, especially at night. According to Medicaid rules, popping back and forth across consumers was breaking the rules, Matt admitted. But they never exceeded their combined allotted hours, and he felt at peace with the sharing. "She got her needs met. I got my needs met."

IV

Experiences and Perceptions of Receiving and Providing PAS

ADLs are basic, life-sustaining tasks everyone does. Nevertheless, each person has unique personal tastes, preferences, values, cultural traditions, and wishes for performing ADLs. These core realities underlie myriad interpersonal complexities in paid PAS, which requires close physical intimacy, often between strangers. Despite its essential functions, paid PAS is low-wage work. The vast majority of PAs are women, many are racial or ethnic minorities, and a substantial number are immigrants. Thus, PAS consumers and their PAs frequently have different socioeconomic backgrounds, cultural heritages, primary languages, and lived experiences, complicating efforts to build respectful, trusting relationships—critical to the physical and emotional safety of both consumers and PAs. Part IV explores these complexities. Chapter 9 describes multilayered relationships between consumers and PAs, Chapter 10 explores the cross-cutting concepts of trust and respect, and Chapter 11 examines physical and emotional safety. Finally, Chapter 12 acknowledges that money matters—low wages and meager employment benefits—can stoke the fragility of relationships between many consumers and PAs. These topics do not have clear boundaries. Many issues cut across two or more chapters.

9

Relationships and Intimacy

I feel extremely grateful to people who have worked for me for
a long time and are constant. . . . People don't treat me like an
employer. They treat me like a family member that they have
an obligation to. Those relationships are very important to me.
If something happens to them, I'm their go-to person. . . . They
come for Christmas dinner, and we do birthdays. . . . I know it's a
business relationship—it has to be that at some level because they
get money every week. And they do stuff for me that I ask them to
do. But it's also this other dynamic that I know is real.

—SUZANNE, private-pay consumer, self-direction

There's a stereotype that people with disabilities are just useless
leeches on the system. That's not true in my experience at all.
They're executive directors of nonprofits, they're artists, they're
lawyers, they're professors. They go out and work. If they don't
have my help, they can't do that. . . . There's value in being able
to help other people. . . . If you're good at it, a lot of clients aren't
going to care if you're queer, a person of color, or even if you have
your own disability. That's the thing that benefits me. . . . I've been
able to be more open about my own mental health issues. . . . I can
be like, "Hey, I'm having a really high anxiety day today." . . . It's
honestly a feeling of mutual respect from my clients that probably
keeps me doing it.

—ABBY, PA, hired by Medicaid consumers under self-direction

ADL supports involve physically intimate, private interactions generally between two people. Over time, paid PAS consumers and their
PAs develop an interpersonal dynamic or relationship of some sort.
For both consumers and PAs, the nature of this relationship carries significant implications. For consumers, these relationships determine their ease
and confidence about living daily as they wish, substantially affecting their
quality of life. For PAs, feeling respected and valued by consumers is essential
to finding personal gratification and worth in their jobs.

All interpersonal relationships are multidimensional and complex. Multiple
factors shape these relationships, including levels of trust, respect, empathy,

comfort with difference, readiness to reveal and transcend vulnerabilities, and open communication to identify and resolve conflicts. In health care delivery, therapeutic relationships between health care professionals and patients are distinct, marked by "the inherent power differential that exists between a client and a practitioner. . . . The relationship is asymmetrical; those looking for help are placed in a position of vulnerability, whereas the professional assumes a position of power."[1] Because of patients' potential vulnerabilities, health care professions delineate ethical boundaries between clinicians and patients—which vary over time, clinical specialty, culture, and geographic region—that should remain inviolate to protect patients and maintain safe, empathic, and healing therapeutic relationships.

The context of paid PAS complicates these dynamics. Some pioneers of the independent living movement aimed to separate ADL support tasks from emotion, rejecting the notion of caring: "For them, the PA model meant a cash service, controlled by the disabled person, in which workers performed the tasks which the disabled person could not do—self-care, domestic tasks, driving—with no need for emotions such as gratitude. In this way, disabled people could become socially independent and regain control of their lives."[2] Consumers would have authority to hire, supervise, and fire their PAs, albeit simultaneously depending on them for essential supports. However, the bright professional boundaries envisioned by early independent living advocates fall apart as soon as consumers and PAs begin interacting. Because of the intimacy of PAS, emotions and interpersonal feelings inevitably emerge. Especially for consumers without ready family or friends, paid PAs may become their primary human contacts, bulwarks against isolation and aloneness—another complex dynamic.

In contrast, for PAs, their workplace is the consumer's home, where they are often alone with a consumer who is physically vulnerable albeit their boss or the person directing their actions, sometimes minute by minute. Some consumers resent the PA's presence (i.e., which personifies their need for assistance) or reject core aspects of the PA's identity (e.g., race, ethnicity). Nevertheless, PAs have essential tasks to perform. As Suzanne and Abby suggest, reciprocity—when consumers and PAs mutually benefit—can become the foundation for strong and enduring consumer-PA relationships. Thus, "personal assistance involves a dynamic blend of social and professional roles, with fluid relational and procedural boundaries. . . . PA relationships develop over time through shared experiences and common interests."[3]

This chapter explores various dimensions of consumer-PA relationships, including intimacy. These relationships are often opaque, with deep, hidden currents of feelings. This chapter draws examples primarily from six consumers and five PA interviewees (Box 9.1).

Box 9.1 PAS Consumers and PAs Quoted Frequently in Chapter 9

Consumers

- **Ariana**, late fifties, Hispanic, arthrogryposis; has had a live-in PA for a dozen years under hybrid program "agency with choice"
- **Linda**, early sixties, White, quadriplegic from multiple sclerosis; uses Medicaid-funded self-directed PAS; Mark's girlfriend for nearly 30 years
- **Matt**, mid-fifties, White, quadriplegic, spinal cord injury 30 years earlier; shortly after injury had agency PAS but for the last 20+ years, has used Medicaid-funded self-directed PAS
- **Mark**, late fifties, White, quadriplegic, spinal cord injury 40 years ago; uses self-directed PAS; Linda's boyfriend for nearly 30 years
- **Michael**, early sixties, White, quadriplegia from primary progressive multiple sclerosis; uses both agency and self-directed PAS
- **Natalie**, early fifties, White, quadriplegic from spinal muscular atrophy; self-directed PAS with public funding, including Medicaid
- **Suzanne**, mid-seventies, White, postpolio syndrome; private-pay, self-directed PAS

Personal assistants

- **Abby**, early thirties, White, has provided PAS for 12 years, self-identifies as queer and bisexual, primarily works through Medicaid self-directed program
- **Aida**, early fifties, Cape Verdean (immigrated as small child), has provided PAS for four years under self-direction private-pay consumer, gray market
- **Chandra**, mid-fifties, East Indian, immigrant, has provided PAS for 30 years through agency
- **Isaiah**, mid-fifties, Black, has provided PAS for 40 years, usually through agency
- **Marion**, age fifty, Black, has provided PAS for 20 years, both through agency and private-pay consumer
- **Trina**, early fifties, Black, has provided PAS for two years through agency

---

Nature of Relationships

Paid PAS requires intimacy and trust and extends over time, making it "likely [to] break down personal, social and professional barriers."[4] During their ongoing interactions, the amount, nature, and content of communication between consumers and PAs largely shapes the contours of their relationship. Communication is critical for negotiating the complexities of interpersonal dynamics. However, many factors affect communication between consumers and PAs, starting with those shaping the power balance between them, such as sociodemographic, language, and cultural attributes. At the most basic level, discordance in language between consumers and PAs significantly increases risks of troubled relationships. The 2007 National Home Health Aide Survey (see Chapter 6) found that 35% described difficulties communicating with their clients because of language barriers; furthermore, workers reporting language barriers experienced four times as many injuries from patient violence as did other home health aides.[5] For consumers, their absolute need for PAS, provided as they wish, puts a premium on excellent communication. Relationships between consumers and PAs depend largely on how each individual navigates:

- **Boundaries** of the relationship
- **Setting agendas** within the relationship
- **Power dynamics,** having their interests take precedence
- **Locations,** having the consumer's home as the primary workplace[6]

Perspectives of PAS Consumers

For consumers, their relationship with each PA falls along a continuum from exclusively professional to intensely personal. Consumers differ about whether they seek PAs with certain personality traits, such as being friendly, sociable, or good company, and they recognize that paid PAS work is not for everybody. At a minimum, the job requires reliability, timeliness, the ability to follow instructions, a genuine interest in people, and an ability to communicate clearly. Relationships take time. "Once PCAs get to know me as a person, and I get to trust them as a person, then I can get this sense of comfort," said Matt. "I don't want them thinking of me as just this medical basket case. I want them to see me as a person first."

Keeping It Professional—At Least at First

Many consumers emphasize maintaining professional relationships with PAs. "We do have fun, but we also keep it professional at the same time," said George, who works with four PAs. "They understand that I am their boss." Natalie sets clear boundaries, distinguishing professional time, when ADL support occurs, from off-clock hours with PAs who are also good friends. Keeping the relationship professional is especially important at the start, as consumers assess the skills and overall performance of a new PA. The first priority is making sure PA candidates can do the job safely and efficiently. One man advises consumers to emphasize this professional relationship and job expectations when recruiting PAs:

> You've got to be honest with people that you're interviewing. Be honest about what your needs are. That's very critical. Treat it as a business relationship. At least initially it needs to be that way. The people need to understand what time they've got to be here, what they need to do, what time they're going to be done, and what they're going to be paid. Stick to that. But exercise the golden rule: treat people like you want to be treated.

Maintaining a professional distance is especially challenging when consumers hire family members or friends as paid PAs. In this context, preferences and circumstances vary widely. A study from England found that consumers expressed multiple concerns about hiring family members or friends: the difficulty of firing someone who performs poorly; an informality and conviviality in the relationship that results in lower-quality care; impediments to consumer control over PAS; and, in rare instances, opportunities for theft.[7] When consumers fire a family member, the action can strain relationships not only with that person but also other relatives, possibly for years.

Another complex dynamic involves consumers who have required PAS support all their lives. Interactions and relationships that are reasonable for young children might be patronizing and inappropriate for adults. People with disability who were encouraged in passive dependency during early childhood may seek independence and control as teenagers and adults. In a study exploring PAS and women with disability, one participant observed that

> I wasn't able to say, "knock it off" to my family who was doing my personal care. I thought it was normal to be tossed around in my chair. To have a comb dragged through my hair so it comes out. To be left on a toilet for an hour. It took me about five years of hiring people, when I realized I didn't have to accept those things. Because of that experience growing up, I feel more vulnerable to allowing it to happen now. Now I feel I have the power to say, "No, this isn't going to be OK."[8]

Like Family and Friends

Many consumers describe close relationships with one or more of their PAs, friendships or family-like relationships, as for Suzanne. Matt believes that developing friendships with PAs is key to consumer-directed PAS: "For a friend you'll do anything, right?" Nonetheless, Matt acknowledges that even with PAs who do not become his friends, "there's still a relationship." Although consumers recognize the professional premise of paid PAS, long-standing relationships often evolve into closeness and mutual concern. "My best PA was my PA for almost 15 years," said one woman. "But she got sick, so she had to stop working for me. It was hard. Her family became part of my family."

Mark became quadriplegic from a spinal cord injury 40 years ago; he is now in his late fifties, with a full-time professional job. One of Mark's PAs has worked for him for more than 20 years. When the PA started, he lived in the same urban neighborhood as Mark; he now lives in a town nearly 40 miles south of Mark's apartment. Nonetheless, the man arises early, driving that distance to provide Mark's morning ADL support four days each week. After leaving Mark, the PA visits another PAS client closer to his home. Describing his relationship with this long-term PA, Mark said, "Kind of like a husband and wife. We can get crabby with each other sometimes, but you know there's a lot of love there. So, it's back and forth. He knows the whole history."

Desire for Privacy

Some consumers need many hours of PAS daily to meet their needs. However, having PAs constantly around, often in small spaces, can be taxing. Albeit acknowledging the necessity of PAS, consumers nevertheless complain about lacking privacy and peace and quiet in their homes. Consumers worry that PAs can overhear their conversations with family or friends, especially about sensitive topics, including difficulties with their PAs. Sometimes PAs hover in rooms as consumers greet family or visitors and want privacy. When PAs fail to recognize cues to leave, consumers must directly ask them to go, which comes naturally to some consumers but feels rude and awkward to others.

Although PAs work hard, down times occur—when PAs must be available (e.g., to respond to periodic needs), but otherwise there is little to do. Proactive PAs seek out IADL and other tasks, making sure all light housework, laundry, and meal preparation are done; less motivated PAs perform only immediate household chores. But at some point, after the refrigerator is organized, floors mopped, and sheets and clothes tidily stashed away, hours can stretch on, and PAs must find their own amusements. Some are quiet, such as students studying (e.g., often at community colleges) or others reading magazines, books, or religious texts. More often, when PAs watch television, play videos or games on tablets or smartphones, or talk on the telephone—they are noisy. The din can annoy consumers, but having PAs wear earbuds or headphones or close the door might prevent them from hearing consumers calling for assistance.

Privacy concerns rise as daily PAS hours increase. Ariana, who is in her late fifties, wanted a live-in PA but worried about her personal privacy. She has a very small home, but she has some land out back. Ariana purchased an RV and parked it behind her house for her PA to live in. "She has her own life," said Ariana, "her own space, and I've got mine. And who wants to live with their job?" Ariana and her PA had not yet figured out how to communicate with each other in the middle of the night if Ariana needs help.

In contrast, Matt lives in a high-rise, public housing building for older people and individuals with disability. He has a two-bedroom apartment and sometimes has had a PA occupy his second bedroom. However, in one disastrous instance, the relationship disintegrated. The roommate stopped performing PAS tasks and invited questionable strangers to stay overnight; one stole from Matt, and others made tenants on Matt's floor nervous. Building management told Matt he had to evict the man. Dislodging a disgruntled roommate is difficult and emotionally draining. Matt's PA-roommate left only after he himself got sick and needed hospitalization. This situation left Matt severely shaken.

Even with nonresident PAs, however, Matt admits he doesn't have much privacy. His PAs must go onto his computer, access his checkbook, and help with many tasks he would rather keep private. Nevertheless, Matt's relationships with most PAs are "interdependent. I know a lot of stuff about them that they don't share with other people." Like Suzanne, Matt has deep local connections that allow him to help his PAs. Recently, one of Matt's PAs had a client "who didn't pay him for several days. I said, 'You tell me if he doesn't pay you, because I'll make sure that this is dealt with.'"

Perspectives of PAS Workers

PAs value their relationships with consumers. But the realities confronting PAs and consumers differ fundamentally. Consumers with significant disability cannot choose to stop PAS. For PAs, performing the job is generally their choice, albeit sometimes driven by pressing financial or personal demands. Paid PAs vary widely in their attitudes toward their work, largely based on their relationships with their clients. A survey of 964 nonprofit agency workers in Chicago asked them five questions about these relationships:

- "Do you think of patients as family?"
- "Do you take better care of your patients than you do of yourself?"
- "Do you make yourself available for patients to call you at home during your scheduled time off?"
- "Do you worry about your patients when you are away from them?"
- "Do your patients think of you as family?"[9]

The responses sorted into four groups.[10] The "nonfamilial" group (40%) reported low support for family-like relationships with their clients. The "overly concerned" group (14%) reported worrying about their clients when away from them, despite not thinking of their clients as family. The "boundary-keeping" group (22%) saw relationships with their clients as somewhat like family but were unlikely to worry about them when away. The "overly involved" group (24%) endorsed all five questions, indicating intensely engaged relationships with their clients.

The English study of PAs and consumers found that "Personal assistance is a unique social relationship, which subverts typical interpersonal boundaries. Disabled employers and PAs often hold divergent views and preferences concerning the status of their relationships."[11] Similarly, the 20 PA interviewees often reported long-term employment and deep relationships with individual consumers, but the PAs expressed different views of the nature of these relationships than did the 21 consumer interviewees. For PAs to protect their personal boundaries and ability to do their jobs, the professional relationship dominates the personal.

Finding the Right Fit

"A lot of what works and what doesn't just comes down to chemistry," said Abby. "It's that personal. You get really intimate with people, and sometimes your personalities just don't mix." For Abby, success requires finding the right fit with her consumer. Most PAs view paid PAS relationships as primarily professional, with fundamentally different expectations than in personal relationships (e.g., informal caregiving they provide to relatives). These PAs bring a professional mindset to establishing relationships with new consumers. They recognize the need to put the consumer's preferences first, and they are willing to tolerate attitudes or demands from consumers that they might not accept in other contexts.[12] They do not quit when challenged but instead expend extra effort. One PA described having to "check her attitude" after she considered leaving a new consumer over small personality clashes. His complaints frustrated the PA in the morning, but she felt better in the afternoon, having realized that she didn't want to quit over "the little things." Months later, the PA was still supporting this consumer. Nevertheless, establishing good working relationships with PAS clients can consume considerable time and effort.

Not Necessarily Like Family or Friends

In contrast to some consumers, many PAs did not describe friendships or family-like relationships with their clients. With two years of experience, Trina is a relative newcomer to paid PAS. She keeps relationships with consumers professional, strictly following agency rules about what tasks she can perform. "I do what I'm allowed to do," said Trina, who worries about injuring herself. "But if it's my mom, or my sister, or my husband, I probably would pull my back trying to help them if they was elderly or disabled. That's love. That's family. So, there's a boundary." Trina cautioned, "If you're treating everybody like family, if you don't have no boundaries, your own health suffers."

When consumers view PAs as family, these presumptions can lead toward exploitation, as consumers ask PAs to do more, stay longer hours, or perform nonstandard tasks. PAs work behind closed doors, generally alone. This isolation can set the stage for additional demands, especially when boundaries between personal and professional relationships erode. Some PAs are drawn into working harder than they can sustain: "emotional attachment can precipitate a personal dedication which far exceeds what might reasonably be expected."[13] Furthermore, to avoid insatiable and intrusive curiosity from some consumers, certain PAs strive to keep their personal lives private. While PAs may learn details about their client's life as part of their duties, PAs themselves often try to reveal little personal information, even in friendly chats with consumers.

Other PAs are open to friendships. Isaiah believes that friendship is essential in providing PAS, especially with women clients—to reassure them he is safe. Abby likes becoming friends with her consumers because of reciprocity; she also maintains friendships with clients she no longer serves. Aida was the only PA interviewee who said her clients "become a part of your family," explaining "you cannot spend four hours a day with a human being and not somehow be affected one way or another, good or bad. There's no way."

Communication Mechanics

PAs stressed the importance of communicating with their clients. "You need to promote a good communications relationship," said one PA, "because you have to know what that consumer's needs are. And you have to know how you're going to deal with them, have problem-solving skills." Sometimes, however, because of their underlying disability (e.g., cerebral palsy, severe muscular dystrophy, certain spinal cord injuries, amyotrophic lateral sclerosis), consumers cannot reliably communicate their needs verbally, and PAs must try to interpret consumers' nonverbal cues.

Michelle (see Chapter 7) worked for four years with a nonverbal client with cerebral palsy. "He couldn't speak," Michelle explained. "He could make contact or communicate with his eyes using a device and moving his head." Eye tracking and gaze interaction assistive augmentative communication devices allow nonverbal people to communicate using eye movements (i.e., the devices detect where consumers look, such as at an alphabet letter, to spell a word or a preprogrammed tile or image to convey a thought, concept, or command). Michelle's client could also shake his head to indicate "no." Learning to communicate this way took her time, but Michelle now considers herself an expert.

Intimacy

PAS requires close physical proximity between consumers and PAs. For bathing, toileting, and dressing, the consumer is completely or partially naked. Physical nearness breeds intimacy—feelings of familiarity or closeness. Whether this intimacy is welcome or barely tolerable varies for individual consumers and PAs within consumer-PA dyads. These feelings directly affect the nature of their relationship and power dynamics. PAS consumers have little choice about permitting this physical closeness, which breaches norms of socially acceptable spatial boundaries between strangers. In contrast, PAs who would find this physical intimacy with strangers distasteful can avoid PAS jobs—they have a choice. PAs often express comfort with or detachment from this aspect of the job, because of their other life experiences or values.

Perspectives of PAS Consumers

Consumers requiring ADL support have no choice. To be bathed, toileted, or dressed requires complete or partial nudity, heightening feelings of vulnerability for some consumers and complicating complex consumer-PA power dynamics. Even feeding and assisting with mobility (e.g., performing transfers, positioning consumers into a wheelchair) require close physical proximity, although typically the consumer is clothed during these activities. Feeding has its own specific dynamic, with PAs selecting exact bits and amounts of food to convey to the consumer's mouth. Consumers have several common views of intimacy with paid PAs.

Consumers' Situations and Feelings Differ

Different people have different levels of comfort with physical intimacy and nudity. "Feelings accomplish nothing," said Ernie, when asked how he feels about intimate tasks. "If I need it done, then I need it done." Mark acknowledges that having had hundreds of PAs of different genders see him nude is "strange." But he feels his body's physical sensations caused by his spinal cord injury "make it less strange. I have the physical sensation like I'm wearing a suit of armor right now." Mark feels that this armor-plated sensation contributes to his perceived detachment about physical intimacy. Sometimes he asks PAs to cover him with a sheet because he is cold, not because of shame.

"I'm not a shy person," said Natalie. Her PAs have different gender identities or are in gender transition, which she considers when giving instructions, generally using explicit language.

> Just because they have a different gender identity, it doesn't mean they know your specific anatomy. So, doing personal care, saying, "Okay, you have to open the labia up and wash me well. Wipe down," may or may not be comfortable for someone. But I found that discomfort happens with all different genders, depending on how someone was raised. . . . I use very explicit language without being squeamish or apologetic, [instead of] cheeky terminology like "my privates" or "down there." I'm just very explicit. It gets some of the social stigma out of it. It's just a mechanical tool.

Linda, who is quadriplegic from multiple sclerosis, is shy. "I don't feel assertive, outspoken," admitted Linda. She knows she should speak up in some situations, "but I've never been like that my whole life." Medicaid allots Linda 70 hours per week of self-directed PAS. She only feels comfortable with intimacy when she has friendships with PAs, where she and the PA "treat each other like equals." Linda therefore has difficulties finding suitable PAs. She would never consider a male PA: "No guy is touching me."

Some Tasks Are More Intimate Than Others

Certain tasks feel especially intimate, heightening consumers' discomfort. One man with a recent spinal cord injury particularly objected to inserting a rectal suppository to initiate bowel movements. "I resisted doing it during my first three months of rehab," he said. "It was all really shocking and jarring." But to maintain his health, he has to use suppositories. "I'm still not comfortable with it, but I don't have a choice, right?"

Managing hygiene around menstrual periods raised strong reactions among most women, even those who were postmenopausal. One woman got injections of Depo-Provera (long-acting contraceptive containing progestin, which lessens or sometimes halts menstrual blood flow) to avoid confronting the issue with her primarily male PAs. Linda, now in her early sixties, was menstruating when she first started using PAS. She described her periods as "gross, disgusting." She stopped using tampons, not wanting PAs to insert them, but that meant she used pads to absorb menstrual blood. "As I explained to my PCAs," Linda said, "I'm sitting in blood all day."

Like Linda, Ariana always wore pads and eschewed tampons, because "I didn't want anybody going that far into my body." Nonetheless, unlike Linda, who refuses to hire male PAs, Ariana had a male PA—a "full-on male"—for about six years.

> That was really difficult. . . . He was a seasoned attendant. He had worked with men and women. That's what he had done his whole life. . . . His girlfriend was in a wheelchair, and she was a friend of mine. So, when he would have to put a pad on me, that was kind of unsettling at first. It wasn't weird for him as much as it was for me. And I've had other male attendants, but they were gay, and so that seemed more comfortable somehow. . . . But it's embarrassing, either way.

Natalie, who is perimenopausal, is not embarrassed by her periods, using pads because tampons are insufficient for her heavy blood flow. Nonetheless, Natalie admitted feeling certain tasks are especially intimate:

> In my experience, the intimate care is not so much the bathing and the bathrooming. It's really the tasks that we're in each other's face. Brushing teeth, putting on makeup, which I don't do very often but once in a while. My male friends say shaving is a really big deal, to have somebody in your face. Doing transfers where you have to hug each other. Those are the real intimate things.

Consumers Feel Comfortable If Workers Seem Comfortable

Consumers reported feeling more comfortable with intimacy if their PAs also seem comfortable. One consumer with self-directed PAS sought PA candidates with this sense of comfort. However, he prioritizes being "reliable and respectful and seeming like they want to be there with you." About intimacy sensitivities, he feels that "almost everybody gets over that part really quick, if they're the kind of person who wants to do PAS work."

Perspectives of PAS Workers

Most PAs report they are comfortable providing intimate ADL supports—it comes with the job. Many described having assisted family members with personal care, giving them a clear-eyed understanding of PAS tasks. "After helping my grandfather, it got to be this normal, everyday thing to me," said Isaiah. "Because he can't do it for himself, someone has to do it for him."

Some PAs empathize with consumers and think about how they would want to be treated if they needed ADL support. "If someone had to do it for me," said one PA, "I'd want them to care for me as their daughter." She wouldn't want a PA who would let her remain soiled. "It's a natural thing, and that's why I enjoy my job so much. I enjoy making them feel good." Abby and her consumers jointly set boundaries for providing intimate assistance, striving to maximize the consumer's comfort. "How I see it is, what if I had a disability and I needed to have somebody help me to go to the bathroom?" asked Abby. "What would I want? I don't necessarily want to have a conversation the whole time." PAs mentioned strategies they use to be sensitive to consumers in physically vulnerable positions. For example, one PA described wrapping towels around consumers who wanted to stay covered during sponge baths.

A few PAs admitted discomfort with providing intimate assistance. Nevertheless, they needed to support their families, and PAS jobs have some important attractions. When Chandra, who has provided PAS for 30 years, started this work, "I had no choice because my children were small, and I could not afford babysitters. This is the only job that is flexible." Working for an agency, Chandra is now selective about which consumers she'll support, partially on the basis of the nature of the tasks they need done. She wants to ensure she feels comfortable with her clients. Her long-lasting agency job now gives her flexibility to refuse serving clients she doesn't like.

Conflict

Conflicts are almost inevitable in human relationships, including between consumers and PAs. The nature of the conflicts varies widely, as do the implications for both consumers and PAs. Conflicts can be especially complicated when family members or friends provide paid PAS. Many conflicts reflect complex interpersonal dynamics and can put consumers into vulnerable positions, as in these two examples:

- Many years ago, a gray market PA thought Michael seemed thin and needed to gain weight. The PA ignored his preferences for meal preparation (e.g., adding more oil than Michael likes), and she piled his plate high with food. Insisting that he "clean his plate," she pushed spoonful after spoonful into his mouth. Michael worried that if he did not comply, she would stop providing PAS. He gained unwelcome weight, which made him feel poorly and compromised his wheelchair seating. (Rehabilitation power wheelchairs, like Michael's, are custom built to consumers' body measurements, such as pelvis width and femur length. Upon gaining weight, people may no longer fit properly in their wheelchair, increasing pressure injury risks.)

Michael finally told the PA to leave after she transgressed another personal boundary in their interactions.

- Ariana follows a low-salt diet. Despite clear instructions, her morning PA excessively salted Ariana's breakfast eggs. The PA protested that she personally likes lots of salt on her eggs, but Ariana repeatedly reminded the PA that the eggs were not for her. "We're having a fight over eggs. I can't believe this," Ariana recalled saying to herself. She finally had to position herself at the stove, watching while the PA made eggs and saying, "don't put in salt." Although Ariana needs her eggs properly prepared, she worries about conflicts escalating and the PA quitting, leaving her without assistance.

Consumers and PAs have somewhat different strategies about how to handle conflicts, although both groups value communication as the key to finding solutions.

Perspective of PAS Consumers

In addressing conflicts, consumers must make a complex calculus, first determining whether they want to retain the PA. Consumers needing to recruit their own PAs are more vulnerable to this concern than people using agency PAS. Those consumers could ask their agency to send a different PA or to help resolve the conflict.

Making Accommodations That Assist PAs

Entirely avoiding emotional discomfort and conflict is impossible, and when friction occurs, in most circumstances, consumers are anxious to deescalate the situation and maintain good working relationships with their PAs. As is consistent with the notion of reciprocity, once they understand their PAs' concerns, consumers often try to make accommodations to better meet PAs' needs. Sometimes, the issue is clear-cut. One consumer relinquished her two beloved cats when her PA developed an allergy and issued an ultimatum: "It's either me or the cats." She chose the PA.

Especially in self-directed PAS, finding the reciprocity sweet spot with their PAs is critical for consumers to maintain their staff. Tom believes it is essential—and in his best interest—to be good to his PAs:

I think how you treat your workers is very important. It's not just for security. It's important to do right by them to make sure that you're not taking advantage of them. To make sure that you're communicating with them. To make sure you're being reasonably flexible towards them. A lot of PAs will take advantage with the flexibility. . . . But then there are other people who will be part of making things work.

Ways consumers can make accommodations for PAs include:

- Being flexible about scheduling conflicts, especially emergencies and unexpected childcare needs
- Giving PAs vacation time, when requested in advance
- Helping organize PAs' transportation during off hours, especially where public transportation is inadequate
- Recognizing and accommodating PAs' religious preferences, such as not scheduling hours on their days of sabbath or religious observances

It is important for consumers to apologize when their behavior toward PAs crosses the line. One consumer spent her career in nursing, and she has high expectations for her PAs. On occasion she feels that PAs don't follow her instructions, and she has no alternative but to fire them. These situations can become tense. With one PA, "We got into a hollering match, and I told her to get out my house." However, the consumer recognized she has a temper and can speak aggressively to her PAs. When PAs complain about this, the consumer "makes amends to them right then. I can be upset; I'm human; I'm not perfect. If I've done something that they didn't feel right by, I apologize to them right then."

Giving Others Responsibility to Resolve Conflicts

Consumers with self-directed PAS sometimes arrange their multiple PAs into teams (see Chapter 8). The team's primary goal is ensuring that consumers receive reliable coverage. For example, Ernie, Matt, and Natalie expect their PAs to negotiate among themselves to find coverage when PAs are sick or want vacation time. The burden of communication and handling scheduling conflicts thus shifts from the consumer to the PA team. Although assigning this scheduling responsibility to their PAs seems antithetical to consumer self-direction, Ernie, Matt, and Natalie view the approach as efficient. It also gives their PAs a sense of control and flexibility over scheduling—a critical factor in job satisfaction.

For consumers with agency PAS, the options for shifting responsibility in conflict situations are sometimes complex. For example, several years ago, Michael had one agency PA who was routinely 20 to 30 minutes late each morning, typically blaming heavy traffic. Because he needs two PAs to get him up and showered, that meant Michael had to pay another PA to wait

20 to 30 minutes for the late PA to arrive. Complaining to his commercial franchise agency about this PA's lateness made no difference. The PA always promised to do better, and because the agency wanted to retain its employees in a tough labor market—and this PA was otherwise competent—the agency did not strictly enforce her designated arrival time.

Conflicts among PAs

Consumers with numerous PAs might find them arguing among themselves, primarily about household tasks like who takes out the trash, mops the floor, or cleans the bathroom. One consumer requires periodic suctioning of secretions, and none of his multiple weekday PAs wants to clean the suction device, which smells foul. So, the secretions build up until one of his weekend PAs, who is willing, takes the device apart and cleans the container.

Mark has a team of PAs, and he witnesses them arguing about "petty kinds of things." Mark prefers for his PAs to negotiate among themselves about who does what. However, he knows which tasks each PA does well, and if conflicts among PAs persist, he intervenes:

> I had one woman who loved to do laundry. She thought the way other people did the laundry was wrong, and sometimes it was. Sometimes people would leave stuff in the washing machine. Someone could do three loads in one shift, and other people couldn't get one load done. So, she did the laundry. Other people like to do the dishes or like to cook, or other people are more mechanically inclined. So, if I want to do some mechanical things, I wait for a certain person.

Mark and Linda have dated for nearly three decades, but they have never lived together. Occasionally, one of them stays overnight at the other's place, precipitating complex interactions or outright conflicts among their PAs. "When you boil it down," said Mark, "some of it's jealousy. Some of it's Linda's easier to work for than I am," in terms of ADL needs. "So, Linda could be done in a half hour if she just wanted to get to bed. Me, on the other hand, it might take an hour, an hour and a half. Or if I'm doing a longer routine, it could take hours and hours." Mark's and Linda's PAs ask how much each is paid, how many hours they work, "and you get equity issues. Like did the person do the dishes? Did somebody leave the laundry?" Showdowns among the PAs can get testy:

> Lots of drama. One of my PCAs stood up to one of Linda's PCAs. There could have been a street fight, as far as I know. The woman [Mark's PA] threatened to leave. She told me to find somebody, start

looking. She had a lot of hours, so I quickly started looking. I found people to fill in, and I told her, "If somebody doesn't want to work, I don't want them working. I'd rather get them right out." Then she backed off. . . . But it's a survival game. Who can I get in when I have an emergency? . . . Lately, some people haven't left me in good standing. I've got one or two problem PCAs who have made it bad for the other PCAs, kind of pushed folks.

Terminating Employment

Threats to safety, dishonesty, and breaches of trust represent bright lines. Consumers typically fire PAs who cross these lines. Not showing up for a shift without first notifying the consumer is also unacceptable. But, before firing PAs, consumers typically explore whether extenuating circumstances caused the unexpected absence. "I'm patient if there is a reasonable excuse," said one consumer. "If it's no show, no call, that may require a decision on my part the PCA won't like."

Natalie has had "to fire lots of people." Like others, she typically tries to understand what motivates the PA's behavior before deciding about terminating employment. Natalie believes that some PAs feel guilty about quitting:

> There are some people who are just doing their crappy job, and I'll say, "You know, it seems like you don't really want to be here. You're distracted. It seems like this isn't the right job for you. Is this true?" And often I'm able to negotiate an agreed-upon end date. A lot of people don't know how to quit. They're afraid to make you mad. They feel like they're being a bad person for not liking doing the work.

Natalie described one PA who was "absent, no call, no show" on three consecutive Monday mornings. Although he had excuses, Natalie felt it wasn't going to work, and she decided to fire the PA, after lining up a replacement. When she fired him, however, "he begged and begged and begged for his job. He cried, and I just couldn't do it." Later, the final straw came with a cooking debacle. "He said he knew how to cook," Natalie recalled, "and then I found him putting Styrofoam into the toaster oven" (high heat causes Styrofoam to melt). Afraid for her safety and weary of his unreliability, Natalie fired the PA.

Perspective of PAS Workers

Conflicts can cause PAs to refuse to work with specific consumers or to burn out, quitting PAS work altogether. Agency PAs can contact their supervisors for assistance with difficult consumers or request reassignment. However, PAs working directly for consumers generally do not have an outside arbiter to help resolve conflicts. Over time, these PAs generally develop strategies for negotiating conflicts with consumers, finding their tolerance set point at which working for particular consumers becomes untenable. Early in her career, Abby complied each time one client asked her to stay beyond her scheduled hours, night after night. Eventually, Abby snapped at the consumer but afterward regretted losing her temper. Since then, Abby has learned to recognize her feelings and avoid being drained by unreasonable consumer demands.

Citing agency rules is a preemptive strike against inappropriate consumer requests—and thus potential conflicts (see Chapter 7). Nonetheless, as one agency PA said, "There's a lot of iffy things that happen that have no guidelines, no rulebook." One of Chandra's clients had Alzheimer's disease and repeatedly locked Chandra out of the house when she took out the trash. The agency reassigned her. Trina had one consumer who lived in a cramped studio apartment.

> She's doing drugs from 8:00 in the morning. She wants me to get this pill out of her bag, put it between some paper, find a hammer, crush it with the hammer, make it like dust. Then she wanted the straw to put in her nose and sniffed it. Before that she was smoking marijuana. I had to put my mask on. I said, "I can't be here." The whole time she's dropping the joint on her chest. She's dropping a cigarette in the bed. She's got a whole cigar box full of marijuana. . . . She says it's for medicinal needs and not to get high. She's doing it for pain. But I'm telling her, "It's not in your care plan." It's 8:00 in the morning when I clocked in, but I can't breathe. I called the agency at 9:30 saying I had to get out of there. The agency let me leave. By 9:45 I was gone.

In addition to difficulty breathing, Trina worried that inhaling the consumer's marijuana smoke could cause random urine tests to indicate Trina herself uses marijuana. She has a second job that does random urine drug tests, and she feared losing that job.

Sometimes, PAs devise ways to assist difficult consumers. Chandra's agency assigned her to a consumer who was a hoarder. "Before I came, he had changed aides every week—every week," Chandra recounted. "He had newspapers stuffed in his house from the floor to your knees." The man flatly refused to remove the newspapers, so Chandra started a slow, steady campaign to discard them. "I'll clean, and I'll throw away two every day," recalled

Chandra. After several weeks, when the nurse and social worker came, they noticed the house was cleaner and had fewer newspapers. "I told them, 'Well, if I'm staying here, I have to have it clean.' They gave me an award for that." Chandra's agency celebrated her for her persistence and dedication to improving the consumer's safety.

10

Trust and Respect

Jessica is in her early fifties and has cerebral palsy. She employs two self-directed PAs—one has worked for her for a dozen years and the other for two years—and both are men. She prefers hiring male PAs, considering them as physically stronger than women. Jessica's cerebral palsy causes limb spasticity that prevents her from using transfer devices, like a Hoyer lift. Therefore, her PAs must physically lift her for transfers, such as from her bed to her power wheelchair. When recruiting PAs, Jessica seeks one personal quality above others—trust.

> I have to have a lot of trust because it's very intimate. . . . I just don't let every male assist me. I do three or four interviews before hiring someone. Both of the assistants who help me now, I'd known them before. One is the father of one of my old assistants. His girlfriend also worked for me before, so I got to know him. I got to know his family. . . . In hiring people, if I've talked to other peers and friends who've also worked with them, that gives me more trust. . . . They're helping me with my independence. Without them, I couldn't do it.

———

In her late twenties, Paola, who is now in her early forties, came to the U.S. mainland from Puerto Rico to earn enough to support her three children. After two years, Paola got her own apartment, and her next-door neighbor used a wheelchair. When she visited, Paola watched the PAs working for her neighbor and then started assisting her too, without pay. Nearly ten years ago,

Paola began performing paid consumer self-directed PAS work reimbursed by Medicaid. She believes that "to be a PCA, you have to make your client trust you, and you have to respect your client." Paola described difficulties with a recent client:

> I'm a very honest person, and when I talk to people, that's what I expect from them. . . . The last client that I had was, at the beginning, "I don't trust Spanish people." She was Black American. And I was like, "Oh, I'm good with that. You don't have to trust me. You don't have to like me. Long as you respect me, and I respect you, we going to be good." I think when I said that to her, she kind of liked it. Then after the time passed, it was so different. She really trust me. She was saying, "Paola, you're the first Spanish person that I trust to come in my house, and I feel so comfortable."

Trust

Trust is foundational to good consumer-PA relationships. Trusting relationships between consumers and PAs can mitigate emotional and physical vulnerabilities and relieve discomfort and fear of close physical proximity. Paralleling reciprocity, trust is a two-way street—both consumers and PAs must trust each other for the relationship to work. Relationships without trust are unlikely to survive.

Undercurrents of trust wend throughout discussions of relationships between consumers and paid PAs (see Chapter 9), as well as concerns about physical and emotional safety (see Chapter 11). Trust also encompasses basic decency and moral imperatives. This chapter uses a literal interpretation of trust—concerns about honesty, illegal behaviors, and theft. Examples come not only from Jessica and Paola, but also from consumers and PAs mentioned in earlier chapters.

Perspective of PAS Consumers

Almost all 21 consumer interviewees reported PAs stealing from them at some point—as one long-time consumer said, "more times than I can count!" Many consumers were matter-of-fact about these thefts, viewing them as expected and almost inevitable costs of paid PAS. Mark, who has used self-directed PAS for three decades, believes thefts arise from the "power differential. Sometimes I have the power; sometimes PAs have the power." PAs earn low wages, often work multiple jobs, and frequently struggle to meet basic needs. Thefts, Mark thinks, allow PAs to counterbalance perceived inequities.

Across consumer interviewees, thefts fell into four broad categories: money, food or other basic household goods, clothing, and idiosyncratic items, sometimes with unclear rationales for the thefts. Consumers feel somewhat differently about stealing across these four categories. Sometimes, when clear evidence of the theft and thief exist, consumers react. Otherwise, they tolerate the losses.

Money

Many consumers reported thefts of money, cash or coins, kept around their homes. Consumers often had difficulty saying exactly how much money had disappeared and equal difficulty pinpointing when the cash went missing or who took it. For example, many power wheelchair users have zippered pouches hanging from their armrests where they stash small quantities of money or loose change (e.g., for bus fares). They rarely keep tabs on just how much cash they drop into these pouches. Many people have trouble remembering exactly how much cash is in their wallets at a given time. Therefore, detecting monetary thefts or fingering the culprit is frequently impossible. To avoid substantial monetary thefts, "Don't keep a lot of money around the house," advised Jessica. "Things will go walking."

Clear instances of cash thefts can be the breaking point for consumers, leading to firing the offending PA. George had difficulty developing the self-confidence to manage his PAs, as required by his state's PAS program (see Chapter 5). When he finally got his own apartment, George hired a PA who had been unemployed for a while. Shortly after starting work, she stole his money, and he fired her face-to-face. "I know where my boundaries are," George said. "My eyes are open."

Food and Basic Subsistence Items

Consumers had more forgiving attitudes toward thefts of food or basic subsistence items, such as toilet paper. These types of thefts are common, but noticing when food or household staples are missing is also hard (e.g., consumers might begin wondering when rolls of toilet paper seem to disappear rapidly). Sometimes, thefts are obvious. For instance, one man reported his PA charging a few extra food items on his debit card when the PA went grocery shopping for the consumer.

Although consumers often sympathize with PAs needing food, they want explanations for these thefts. Nevertheless, consumers hesitate to confront PAs suspected of stealing if they lack backup PAS, as did Ariana:

I had an attendant who was stealing meat out of the freezer in the garage that I stocked with meat. I would go out there to get pork chops and be like, "Where are the pork chops? Did we eat them?" I had just bought a big bag of dog food, but we were out of dog food. You start wondering, "Why am I running out of stuff so fast?" Finally, I caught her red-handed. She was stealing pork chops, dog food, and paper towels. I said to her, "Why are you doing this?" I was afraid to be full-out confrontational. I wasn't sure if I was going to have an attendant the next day; she might have to come back. If I didn't need her desperately, I probably would've said, "Get out. You're fired." But instead I said, "Bianca, why are you taking food? If you need a package of pork chops, I'll give it to you. If your dog needs dog food, I'll buy her a bag. I have no problem with that. But just ask me. Why are you stealing?" Bianca continued to deny she was stealing even though she was standing there with the food in her hands.

Clothing

One man didn't notice that some of his clothes were missing, but his wife recognized when his PA wore one of his neckties. "Several pieces of my clothing disappeared," he recalled, "but it wasn't a big deal for me at the time. I just figured, 'Well, my aide must need them worse than I do.' I'm obviously not wearing a lot of ties these days." Stealing clothes is common, although motivations for these thefts varies. Some PAs steal because they need clothing for themselves or family members. Envy prompts other thefts. Jessica described previous PAs stealing her clothes. "I had nice clothes," said Jessica, "so, they would want to wear them. When I would call people out about it, suddenly the clothes would reappear." Natalie recalled that one of her first PAs "asked to borrow $30, and she took a jacket of mine that she'd been admiring. She never showed up for work again."

Linda loves jewelry—nothing expensive, but fun and colorful. She likes making jewelry, too, with big beads and cut glass. Several years earlier when she used agency PAS, one PA stole jewelry she had made. When Linda reported the theft, the agency blamed her, saying she should not keep jewelry, even her handmade trinkets, in her home.

Idiosyncratic Thefts

Linda believes that some PAs come into her house, look around, and ask themselves, "I don't have that much. What do you have here that I might take?" Recent thefts include CorningWare pots and dishware that, although not valuable, have sentimental value to Linda, and a brand-new set of sheets she had bought for her boyfriend, Mark.

Another idiosyncratic theft included Ariana's wedding ring from her first marriage. "It's not something you notice right away," said Ariana ruefully.

"When I left my ex, I put my wedding band in a jewelry box, and I've never found it since. Somebody stole it, but who knows when?" Natalie's long-forgotten marijuana also disappeared. "I was never a big pot smoker," said Natalie, but she stored a small marijuana stash in a plastic bag. One day, when she looked for marijuana, the bag was empty. Natalie didn't think further about it, but her PA who had stolen the marijuana remembered. "I never knew it," said Natalie, "until she was working her 12 steps and called me crying, saying, 'I stole.' It was pretty intense to have her doing her amends thing, crying and crying and apologizing, which was her process that she needed to go through."

Security Cameras and In-Home Monitoring

Peggy, who is in her sixties and disabled by spinal muscular atrophy, had a live-in PA who had started acting in erratic, aggressive ways, scaring Peggy. Anticipating the need to fire the PA, Peggy began compiling a paper file, which she kept in her desk, detailing troubling incidents. One day, Peggy couldn't find the file and panicked, wondering whether she had mislaid it. Peggy then remembered security cameras installed at strategic locations inside her home. When she purchased her home security system, the company offered Peggy not only exterior but also interior cameras at an affordable price. Peggy logged onto her computer and pulled up images from the interior camera. "It shows her walking out of my office with the folder in her hand," said Peggy. "It also shows her leaving the house with my folder. That video was my saving grace."

When the PA returned to the house, Peggy had her sister present for reinforcement. Peggy asked the PA to return the file, the PA denied having taken it, and Peggy told her the security camera had captured the theft. In the ensuing confrontation, Peggy threatened to call the police, but the woman left. "As soon as I fired her, I called a locksmith," said Peggy. "She gathered whatever belongings she could out of her room and had to step over the locksmith to get out."

Use of security cameras, like Peggy's, to monitor activities inside and outside homes is becoming more common as home-based surveillance technologies fall in price and rise in convenience. Nursing homes and congregate living settings (e.g., for people with intellectual disability) often use security cameras to detect and prevent abuse of residents. Some facility operators, however, fear that these installations invade patients' privacy and impede staff recruitment and retention; ethical and moral questions arise when the interests of residents conflict with those of institutions.[1,2] Nonetheless, in-home monitoring devices are increasingly used to support home-based living for people with chronic disease or disability, ranging from daily oversight of health symptoms to safety surveillance (e.g., detecting falls).[3] Peggy asserted emphatically that she informs all her PAs about the in-home video surveillance—she does not want PAs, especially live-in staff, to accuse her of violating their privacy. Being constantly on camera might threaten bonds of trust between PAs and consumers.

Perspective of PAS Workers

Trust is essential to consumer-PA relationships from the PA's perspective too. "You have to respect and trust the person to work for a person," said Isaiah, "and to get them to trust you." Without trust, PAs can feel uncomfortable in their jobs and at risk of false accusations. Many PA interviewees, like Paola, reported consumers not trusting them because of racial and ethnic differences. PAs often sense that consumers expect PAs to steal, making PAs feel they must constantly prove their honesty and trustworthiness. Perceptions that consumers anticipate thefts of even small items can introduce wariness and suspicion into PA-consumer interactions, from the start of employment.

Accusations of theft and other PA misdeeds play out differently for agency and consumer self-directed workers. For example, her agency notified Trina that one consumer had accused her both of eating all the consumer's food and breaking the television. The agency removed Trina from this consumer, whom Trina felt had never liked her. A client of Chandra's accused her of making expensive overseas telephone calls, presuming that Chandra, an immigrant, was calling her homeland. Chandra's agency manager investigated the telephone log the consumer provided, indeed finding lengthy calls abroad but not to Chandra's home country—instead to a country with a similar sounding name. Another agency PA, also an immigrant, had made those unauthorized long-distance telephone calls.

Agency supervisors or managers act as buffers or intermediaries between suspicious consumers and an accused PA. In consumer self-directed employment, PAs have no such mediator. PAs can face legal threats, as did Aida. She took her consumer with Medicaid-funded self-directed PAS to a medical appointment and, afterward,

> As I was going out to look for the [paratransit van], she's inside telling the security guard that I abuse her. . . . When I came back in, the officer pulled me aside and says, "I want to talk to you. She's saying you hit her." I was like, "What? What? I did no such thing. I didn't hit her. I didn't do anything." I went outside, and I called her daughter. . . . After that I was scared out of my wits. I was like, "Oh my God, she could lock me up if she indicates that I did something to her."

The client withheld Aida's paycheck. After the consumer complained loudly to a bus driver that she physically abused her, Aida quit.

Aida thought seriously about leaving PAS work altogether, but she sorely needed the income. "I talked to my pastor," said Aida. Several days later, her pastor told Aida about another woman, also with Medicaid self-directed PAS, who needed a PA. Aida went to work for the woman, "and it was good, until it went sour."

> I really fell in love with her. I felt like she was more than just a client. She became part of my family. She trusted me, and she valued my opinion. She was an artist. She made the most beautiful jewelry you could imagine, and I encouraged her to start selling them. I would go online and make cards for her. I tried to help her. . . . She had a lot of family meddling, like her sisters. Everybody wanted to tell her what to do. She felt like she couldn't make her own decisions. She was fighting to take control of her life.

The consumer's niece started angling to take Aida's job as her aunt's paid PA. Various relatives falsely accused Aida of making errors with the consumer's medications, and one sister assaulted Aida in the consumer's home. Aida wasn't injured and decided not to press charges, but the consumer fired Aida. "She didn't want to and feels bad about it," said Aida. The consumer was caught between her niece wanting the PAS pay and her allegiance to Aida. That happened six months before our interview, and Aida had not yet resumed PAS work. "I got so disheartened," said Aida. "You're helping these people have a better quality of life, and you're put in World War III."

Respect

In addition to trust, both consumers and PAs seek mutual respect in their relationship. Various factors challenge this two-way respect. At the most basic level, consumers are physically vulnerable, without the visible signs of strength associated with commanding respect. On their side, PAs are generally female, racial or ethnic minorities, and frequently immigrants, all traits associated with social disadvantage. Complex dynamics involving gender and race-ethnicity can stall growth of mutual respect in the consumer-PA dyad.

Gender Dynamics

Perspective of PAS Consumers
Almost 90% of PAs are women (see Table 6.1), and most consumers—especially female consumers—prefer hiring women PAs (see Chapter 8). Concerns about mutual respect do arise between women. However, in PAS, concerns

about disrespect are more likely when male consumers have female PAs. Male consumers can sexually harass female PAs, threatening physical and emotional safety (see Chapter 11). Sensitivity to language and interaction style is essential with female PAs, said Mark, "to make sure the consumer's not crossing the lines or perceived to cross the line."

Exactly where that line delineating sexual harassment lies is sometimes unclear, and boundaries may differ for consumers and PAs. At one extreme, some consumers seek sexual intimacy with an uninterested PA. "The rule of thumb is you wouldn't want to have a sexual relationship with a PCA," said one male consumer. But he admitted that, when much younger, he had brief sexual encounters, which he viewed as consensual, with two or three female PAs. From talking with other men with disability, he finds that even today, with heightened sensitivity from the Me Too movement, sexual relationships occur and appear consensual. But he now believes that having sexual relations with paid PAs is simply wrong—distorting or upending power dynamics in an ostensibly professional relationship and possibly imperiling the physical or emotional safety of both consumers and PAs.

Sexual orientation further complicates gender-based dynamics around sexual intimacy. Gay male consumers can make sexual advances to male PAs, just as lesbian consumers can seek sexual encounters with female PAs. Regardless of the sexual orientation of consumers or paid PAs, sexual encounters almost inevitably disrupt movement toward mutual respect within the consumer-PA dyad.

Nevertheless, some consumer interviewees admitted difficulties maintaining professional distance. Carlos, who is in his early fifties, lives in a college town and likes to recruit young women as his PAs. He freely admits enjoying their company but tries never to develop romantic feelings for them. Despite this, Carlos conceded, "You tend to fall in love with caregivers. You tend to develop a bond between you and them. It can get a little sticky in certain situations. . . . When that happens, most of the time they leave and never come back."

In some cultures, certain types of touching—like hugs or cheek kisses— are common rituals of greetings or goodbyes, including between persons who are mere acquaintances. Local norms vary: "greeting a client with a kiss on both cheeks may be acceptable in Montréal but not in Dallas."[4] For multiple reasons, including differences in physical functional abilities, kissing or hugging in paid PAS is more complicated. One man with quadriplegia had a PA who kissed him on his lips every evening as she ended her shift, although he neither invited nor enjoyed the contact. To the consumer, these kisses felt like a power play—she leant down over him, unable to resist because of his immobility. He feared becoming sick (e.g., viral illnesses) from this unwanted intimacy but was afraid to complain. He needed the PAS and didn't want her to quit.

Another man found comfort in ritualized physical contacts. He has a low-level spinal cord injury and can do most tasks independently, except for his bowel regimen. He pays privately for PAS and so he aims for efficiency with his long-time PA:

> In the morning, when she first gets here, it's just, "Good morning, how are you doing?" And then we get on with business. . . . A couple of years ago, at the end of the morning, she would give me a hug. That was great because at the time I wasn't getting a lot of hugs. I don't care who you are, human contact is very therapeutic and beneficial. Then it's just become part of our routine, that she gives me a hug and a little kiss as she leaves. And I wish her a happy day, and we're good.

The consumer and PA have settled into a mutually supportive and respectful relationship, sharing some personal information about family matters: "We've become pretty good friends and confidants to a degree. . . . I'm extremely blessed in that regard."

Sometimes consumers and PAs have widely varying perspectives on what constitutes disrespectful or inappropriate behavior. For example, Mark recently joined a video streaming service through his cable provider and was excited to sample new shows. Responses from some female PAs caught him off guard:

> I like the historical dramas. But when I turn the TV on, I can't change the station. I need the PCA's help. Some of these historical dramas have a lot of nudity in them, nudity and violence. It seems the nudity concerned one of the PCAs. . . . So now I'm trying to find these shows that don't have any nudity or something that might upset my PCAs. Lately, I'm trying to make sure that I don't offend anybody.

Mark treads carefully, uncertain of trigger points affecting his female PAs.

Finally, some consumers might want PAs to provide sexual facilitation, assisting consumers in sexual activities. Certain providers specialize in sexual facilitation for individuals with disability. Their identities and skills spread by word of mouth, and interested consumers hire them to accommodate specific sexual encounters. Asking their usual PAs to perform these tasks can cause discomfort, friction, or outright rejection. Such requests can precipitate moral dilemmas for PAs who feel uncomfortable performing these tasks, have concerns about privacy, or find the sexual requests incompatible with their moral standards.[5] These situations raise questions about how far self-direction can go in actualizing consumers' preferences, when consumers direct PAs to do something that PAs find morally objectionable.

Perspective of PAS Workers

PAs value feelings of mutual respect with their consumers, although many come from historically disadvantaged backgrounds. PAs often endure lewd remarks, inappropriate touching during intimate tasks, and outright sexual harassment. Consumers making overtly sexual advances marks a bright line for many PAs, leaving them feeling disrespected and unwilling to continue supporting the offending consumer. For example, Chenoa is in her mid-forties, Native American, and has not graduated from high school; she has worked about a dozen years in Medicaid-funded self-directed PAS. At one point, a male close friend became her client. Over time, the man began expressing romantic feelings for Chenoa that she did not reciprocate. Nevertheless, because of their prior friendship, Chenoa felt committed to remaining his PA, although giving him the customary sponge baths became intensely uncomfortable. Not only did he pressure her sexually, but also he repeatedly tried grabbing her leg. Finally, Chenoa left the consumer when he urged her to move in with him.

Chandra has spent 30 years providing paid home-based PAS. She stayed in the job only because it offered the flexibility she needed to raise her children. Otherwise, she would have preferred a different career—primarily because of low wages but also because of difficult consumer attitudes. Chandra contrasted two scenarios. "Sometimes the patient is a miserable person," Chandra said. "It's like they just want to tick you off. You want to quit and go home." In contrast, "sometimes you find a very loving, kind person." Chandra feels that consumers need "to know how to speak to the aide in the right tone and with respect. They're coming there to help you." Otherwise, when consumers "start abusing the aide, that person's going to want to run."

Occasionally, what PAs perceive as disrespect might result from consumers' frustration about being unable to perform basic tasks on their own. One agency PA had a severely disabled consumer with multiple sclerosis who seemed to have a chip on her shoulder:

> She was very, very challenging. . . . She has family, but nobody wanted to deal with her because of her attitude. But she likes me. We had our ups and downs. Not where we fist fight or nothing like that, but we had lots of disagreements. She was very set in her ways because she couldn't do nothing. She can't walk. She can't bathe herself. She can't feed herself. She can't even get up on her own to go to the bath-

room. She wears diapers. I had to change her every time I turned around. . . . I had to say to myself, "I don't like this. I don't want to do this." But in the same token, I don't want to give up. I don't want to make an excuse. . . . It was very, very challenging with her, very. But I stuck with it. I did not give up because I said to myself, "What if this is my mother or my grandmother that need help, and I turned my back on them? That's not right. God won't forgive me for that." I helped her out to the best that I can.

Race and Ethnicity Dynamics

Perspective of PAS Consumers

The majority of home-based paid PAs are racial or ethnic minorities (see Table 6.1). Racial or ethnic concordance or discordance between consumers and PAs inevitably affects power dynamics and the nature of relationships. One man described feeling culture shock when he moved from a state with few minority residents, where all his PAs were White, to a southern state, where all his PAs were Black women. He feels he and his current PA respect each other, but "It's not been something that we've talked about. . . . I've always been a fairly open minded and liberal thinking person. I never really had any racial animosity towards anyone. But I'm a 'Yes ma'am,' 'no ma'am,' 'thank you,' 'please' kind of guy, and that goes a long way."

Many Americans acknowledge difficulties talking openly and revealing feelings about race and ethnicity. Only one interviewee expressed a clear preference for the race and ethnicity of her PAs, openly admitting wanting ethnically concordant PAs:

> I am of Hispanic origin. I consider myself a Mexican American or Hispanic. I am a second-generation American. . . . I don't want to sound racist, but I am more comfortable with my own ethnic group and women than I am with a Black person. I don't know why I find their work ethic to be different. But on the other hand, I've had some very loyal attendants here and there that were Black, so that's not even true. But when I'm hiring and a Hispanic woman is one of the applicants, that's probably the one I'm going to go for.

Other consumers recognized the complex history of race and ethnicity in the United States and understood disadvantages facing PAs from minority backgrounds, compounded by the low wages and lack of respect accorded PAS work. Natalie's first imperative on this concern involved improving PAS wages and benefits—"It needs to be a good job that someone can actually

raise a family on." But she admitted, "I don't know how to make it more socially valued without dealing with sexism and racism." Natalie, who is White,
had to confront her own racial stereotypes when interacting with PAs:

> A long time ago, this woman PA was African American. She was also
> legally blind, and I was really young. . . . I had to juggle assumptions
> I made about her, about how educated she was or about what her
> priorities were. She was also very religious. . . . I had to undo stereo-
> types I had about her. I also had to acknowledge I was the White
> woman, telling this woman who's older than me, who's Black, how
> to do things and what I want done. I felt self-conscious. It wasn't her
> responsibility to make me feel comfortable. We worked together for
> three years. . . . I had my rock and roll crap on the radio, and she had
> her headphones on listening to her soul music at the same time. It was
> quite a funny scene. We didn't talk much because we were just listen-
> ing to our music and doing other things that didn't require much com-
> munication.

Suzanne, who pays privately for her self-directed PAS, grew up in a southern state and is sensitive to the racial and ethnic legacies of that region.

> I feel acutely aware of my role as a White person and perpetuating
> racism, just acutely, deeply, fiercely aware of that. At this particular
> moment, three of the people that work for me are African American
> and one is Cuban. . . . And there's been a diverse cross-section of peo-
> ple that have some LGBT identification, et cetera. When hiring, I'm
> going to make a pitch for somebody who's non-White. Even though
> there's this weird dynamic of having people of color taking care of
> a White person, I have this southern legacy. The idea that people
> need work and should be trusted and given opportunities trumps
> that particular dynamic. . . . The folks that are working for me who
> are African American have struggled in their lives and continue to
> struggle and fight against really serious challenges. I'm not making
> the situation any better from a big standpoint, but they're making a
> pretty decent amount of money from me. . . . I think my practices
> are fair and reasonable.

Michael, who is White, lives in a racially and ethnically diverse region,
and his many PAs come from different racial, ethnic, and cultural backgrounds. They include native-born Americans and people from the Carib-
bean, Central America, eastern Europe, and West Africa. He needs two PAs

working together to get him out of bed, toileted, and showered every morning. Therefore, Michael often has two PAs working simultaneously who are from different racial, ethnic, and national origins, with their interactions driven by stereotyping and complicated assumptions about the other PA. PAs from some backgrounds don't respect PAs with other origins. For example, some PAs view people from a certain West African country as lazy, stoking tensions among the PAs about apportioning the workload: who does the laundry, cleans the kitchen, scrubs the bathroom, mops the floor, and takes out the trash? These questions have sometimes precipitated disrespect, heated debate, simmering antipathies, and passive-aggressive undercurrents among his PAs, with accusations hurled about others shirking work. "Racism isn't just confined to White versus Black," Michael observed (an immigrant from Great Britain, Michael is prone to understatement).

Perspective of PAS Workers

PAs who are racial or ethnic minorities often anticipate disrespect and distrust when paired with a consumer from different origins. But by behaving professionally, doing the work, PAs find they eventually earn respect and even loyalty from consumers. Chandra, for example, fully expected that she would be replaced because of ethnic differences with her newly assigned agency consumer, a Latina:

> If you go to a Black patient, they would prefer Black people. Hispanics would prefer Hispanics. I am not Hispanic, but I know how to speak Spanish very well. . . . The client said, "But you're not Hispanic. You would not understand my way of life." I said, "All right, I will hold on until they find you a Hispanic." And she saw what kind of person I was; she started to get to know me little by little. I lasted there for four years because she got used to me, and I was doing the things she wanted me to do. We had no fights; we had no arguments. It came to a point where she couldn't do it without me.

Isaiah acknowledges that he was nervous to start PAS work because his agency assigned him clients in a predominantly White neighborhood of a racially divided city—he is African American. He senses most of his clients are prejudiced when he first appears, but he behaves professionally, and they get to know him for who he is very quickly. He says he has never been blatantly disrespected as a PA because of his race. A woman PA, also African American, said that she has never felt discriminated against but admits having difficulties coming to terms with providing PAS supports, sometimes feeling like "the help."

Some PAs have confronted overt disrespect and discrimination because of their race. Marion, who is African American, had one White male client who refused all her offers of assistance. Her agency assigns PAs for a minimum of three hours each session, and on her third visit to him, she completed the primary task—taking him to an appointment—within an hour. Noting she still had two more hours to work, she asked, "'Is there anything that I can do? I don't mind taking out the trash. I don't mind laundry.' I saw dishes piled up and trash everywhere. He said, 'I don't need your help. No. You could just leave.'" Marion called the agency, suggesting he probably would prefer someone else. Several weeks later, the agency again assigned Marion to this consumer, who had called asking specifically for her. Although Marion was reluctant, she agreed to go:

> He actually apologized. He said, "I'm sorry. I had a lot going on, and I really don't want you to think I was racist. I had a bad experience before, I guess, with African Americans." So, when he saw me, it was just, "Ugh. Not another one." It was like that without getting to know me. So, he apologized, and I think I went to him maybe a total of 10 times.

Mona (see Chapter 1) is African American, and her perceptions of racial dynamics and disrespect are complex:

> When I walk into a home of a Black person or someone who is Hispanic, they treat you like you are a servant. They let you know that. And when it comes to the race aspect with older White people, I use a little bit of what's called psychology. You got to look at where they come from. It's like in the movie *The Help*, with my White client with dementia [the mother of brothers Bob and Dan], she identifies with that. Oh, my Lord. But you know the roles. Black helpers know what their role is with the White person in the home. You know what you should and shouldn't be doing. But at the same time, it's only because of where they come from, how things used to be. And they're old. It's hard to break them out of that.

11

Physical and Emotional Safety

S am is in his mid-fifties and quadriplegic from muscular dystrophy. For many years, he has hired PAs under Medicaid self-direction (see Chapter 8). Aiming for reciprocity—win-win opportunities for both Sam and his PAs—he employed people whom others might avoid, individuals with histories of substance abuse or serious mental illness. Sam's choices reflect his "liberal values. It appeals to me as a human being." But when his PA's mental illness suddenly recurred, incapacitating her, Sam first ensured she received necessary medical attention, and then he fired her. The PA was stunned, upset about losing her job. However, Sam feared for his safety. Although the PA never overtly threatened him, her inability to reliably provide essential ADL supports posed imminent risks to Sam's health and was enormously stressful and emotionally draining. Sam recognized how others might judge his firing this PA, but he defended his action:

> Being taken seriously as a boss is hard. The power dynamic is fascinating. You're the boss while you're naked and laying down. This is not a good power dynamic—normally you're not in control when you're naked and laying down. It takes a lot to maintain and exert control of the situation when you are physically vulnerable. . . . When I fired my PA with mental illness, it sounds cruel. It's really hard to be cold. But for my own safety, I had to do it. I can't help anyone else if I'm in danger.

Chandra's agency sometimes holds in-service training sessions for PAs about how to handle threats to their safety, dangers she views as widespread. Chandra recounted a recent local story about a consumer's grandson, who was released from an inpatient psychiatric unit and later stabbed his grandmother's PA several times: "The aide got away by running out the door and screaming." In her long experience, Chandra has felt threatened in clients' homes, generally not by the consumer but by other household members, such as "their son or grandson who's out of jail. That's scary, that's scary. They're in that apartment with you, and you're spending many hours there." One time, substituting for another agency PA, people "were selling drugs from that apartment. Listen, I'm not stupid. What are people knocking on the door every 10 minutes for? I was really, really scared. I didn't go back there the next day."

Some dangers arise unexpectedly. "There was this lady in an electrical wheelchair," Chandra said. One day, the consumer left home and rode her power wheelchair very fast in the street—"she's going like a jet"—while her PA sprinted behind. Suddenly, the PA fell; she'd had a heart attack. After this incident, the agency clarified its policy. "They told us, if that ever happens, do not run behind the wheelchair," Chandra reported. "Just call the agency, and you can go home."

Safety Overview

Both consumers and PAs face safety risks in PAS. Recognizing that fact does not imply a false equivalency, that dangers to consumers and PAs are generally equal. An immutable difference exists: consumers with severe disability who need paid PAS cannot live without safe and reliable supports; in contrast, with the high demand for paid PAS, most PAs can leave a job without major long-term consequences (they will, most likely, easily find another PAS position). Occupational injuries, however, could have devastating lifelong implications, restricting PAs' future employment prospects and perhaps causing permanent disability.

This chapter considers safety hazards for consumers and PAs. For both groups, abuse is a major threat to physical and emotional safety. Extensive experience with abuse of older persons offers helpful insights, albeit focusing on the vantage point of consumers. Elder abuse generally falls into broad categories:[1]

- **Physical abuse:** injuring or inflicting physical pain
- **Emotional abuse:** verbal threats, harassment, intimidation, or psychological assaults

- **Sexual abuse:** touching, fondling, intercourse, or other sexual contacts with individuals who do not willingly consent or are unable to understand, feel threatened, or are physically forced into sexual activity
- **Confinement:** isolating or restraining individuals against their will, without clear medical or safety justifications
- **Passive neglect:** failure to provide basic life necessities, including food, fluids, clothing, housing, and medical services
- **Willful deprivation:** actively withholding food, fluids, clothing, housing, medications, medical services, means of communication (e.g., access to a telephone), assistive devices (e.g., wheelchair, walker), therapeutic devices, or other physical assistance, and thus inflicting physical, mental, or emotional harm—unless an individual with decision-making capacity has clearly indicated preferences to forego these basic supports or services
- **Financial exploitation:** misuse of or withholding financial resources without an individual's consent

Among older adults, abuse is associated with a 300% higher death rate than for people free from abuse.[2] Warning signs of abuse include the following:[3]

- **Physical abuse, neglect, or mistreatment:** pressure marks, bruises, abrasions, burns, broken bones
- **Emotional abuse:** unexplained withdrawal from usual daily activities, sudden decrease in alertness, or unexpected depression; difficult, strained, or tense relationships; frequent arguments between the consumer and caregiver or PA
- **Verbal abuse:** belittling, threatening, intimidating, or verbal attempts to control the consumer
- **Neglect:** poor hygiene, unexplained weight loss, failure to take medications and manage chronic health conditions, unattended medical needs, pressure injuries
- **Financial abuse:** sudden and unexplained change in financial status

Abusive experiences range from neglect to outright physical assault and encompass both emotional and physical threats.

Safety and Paid PAS Consumers

Consumers' attitudes about paid PAs and safety vary by their circumstances. The intimacy of PAS and inherently complex power dynamic between consumers and PAs provide many opportunities for harm, physical and emotional. Low-income consumers appear more likely to experience abuse from paid PAs than higher-income clients.[4] Informal caregivers—family members and friends providing PAS—can also abuse people with disability and older people. Roughly 10% of adults 60 years old and older experience some form of abuse each year; yet only about 1 in 14 of these cases is reported to authorities.[5] Comparable abuse statistics for younger adults and people with disability in general are not available, although multiple studies have documented abuse of people with disability.[6] One study found that 26% of women with disability report sexual violence at some point in their lives, as compared with 15% of women without disability.[7] Among men with disability, 9% report lifetime sexual violence, as compared with 6% among nondisabled men.[8]

Intimate partner violence raises particular concern. It happens more often when one partner has a disability than among couples with no disabled partner; the person with disability is typically the abuse victim.[9] Intimate partner violence against people with disability often explicitly targets points of vulnerability, such as

> being prevented from using a wheelchair, cane, respirator, or other assistive device, or their partners refusing to provide an important personal need, including giving medication or bathroom/shower/dressing/eating assistance. Abuse can also occur during personal assistance; for example, using unnecessary touching, force, or roughness during bathing, dressing, or transfers. . . . [T]hese disability-related abuses may not only affect an individual's safety and quality of life, they can also worsen medical conditions and/or increase overall functional impairment. For example, without regular medication, an individual's problematic health symptoms may increase, leading to longer and/or more severe relapses of a medical problem or causing other complications (e.g., infection, increase in pain levels, and/or malnutrition).[10]

People with disability often do not report these abuses, afraid of losing critical assistance regardless of its injury risks. In these situations, people with disability generally lose their sense of agency or empowerment to mitigate the threats. Exploring the experiences of women with disability, one study found that abusers were typically husbands or male partners. One participant highlighted the irony of her situation—trying to assert independence despite depending on her husband—stating, "You finally say, 'OK, this is it, I'm going to do whatever I can to change this marriage. And by the way, can you bring my scooter to me so I can leave you?'"[11] Medicaid payments to family members serving as paid PAs can perpetuate this abuse, hidden within homes.

Sometimes abuse feels subtle, making consumers question whether they have legitimate concerns. "The closest I've come to physical abuse is people just not paying attention to what they're doing, so they hurt me in the process," said a woman participating in a study of PA abuse. "You're uncomfortable all day because they didn't get your socks or underwear right because they were in a hurry."[12] Neglect or being ignored also constitutes abuse, as another participant observed: "I was abused by this one woman. She didn't say anything abusive. She just disregarded my [directions] no matter what I said."[13] Physical harms need not require assault: "I had an attendant once leave me stark naked on the toilet and walk out. So, I consider that abusive."[14]

Men with disability can also have experiences of violence from family caregivers or paid PAs similar to those of disabled women, as did one man:

> He and I got into the verbal altercation . . . so he thought he would put me in my place by throwing me up on the back of the chair, then letting me hang there. I'm on a ventilator. . . . I had already been off for an hour and a half, and I was getting winded. . . . [H]e just kept screaming at me, [forced me] to apologize to him[,] . . . [me] hardly able to breathe, and I'm supposed to apologize to this guy. He really scared the hell out of me.[15]

Abuse of men with disability can also seem subtle: "It's neglect, passive aggressive behaviors, control, not listening, deliberately not following directions. . . . You may not be aware of it. And if you've lived with it for years and years, it may just go right over your head."[16] Being unreliable can pose danger, asserted one man: "Not showing up is abuse because your life depends on that. It literally does at times."[17] Careless PAs can cause injury, as for one man: "An attendant dropped me because he really wasn't paying attention, and I broke my leg in the fall. Whether or not it's considered *abuse*, it's harmful . . . a lack of focus or attention can result in severe physical damage."[18]

In the study of abuse among men with disability, one man worried that complaining could result in policy makers eliminating consumer self-directed PAS:

> Studies like this are very helpful, [but] in the wrong hands, they could potentially make it look like . . . "we need to jump in there and protect these poor little crippled people." . . . We have to be careful that that isn't misinterpreted by some well-meaning legislator . . . and used against us . . . [to] try to limit and tell us who we can . . . and who we can't have work for us.[19]

Some government programs assist consumers in making hiring decisions. For example, in Massachusetts, the Disabled Persons Protection Commission aims "to protect adults with disabilities from the abusive acts or omissions of their caregivers through investigation oversight, public awareness and prevention."[20] Twenty-six states currently have registries that identify persons who have abused people with disability.[21] Consumers and agencies can check job candidates against these registries before making hiring decisions.

Concerns from Consumer Interviews

The 21 consumer interviewees expressed various worries about physical and emotional safety.

Constantly Feeling Vulnerable

Many people continually feel physical or emotional vulnerability, dreading that, at any moment, their PAS supports could vanish or fall through. Losing supports could be catastrophic, even life-threatening. Ariana, who manages her PAS through a hybrid agency with choice program, observed that

> there is a vulnerability, definitely. I think that's why many people with disabilities come across as tough or mean because you can't let your guard down. You can't let people know that you're scared, because that's when it happens. It's like anything if they smell fear. So, we have to come across as confident, in control. I'm the boss. I'm the supervisor. You're not going to come in and tell me how I should be living.

This simmering unease—about upending daily life and losing control—seems mundane in comparison with overt instances of physical or emotional violence. Nevertheless, constant, baseline anxiety has enormous consequences for consumers, as follows:

- **No-shows.** When PAs do not show up for work, consumers with severe disability can be unfed, unbathed, untoileted, undressed, and in bed all day. If they are without appropriate communication accommodations, consumers may be unable to contact help. If PAs do not appear the next day either, the situation can become dire.
- **Coverage.** For self-directed PAS consumers, maintaining PA staffing, ensuring PAs are reliable and arrive as scheduled, can be time-consuming, exhausting, and stressful.

- **Staffing choices.** For some agency consumers, not having control over the PAs sent to their homes can cause anxiety.
- **Staff turnover.** Frequent PA turnover requires consumers to repeatedly train new workers, an exhausting and time-consuming process. All new PAs have a learning curve as they absorb the consumer's preferences and learn specific and critical support tasks. During that training period, providing ADL supports takes longer, tiring the consumer.
- **Firing decisions.** When a self-directed PA performs poorly, deciding when and how to fire the PA is stressful, sometimes raising concerns about physical safety.
- **Infection control.** Failure of PAs to wear gloves or to wash their hands thoroughly puts consumers at risk of infections. Sometimes, PAs show up with active infections, such as a strep throat. Sending infectious PAs home is the only option—but what if consumers don't have replacement PAs? The COVID-19 pandemic escalated this concern (see Epilogue). The asymptomatic spread of the novel coronavirus meant that PAs who did not feel sick could unwittingly spread the virus to their consumers if they did not follow explicit precautions.
- **Basic hygiene.** PAs not following basic hygiene practices during food preparation, for example, handling food after blowing their nose or touching their face or hair, raises infection concerns, even when PAs are not acutely ill.
- **Rearranging belongings.** PAs frequently move consumers' possessions without telling them, so consumers cannot find objects, large and small—important letters or documents, favorite scissors or cooking utensils, specific grocery items or pieces of clothing, or articles with special personal significance. Losing their possessions can make consumers feel that the sanctity of their home has been breached. Missing bills or important documents can cause practical headaches. Sometimes PAs misplace critical medications or other health-related items, posing health risks.

In addition, as noted previously, PAs can inflict microaggressions on consumers, such as adding excessive salt to food, insisting consumers "clean their plates" during feeding, and unwanted kissing or caresses. These intrusions might seem trivial, unworthy of making complaints. But they can nevertheless leave consumers feeling frustrated, violated, or imperiled.

Injuries

People with severe physical disability are often injured at some point, frequently with no one to blame. For example, Natalie has had many broken bones and

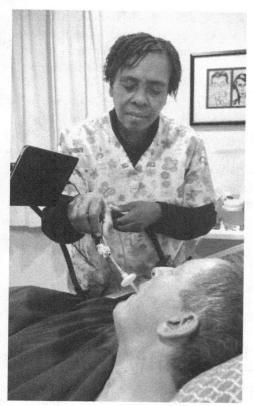

Nelita positioning Michael's sip-and-puff device that operates his tablet computer, December 29, 2019. The tablet with sip-and-puff is Michael's connection to the outside world and to make emergency calls. He also programmed the tablet to operate functions throughout his home, like operating lights, adjusting the thermostat, and playing music. The end of the tube needs to be positioned precisely, so that Michael can sip or puff small breaths into it without the tube poking his face. Training PAs to position this tube requires patience, as does positioning the tube multiple times daily. Mispositioning the sip-and-puff device, through inattention or malfeasance, would be an easy way to abuse consumers who depend on this technology. (Photo credit: Hanniel Dossous)

sprained ankles, which she attributes to her frailty or wheelchair malfunctions, not PAs. Sometimes, PAs are careless when dressing her, causing pain: "Once in a while I'll say to my PA, 'You really need to be more careful.' But it's not malicious." Peggy, who, like Natalie, has spinal muscular atrophy, rolled out of bed while sleeping and broke her hip. Peggy, who has a live-in PA, took several seconds to realize what had happened. She then called her PA, who started trying to turn her, causing more pain. The PA dialed 911, and the ambulance took Peggy to the hospital. She later got a bed with rails to prevent future falls.

Devices like Hoyer lifts and other assistive technologies make some ADL tasks easier and safer for consumers and PAs. Mechanical lifts are especially critical for moving people in and out of bed, on and off toilets or shower chairs, and in and out of wheelchairs. However, no technologies yet exist that replace human assistance for basic ADL supports. Robotics have advanced substantially and can now perform certain household chores, like vacuuming, mopping floors, cleaning windows, doing laundry, and folding washed items.

New technologies provide automated feeding, albeit slowly and clumsily; it remains unclear whether these devices will improve sufficiently to appeal to people needing feeding assistance. Therefore, the most efficient option for ADL supports remains human assistance, despite the inherent risks from human fallibility.

However, even basic assistive devices, like shower chairs, are not fool-proof. Six months after her hip fracture, Peggy fell again. Using a Hoyer lift, her live-in PA was transporting Peggy, who was naked, into the bathroom for her morning shower. As the PA started moving Peggy from the Hoyer lift sling onto her shower chair, Peggy suddenly fell to the floor. She hit her head, causing a concussion, and also broke her femur. Peggy remembers her PA being very calm, checking Peggy, and then calling 911.

> I had two fire trucks and one ambulance and about seven or eight emergency people in the bathroom. I'm naked on the floor with a broken leg. Every time they tried to move me, I screamed. . . . They ended up sliding the [Hoyer] sling up under me, which was very deli-cate. It was a good heave-ho, and they said, "This is going to hurt." Those life experiences have taught me to have a plan in place.

Peggy developed posttraumatic stress disorder (PTSD) after this injury, attributing the PTSD to feeling she had lost control: "I couldn't figure out where we went wrong. I wasn't able to see how I fell. All I know is I was on the floor—it was faster than a blink of an eye. It took me quite a while to struggle with the reality that it wasn't my fault. It wasn't my attendant's fault." Peggy eventually determined that defective design of her shower chair caused the fall (i.e., when her PA positioned Peggy on the chair, leaning forward because of the Hoyer lift positioning, the chair flipped over). Peggy hired a personal injury lawyer and won a lawsuit against the chair's manufacturer.

Exhausted PAs

Many PAs work multiple jobs to make ends meet, leading to such profound exhaustion that it compromises safety. Studies have recognized that health care professionals who lack adequate sleep can make dangerous errors in pa-tient care.[22] To protect patient and trainee safety, starting in 2003, graduate medical education training programs limited physician trainee work hours to 80 hours per week.[23] PAs working two or three jobs can easily exceed 80 hours, leaving them weary, unable to think quickly or remain alert. Espe-cially when PAs assist consumers with medication administration, exhaus-tion heightens risks of errors, just as it does in hospitals. The difference is that hospitals generally have the capacity to recognize dangerous medication errors and treat as needed, whereas in consumers' homes these mistakes can escape detection.

PAs can fall asleep on the job. Especially when consumers do not require minute-by-minute attention, PAs might lie down on the couch in a neighboring room, for example, awaiting the consumer's call for assistance. If PAs fall asleep, they might not hear that call.

For example, one night Michael noticed it was getting late. Despite repeatedly calling her name, his PA had not come into his bedroom to perform final evening tasks (emptying his leg bag, positioning his pillows and blankets)—her scheduled departure time was 10:00 P.M. Using a voice-activated system, he tried telephoning her mobile phone, but unbeknownst to him, the PA had silenced her telephone so that it didn't ring during work hours. As the time ticked by, Michael began worrying. He suspected that the PA, who worked very long hours, was sound asleep, but she was an older woman, and he wondered if she had become ill. About 10:45, he called 911, seeking assistance. When the police officers arrived, they knocked heavily on the front door, arousing the PA, who had fallen asleep on the couch and was disoriented when awoken. The PA's history as an immigrant from eastern Europe who had lived through totalitarian regimes made her defensive when police officers were suddenly on the doorstep. She strenuously denied having been asleep. The police officers left after ensuring Michael's well-being, and the PA continued protesting she had been awake the whole time. Concerned about the PA's safety getting home, Michael encouraged her to stay overnight, but the PA drove off. From that evening forward, the PA became increasingly unreliable and verbally confrontational, and Michael fired her about two months later.

Feeling Hopeless

Depression is a common secondary disability. Feelings of hopelessness and lack of control make consumers more vulnerable to emotional abuse. Social isolation and microaggressions from PAs—including persistent disrespect—can tax the resilience even of consumers who have accommodated to severe disability. Being bedbound, confined to home, with few visits from friends or family, can make consumers susceptible to patronizing or contemptuous comments from PAs. For example, one man, an accomplished professional, spent day after day in bed, surrounded only by PAs, who needed to clean up his frequent bouts of bowel incontinence. His primary PA, a woman in her fifties, performed this essential task, but she addressed the man mockingly, as if he were a child. She made fun of his situation and bullied him.

Shortly after Matt's spinal cord injury several decades ago, his insurer required him to use agency PAS. The agency PA arrived daily with her three-year-old son. After the PA bathed Matt and performed his bathroom routine,

> She would sit in my room and get high all day. Her son was a cute little kid, but he'd come over and taunt me and bend my finger back and say, "Can you feel this?" I would say, "No. I can't feel that." And he'd bend my finger back further. "Can you feel this now?" His mom was watching this, and she would say god-awful things, telling him, "You'll go to hell." . . . She sat in front of the TV, these game shows, talk shows, all these mind-numbing shows. And she stole all the time. She would take food my mom had put in the freezer. . . . It was horrible that I was stuck with her all day.

At the time, Matt only had a manual wheelchair, which he could not operate on his own. He was literally stuck. "Back then, I was a church mouse. I was so afraid. I'd spent almost nine months in the hospital and learned to survive. You just keep quiet. So, I would not say anything to these aides." Matt felt despondent, until several months later, a friend started picking him up and taking him to classes at the local community college. "He saved my life," said Matt. Getting Matt out of his home launched him on the path out of agency and into self-directed PAS. He regained hope.

PAs on the Front Lines

As Peggy's bathroom fall story suggests, PAs are sometimes the frontline defense, taking appropriate action when the consumer's safety is at risk. Peggy's trauma was obvious. However, PAs who are vigilant and know their consumers well can recognize subtle changes that might portend bigger problems. For example, Shauna described what happened when she arrived at the home of her long-time consumer:

> She just didn't seem herself. There was just something totally different about her. Her eyes looked different. She didn't want to get out the bed. She couldn't stand. And when she went to the bathroom, her urine smelled so strong, out of the ordinary. And the way she was talking was just off. It wasn't normal. So, I called 911. They came, and they was like, "You did the right thing because she has a UTI [urinary tract infection]." By then she was just shaking.

Several other PAs described instances where they dialed 911 because something about the consumer seemed off—and the PAs were correct, detecting problems that could have become life-threatening without treatment. One day, upon arriving for work, Isaiah found his consumer on the floor. Isaiah could not lift the man and telephoned 911. "And as a human, you can't do nothing but be concerned," said Isaiah. "I've even sat at the hospital for hours with my clients."

Safety and PAS Workers

Providing PAS is physically and emotionally demanding. According to the National Institute for Occupational Safety and Health (NIOSH):

> Home healthcare workers are frequently exposed to a variety of potentially serious or even life-threatening hazards. These dangers include overexertion; stress; guns and other weapons; illegal drugs; verbal abuse and other forms of violence in the home or community; bloodborne pathogens; needlesticks; latex sensitivity; temperature extremes; unhygienic conditions, including lack of water, unclean or hostile animals, and animal waste. Long commutes from worksite to worksite also expose the home healthcare worker to transportation-related risks.[24]

Home health care workers have lower rates of occupational injuries than workers in nursing homes or residential facilities. In 2018 health care workers in nongovernmental nursing homes or residential facilities had 5.9 nonfatal injuries per 100 full-time equivalent (FTE) workers, versus 2.6 nonfatal injuries per 100 FTE in home health care. (These figures encompass various home care providers, including skilled health care professionals as well as PAs, homemakers, and other aides; statistics by type of worker are unavailable.)[25]

Nonetheless, home care providers confront wide-ranging environmental and nonhuman dangers in their workplaces—the isolated and unregulated environment of consumers' homes. A survey of approximately 1,560 home care agency workers in New York City identified multiple environmental safety hazards in their clients' homes, including cockroaches, 33%; mice or rats, 23%; animal hair, 21%; excessive dust, 19%; threatening pets, 17%; messiness, clutter, or loose rugs (i.e., trip hazards), 17%; irritating chemicals, including bleach and cleaning agents, 17%; peeling paint, 15%; unsanitary conditions, such as dirty toilets, 12%; mold or dampness, 10%; temperature extremes inside the home, 9%; loud or irritating noises, 4%; and guns, 2%.[26] However, home health care workers often lack basic protective equipment, with 11% reporting absence of disposable gloves, which would also protect consumers' safety.[27] These percentages come from agency home care workers in New York City, where environmental hazards might be especially common. Nonetheless, other locales, such as homes in rural areas, might also pose significant albeit different specific threats.

NIOSH has identified broad areas where home health workers face occupational hazards:[28]

- **Back injuries and musculoskeletal disorders:** injuries of muscles, tendons, ligaments, nerves, joints, cartilage, bones, or blood vessels of the back or extremities caused or aggravated by lifting, pushing, or pulling during work tasks. Moving consumers with functional impairments, who cannot assist the lifting process, increases the likelihood of PA injuries—as does moving people who are obese. Small or cramped spaces in consumers' homes complicates efforts to move consumers. Home health care workers can spend 40 to 48% of their time in poor posture positions, such as being twisted or bent forward, which may cause neck, back, and shoulder problems.[29] Using hoists or other lifting devices can reduce workers' injuries during consumer transfers by 39 to 79%,[30] but these technologies are not universally available in homes or appropriate for certain consumers.
- **Occupational stress:** "harmful physical and emotional responses that occur when the requirements of the job do not match the capabilities, resources, or needs of the worker."[31] Home care workers experience occupational stressors similar to those of others in health care, including the deaths and severe illness of clients, workload and time pressures, and problematic consumer behaviors, including aggression, lack of cooperation, and irritability. In addition, "home healthcare workers may have to deal with stressors that healthcare workers in hospitals or other inpatient healthcare settings do not: their work is not directly supervised, they generally work alone, they might travel through unsafe neighborhoods, and they may have to face alcohol or drug abusers, family arguments, dangerous dogs, or heavy traffic."[32] Furthermore, PAS consumers may not sufficiently insulate PAs from these threats or support PAs confronting inappropriate demands from other household members.
- **Violence:** threats of or actual physical assaults by people or animals. Unlike institutions with onsite security staff or systems,

home care settings have no safeguards against workplace violence. In 2006, 5.5 per 10,000 full-time home health care workers experienced nonfatal assaults, more than twice the rate for all U.S. workers.[33] Complicating these risks are consumers' complex mental health conditions, alcohol or substance abuse, poverty and unmet needs, chaotic family dynamics, and weapons in the home. Violence in home health care settings is underreported for multiple reasons, including PAs fearing retribution or accusations that they were at fault, embarrassment, or beliefs that dealing with violence is part of the job. Workplace violence can inflict heavy costs on home health care, ranging from emotional distress to disabling injury to death.

- **Latex allergies:** allergic reactions to products made from dry natural rubber latex. Latex allergies typically arise after repeated exposures to latex products and range in severity, including skin rashes, hives, itchy eyes, runny nose, sneezing, scratchy throat, asthma, and rarely shock (other symptoms typically precede shock). Many products that PAs touch contain latex, primarily gloves but also urinary catheters, stomach tubes, adhesive tape, and components of ventilation equipment. Latex gloves containing powder are more likely to cause allergic reactions: when people remove these gloves, they breathe in powder particles released into the air. The U.S. Food and Drug Administration requires all products containing natural rubber latex to be labeled. If workers are not handling infectious materials, using nonlatex gloves is advisable.

NIOSH also describes risks associated with needlesticks and bloodborne pathogens,[34] which might affect PAs who are providing health care services, such as injection medications or wound care. NIOSH provides a checklist for home care workers to consider in assessing safety risks of job placements (Table 11.1).

Safety concerns identified by NIOSH parallel worries raised by PA interviewees, described throughout this book. Examples include unsafe neighborhoods, poor lighting and broken elevators in high-rise buildings, apartments crammed with hoarded newspapers, and consumers or household members with threatening attitudes. PAs also echo NIOSH's warnings about threats from animals. One PA recalled her first agency consumer: "He had a big pit bull and a lot of other animals. And his place had a bad odor. I couldn't help him out because the dog was in my way. I called my company and said, 'Listen, I can't stay here. I'm scared of dogs.'"

Some PAs make valiant efforts—at risk to themselves—to protect their consumer from injury. Marion recalled driving a client to her primary care

TABLE 11.1 CHECKLIST: MAXIMIZING SAFETY FOR HOME CARE PAs[1]
Initial and annual training should address:
Preventing musculoskeletal injuries
Preventing slips and falls
Recommendations for performing ADL/IADL support tasks ergonomically and obtaining ergonomic equipment
Infection control and prevention procedures
Performing hand hygiene and proper use of gloves and other personal protective equipment, as needed
What to do if home is unsanitary or unsafe (e.g., lacks potable water, insect infestations, lacks heating or cooling, weapons not stored safely, threatening animals)
What to do if PAs believe they are in danger
Identifying workplace stressors and reducing stress
Recognizing consumers' angry or aggressive behavior and verbal abuse
How to respond to verbal abuse and calming an angry consumer
What to do if PAs feel uncomfortable in the consumer's community
Recognizing illegal drug activity
Making appropriate decisions in response to threatening weather
Safe transportation to and from workplace (e.g., if driving to work, wear seat belts, use hands-free communication; if public transportation, have updated schedules and access to real-time service alerts)
PAs should know:
How to report safety concerns in physical environment of workplace
What to do if they are injured on the job
What to do if they feel threatened or verbally abused by consumer
Symptoms of latex allergy and appropriate response
PAs and home care settings should have:
Appropriate gloves, preferably nonlatex, and other personal protective equipment, as needed
Low-heel, slip-resistant, sturdy shoes
Safe and hygienic workplace
Appropriate ergonomic equipment
Weapons stored safely
Animals restrained within or outside the home, as needed, before PA arrives
Cell phone with reliable signal
GPS or good, up-to-date local maps for finding homes of clients

Source: Adapted from National Institute for Occupational Safety and Health, Centers for Disease Control and Prevention, U.S. Department of Health and Human Services. NIOSH hazard review: Occupational hazards in home healthcare. DHHS (NIOSH) Publication No. 2010-125. U.S. Department of Health and Human Services; 2010:49–51. https://www.cdc.gov/niosh/docs/2010-125/pdfs/2010-125.pdf?id=10.26616/NIOSHPUB2010125
[1] This table does not include factors related to clinical tasks, such as handling syringes and infectious materials.

doctor's office. They were running late, and the consumer was anxious that the doctor might refuse to see her. Marion felt rushed. As they got out of the car in the parking lot, they both lost balance as Marion tried to position the consumer in her wheelchair:

> I thought, "Oh, my God. We're both going down. We're going down." But when I went down, I twisted and was able to place [the consumer] on the frame of the car. I was totally on the ground. I said to someone, "Please get the nurse." The nurses came out, and they assisted me and asked if I needed any help. I said, "I will be fine. Just help me into the car." I stayed in the car while the nurses took [the consumer] to see the doctor. . . . [The consumer's] aunt came and drove us home. I could not move. I took some pain pills. I was out for a week.

Finally, home care workers have high rates of workplace physical or emotional violence. The survey of approximately 1,560 home care agency workers in New York City found that 28% reported verbal abuse from their clients, 11% noted neighborhood violence or crime, 9% experienced racial or ethnic discrimination from the client or client's family, 8% encountered threats of physical harm, and 5% reported drug use in the home.[35]

Another survey questioned roughly 1,210 consumer self-directed home care workers in Oregon about a wide range of abusive experiences. Findings included being yelled or sworn at, 42%; verbal aggression, 35%; clients crying to make workers feel guilty, 29%; threats to throw something at workers, hitting workers, smashing or kicking something in workers' presence or displaying loss of control, 21%; being exposed to sexually explicit materials or comments, 21%; being cornered or put in positions difficult to escape, 19%; being targets of rumors of sexual promiscuity, whistled or leered at, teased sexually, having sexual compliments, 17%; having someone try to hit worker but failing, being kicked, bitten, hit with a fist, pushed, grabbed, shoved, or slapped, 14%; gender-based insults, sexist remarks, 14%; having someone breech their personal boundaries or being pinched, patted, or hugged in uncomfortable way, 11%; being fondled in sexually explicit way, 3%; having someone unnecessarily expose themselves, 3%; having someone handle a gun or knife in a threatening way, 2%.[36]

Being exposed to violence or abuse in their workplace can harm home care workers long-term and make them reconsider working in the field. NIOSH surveyed almost 700 home health care workers and found that their personal or job characteristics—age, gender, race, job title, and hours of work, and whether care tasks used needles—did not affect their likelihood of workplace violence.[37] However, the 35% of workers reporting language barriers with consumers had four times more injuries from patient violence than did other home health aides.[38] A survey of nearly 1,000 agency home care workers in Massachusetts found that workers older than the median age of 48 years were about 40% less likely to experience verbal abuse than younger workers.[39] Various factors were significantly associated with workers' reports of verbal abuse: workers hired directly by consumers were about 25% less likely to report verbal abuse; workers with too little time to perform prescribed tasks were 60% more likely to report verbal abuse; those using a mechanical transfer device were 36% more likely; and those working in homes with cramped spaces were 92% more likely.[40] Situations with language differences between home care workers and clients were 16% more likely to have workers reporting verbal abuse.[41] Consumer characteristics associated with higher rates of reported verbal abuse included dementia, 65% higher than with consumers without dementia; mental illness or psychological problems, 58% higher; mobility impairments, 73% higher; and with a consumer who smokes indoors, 29% higher.[42]

Regardless of their personal attributes or job experiences, encountering workplace violence or abuse can have lasting and serious consequences for home care workers. The Oregon survey of self-directed home care workers found that experiencing workplace violence or sexual harassment substantially increased workers' fears of future similar events and significantly heightened rates of stress, depression, sleep problems, and work burnout.[43] These findings raise questions about how to protect workers' safety while supporting consumers' needs. Clearly, PAs should not be subjected to abusive or violent clients or dangerous work environments. Nonetheless, consumers abusing PAs may have conditions, including mental health disorders, that require PAS support. In delineating rules for their consumer-directed PAS program, Oregon confronted these conflicting imperatives:

> Under Oregon's consumer-driven model, a homecare worker leaving the home of a person who requires 24/7 care is considered abandonment and can result in the loss of the homecare worker's provider number (which can never be reinstated) and loss of employment. . . . The Oregon Homecare Commission [later] added a provision to allow the homecare worker to leave if she or he felt at risk of serious injury. When establishing such provisions, it is important to also provide clear guidelines on appropriate procedures for leaving the home (e.g., notifying the consumer-employer's family/emergency contact, and/or requesting a welfare check by the local police) and on documenting the situation/use of the procedures so that if the homecare workers [sic] actions are called into question, there is a record.[44]

Clearly, these complex situations raise the urgency of training both consumers and paid, in-home PAs about appropriate behaviors and expectations within the consumer-PA dyad.

Pandemic Threats

Finally, in 2020 across the U.S. population—and worldwide—the COVID-19 pandemic brought nearly universal feelings of vulnerability, anxiety, and fear. Within the consumer-PA dyad, these emotions reflect reality: PAs could bring the novel coronavirus into consumers' homes, and consumers or their household members could infect PAs. Especially at the pandemic's outset, even hospital staff lacked adequate essential PPE, such as N95 masks, gowns, and gloves. PPE was even scarcer among home care providers and virtually absent for PAs. In addition, testing for coronavirus was limited, especially for people with disability unable to access testing centers (e.g., pop-up drive-through facilities), impeding efforts to identify asymptomatic but infected people who could spread the contagion. Numbers are currently unknown, but anecdotal reports describe people with disability dying without care in their homes from COVID-19 and both informal and paid PAs dying after coronavirus exposures from consumers. Fully examining and addressing the complex implications of pandemics for in-home paid PAS is essential—experts warn that new global pandemics are almost inevitable. The threats to both consumers and PAs are stark.

Money Matters

As described in Chapter 9, some independent living movement pioneers envisioned insulating paid ADL supports from the complexities of human relationships, treating PAS as "a cash service . . . with no need for emotions such as gratitude."[1] Of course, given the nature of ADL support, this vision collapsed. Ironically, perhaps, the fact that paid PAS involves monetary transactions—by cash, payments from a third party (e.g., Medicaid), or through an agency—has its own interpersonal consequences. Wage levels convey respect and societal value. Yet in 2018 the median hourly wage for home-based PAS was only $11.40,[2] and the median annual income for home care workers was just $16,200.[3] However, the personal and emotional value consumers ascribe to these essential services and the value society places on PAS, as measured by wages, are almost polar opposites. Natalie observed that

> home care work is not socially valued. It's not like, "Oh, look you're a nurse. That's really cool," or, "Oh, wow, you're a paramedic." I know paramedics are paid horribly as well, but paramedics have more social standing than a home care worker. I think that it's partly misogyny. This work is largely done by people of color, and it's often done by people with lower education levels. It's considered unskilled labor. . . . We need good wages, benefits. It needs to be a good job that someone can actually raise a family on.

This issue assumed special urgency during the COVID-19 pandemic when home care workers, including PAs, were expected to show up for work but were not paid hazard pay as essential workers, despite obvious risks to their health from their jobs.[4]

This chapter explores how low wages and benefits for in-home PAS affect relationships, including feelings of obligations for social justice between consumers and PAs. Certainly, some PAs are drawn to PAS by more than their paychecks. PAS fulfills an inner need to help other people. Nevertheless, low wages remain an omnipresent backdrop and can affect the quality of PAS consumers receive, as well as PAs' satisfaction with their work lives.[5]

Dynamics and Definition of Employment

When considering wages and other job benefits, the first question is whether PAs are agency employees, employees of a consumer, or independent contractors—someone running a small business providing PAS. Agencies are responsible for paying federal and state taxes for their employees and complying with other local and federal labor regulations. For gray market and consumer self-directed PAS, the situation can be somewhat unclear. In these contexts, several factors establish the employment relationship between consumers and PAs, as delineated by the U.S. Internal Revenue Service (Table 12.1).

When consumers hire people to work in their private homes, including as caretakers, health aides, or private nurses, the U.S. Internal Revenue Service views these workers as household employees: "The worker is your employee if you can control not only what work is done, but how it is done."[6] In contrast,

> If only the worker can control how the work is done, the worker isn't your employee but is self-employed. A self-employed worker usually provides his or her own tools and offers services to the general public in an independent business. . . . If an agency provides the worker and controls what work is done and how it is done, the worker isn't your employee.[7]

The U.S. Internal Revenue Service issues annual rules on whether employers must pay employment-related taxes for employees. For instance, if an employer paid cash wages of $2,000 or more in 2020 to an individual household employee, such as a PA, the employer must withhold and pay Social Security and Medicare taxes totaling 15.3% (half paid by the employer and half by the employee).[8] Under the definition of employees—that employers control both the work that employees do and how they do it—most PAs, especially under consumer self-direction, are clearly employees. If, however, consumers treat PAs as independent contractors, consumers must submit a tax Form 1099-MISC, Miscellaneous Income, for each contractor paid at least $600 during that year.[9] Table 12.1 shows other tax requirements and

TABLE 12.1 U.S. Internal Revenue Service Distinctions Between Employees and Private Contractors for Self-Directed Personal Assistants

	PA as employee	PA as private contractor
Definitions	IRS rule: "the worker is your employee if you can control not only what work is done, but how it is done. . . . If an agency provides the worker and controls what work is done and how it is done, the worker isn't your employee."[1]	IRS rule: "an individual is an independent contractor if the payer has the right to control or direct only the result of the work and not what will be done and how it will be done."[2]
IRS tax forms	W-2	1099-MISC (miscellaneous income)
Job requirements and standards	Employer (consumer) determines job requirements and standards that PA must meet.	Worker (PA) controls job requirements and standards and provides own tools for performing the work.
Social Security and Medicare taxes	Employer (consumer) pays half of Social Security and Medicare taxes, and employee pays the other half. Wages paid to the following do not count: spouse, child under the age of 21, parent, or employee under the age of 18.[3]	Independent contractors must pay their own Social Security and Medicare taxes, in the form of a self-employment tax.[4]
Federal unemployment taxes	Employer (consumer) pays federal unemployment taxes on a specified amount of income and might also owe state unemployment taxes.[5]	Independent contractors are not required to pay federal or state unemployment taxes.
Eligibility for unemployment benefits	Yes	No

Eligibility for workers' compensation	Employers (consumers) must carry a workers' compensation insurance policy that meets state-specific labor laws. Policy may provide protection for both the consumer (e.g., PA forfeits right to sue consumer for workplace injury) and the PA (e.g., coverage for medical expenses).[6]	No
Paid time off	Depends on state-specific policy	No
Paid family leave	Depends on state-specific policy	No
Paid sick time	Depends on state-specific policy	No

[1] Internal Revenue Service, Department of the Treasury. Household employer's tax guide for use in 2021. Publication 926, Cat No. 64286A. Department of Treasury; March 5, 2021:3. https://www.irs.gov/pub/irs-pdf/p926.pdf

[2] Internal Revenue Service, Department of the Treasury. Independent contractor defined. Accessed May 28, 2020. https://www.irs.gov/businesses/small-businesses-self-employed/independent-contractor-defined

[3] Internal Revenue Service, Household employer's tax guide, 5.

[4] Internal Revenue Service, Department of the Treasury. Self-employed individuals tax center: What are my self-employed tax obligations? Accessed May 31, 2020. https://www.irs.gov/businesses/small-businesses-self-employed/self-employed-individuals-tax-center#Obligations

[5] Internal Revenue Service, Household employer's tax guide, 5.

[6] Internal Revenue Service, Department of the Treasury. Internal revenue service manual. Section 6.800.1 Workers' Compensation Program. Last reviewed or updated September 10, 2017. Accessed May 28, 2020. https://www.irs.gov/irm/part6/irm_06-800-001

[7] The Federal Family and Medical Leave Act applies only to employers with fifty or more employees.

employment benefits for employees and independent contractors. PAs hired as employees generally have greater job benefits than those treated as independent contractors.

Some consumers have control over the wages and benefits they can pay their PAs, but many do not (e.g., must pay wages set by their Medicaid program). Relatively few consumers are wealthy enough to personally pay their PAs high wages and benefits. Thus, the discordance between low wages and consumers' absolute need for PAs' services is a generally unspoken, sometimes uneasy, context to all interactions between consumers and PAs. In moments of frustration, safety concerns, or other stresses of PAS, low wages and terms of employment can become a flash point for PAs—who might decide that it's not worth it, their wages and benefits do not compensate them adequately for the job's demands. Recognizing this dynamic, consumers might forgo raising concerns about a PA's job performance, afraid their PA would walk out, leaving them stranded.

Paying high wages, bonuses, or other job benefits could paper over some tensions, but few consumers have the resources to do so. Some consumers therefore live with rueful recognition that the PAs providing their critical ADL supports are not paid enough, but there is little they can do about it. They may try to find opportunities for reciprocity, where they can benefit PAs in different ways (see Chapter 9). Other consumers reject this guilt and blame broader societal values and social safety net policies for failing to provide living wages to these essential workers. Either way, the situation can breed subliminal or conscious anxiety and discomfort.

Most consumers do not reveal their private financial matters to their PAs, viewing that as confidential personal information. Some PAs do write checks for consumers or use the consumer's credit card to make purchases. A quick, online search identifies scattered instances of PAs charged with embezzling large sums from consumers, who are generally characterized as older people with dementia. Typically, these check or credit-card transactions occur under the consumer's scrutiny. Not knowing details about consumers' assets, especially consumers with Medicaid, may give PAs the false impression that consumers have enough money to pay more, especially when stereotypical class differences exist between consumers and PAs (e.g., consumers living in middle-class neighborhoods, in nicely furnished and spacious homes).

When consumers who once had middle-class lifestyles qualify for Medicaid (an arduous process), their remaining assets are typically held in various trusts (e.g., Special Needs Trust, Qualified Income Trust) and can be spent only on items regulated strictly by the state. In addition, when Medicaid beneficiaries die, states have the first claim to their assets, to recover whatever the Medicaid program spent on their medical care, LTSS, and other supports. Medicaid programs may not allow consumers to pay their PAs bonuses or time-and-a-half pay for overtime or covering holidays—restrictions PAs might not understand. Admitting these financial constraints might embarrass or pose internal conflicts for some consumers, especially those who see themselves as social justice advocates or strong believers in workers' rights. Even if PAs understand these rules and consumers' resource constraints, PAs might feel that is not their problem—they deserve fair wages and overtime pay.

Perspectives of Consumers

Most consumers recognize the low wages PAs receive. However, some consumers are more insulated from this situation—for example, by having a payor such as Medicaid set payment amounts—than other consumers (e.g., agency clients).

Private Pay and Agency PAS

In the gray market—where consumers make private arrangements with PAs, without tax or other employment filings—consumers and PAs ideally negotiate arrangements that are largely acceptable to both. Even so, consumers and PAs must sometimes navigate complex and competing interests. For example, hiring noncitizens who cannot legally work in the United States is illegal. If consumers hire workers to provide ongoing PAS, the consumer and PA are supposed to each complete their respective part of the U.S. Citizenship and Immigration Services Form I-9, Employment Verification. This requires employers to verify that workers are either U.S. citizens or have legal authority to work in the United States.[10] Undocumented workers, desperate for income, may seek PAS jobs in the gray market; consumers, anxious for PAS, might see undocumented workers as an inexpensive option. This situation—hidden from authorities—is fraught with opportunities for abuse.

Suzanne pays her PAs privately, letting them decide whether they prefer under-the-table (i.e., gray market) or over-the-table payments. With the latter option, Suzanne is their formal employer, obligating her to pay Social Security and Medicare taxes (and withhold these taxes from the PA's paycheck) and file tax documentation. In addition, the state may require consumers like Suzanne to pay state and federal unemployment taxes and provide workers' compensation coverage, in case a work-related injury occurs. Suzanne feels a fiduciary responsibility to her PAs and encourages them to take a long view, believing that over-the-table compensation is better for most PAs over time. Nevertheless,

> I give them an option. Obviously, it's more money for me to pay them over-the-table, but I'm perfectly willing to do that if people prefer it.

I encourage them to do it, because the young ones especially don't understand the implications of not doing it. . . . Most of them really don't want to do it for various reasons. Some people have subsidized housing. They're holding their lives together with other kinds of supports that the reported income would jeopardize. So, it's their call. I will do whatever they want.

Suzanne and her PAs both keep track of hours worked and "square it up at the end of the week." She trusts her PAs to be accurate.

Some consumers pay agencies privately for PAS, such as Michael, who for many years paid a commercial franchise hourly fees (see Chapter 7). While he paid $21 or $22 per hour, Michael speculated his PAs at the time received maybe $12 or $13 hourly. The franchise agency required PAs to clock in and clock out using Michael's landline telephone to accurately record the hours worked. Michael did not have resources to supplement his PAs' wages, but he tried to help his PAs in other ways.[11] For example, more than a decade ago, Serge, who is Haitian, covered evening hours for Michael through the agency; they communicated in French. Michael saw a chance to assist Serge after the devastating January 12, 2010, Haitian earthquake. Serge's wife was visiting relatives in Haiti when the earthquake struck. As Michael wrote,

> She sustained minor injuries. Serge was desperate to bring her back to the United States. Unable to speak English, he couldn't make the necessary inquiries with the airline and organize her flights. This is something that I could do for him.
>
> I was able to get her on a flight from Santo Domingo, and she has now returned to the United States. Serge is grateful for this help. But so am I grateful to Serge and my other personal care assistants. The job they perform—the assistance they provide—allows me to live as normal and fulfilling a life in my own home and community as I can.[12]

Medicaid and Other Public Programs

Consumers who receive PAS under Medicaid or other state-funded programs confront not only limits on what they can pay their PAs but also restrictions in the number of hours allowed (see Chapter 8) and sometimes where they can receive services (e.g., whether only within homes or also outside homes). These provisions vary from state to state and across different Medicaid programs. As described in Chapter 3, consumers who receive both employer and budget authority from Medicaid may be able to offer higher wages, enabling them to hire PAs to perform skilled services. However, Medicaid specifies consumers' total monthly budgets. Therefore, if raising PAs' wages brings the monthly total above the allotted budget, consumers would need to cut the number of PAS hours to avoid cost overruns. In some states, Medicaid imposes additional restrictions on budget authority (e.g., disallowing time-and-a-half wages for holidays).

Among interviewees with Medicaid, most consumers expressed discomfort with the low wages and benefits their PAs received, but they had no control. "It's out of my hands," said Ernie. "They are all underpaid." Hourly PA wages varied across states. The highest wage was $15 per hour in Massachusetts, where 1199 SEIU (the union representing PAs) played a prominent role in negotiating PA wages with Medicaid. Ernie's state borders Massachusetts, but his Medicaid program pays only $11 an hour for new PAs, and his state has raised wages just once in the past 13 years. The lowest hourly wage reported was $10 an hour, and the consumer reporting this low rate acknowledged that his PAs could not survive on that amount: "They all have other jobs."

Consumers living in high-cost areas sometimes have trouble finding PAs for Medicaid-level wages. Natalie lives with her long-time boyfriend, but they never married because his income would have disallowed her from Medicaid eligibility. Nevertheless, his income gives Natalie the flexibility to pay her PAs extra dollars to supplement the low Medicaid wages. "The average one-bedroom apartment in my area is $2,000 per month," said Natalie. "I pay my PAs $19 to $20 an hour. Medicaid pays only $12.50 an hour." Natalie's program terminates employment of PAs who ask consumers for higher wages than Medicaid's rate.

> But there's no stipulation that restricts me from offering that. I haven't been challenged, and I don't see any reason to challenge me except that other home care recipients don't like it when some of us are able to pay more than others. It makes that harder for them. I'm not hiding the fact that I do this, but if there was a challenge, I'd say, "I get to do whatever I want to do with my earned income." I don't do it via payroll. I do it as a tip. I 1099 those. I 1099 everybody, and I document everything. I'm not paying anybody under the table, as much as people want me to.

Natalie uses "1099" as a verb—1099 is the U.S. federal tax form used to report miscellaneous income that is not payroll or salary income, such as payments to independent contractors (see earlier in this chapter).

Another issue is that consumers sometimes need more hours than Medicaid or their state program allows. Strategies that provide extra income—or benefits equivalent to income—can help address this concern. For example, based on an annual assessment performed by the state, her public program allows Ariana 29 hours per week of PAS. Ariana feels she needs more hours, and to compensate someone to provide extra hours, she placed an RV in her backyard to house a live-in PA rent free. She reasoned that the RV gives her PA desirable privacy. Furthermore, Ariana believes that providing free housing and paying for food would compensate her PA for low wages and work hours beyond those covered by her public program. Another consumer also covers basic living expenses for her live-in PA. "I've placed a value of $1,500 a month on this benefit," the consumer said. "We're looking at room, food, amenities, Wi-Fi, cable." Her PA gets $11 an hour from the public program.

Finally, some programs cover only in-home PAS. When consumers need support outside their homes, they must pay privately, even in emergencies. For instance, Jessica's PAs must clock in and out, using Jessica's home telephone—documenting not only their work hours but also their location (i.e., in her home). Jessica uses a battery-powered wheelchair, which is usually reliable but can stop suddenly because of electronic problems, such as low battery charge or loose wiring. Power wheelchairs are heavy, and wheel mechanisms must be disengaged, allowing the power wheelchair to "free wheel," before someone else can push it. One day while out by herself, Jessica's wheelchair malfunctioned.

> My chair died. It just died, and I was in the middle of the street downtown. Luckily, some people pushed me off to the side, and I had to call my assistant to push me home. He was close to his house. So, he could get to me faster, I called him a cab and paid for the cab. Then we took the cab home—my city has good wheelchair taxis. But then once we got to my house, I paid for another taxi to get him home.

Jessica also paid her assistant for his time. Whenever Jessica had her PA assist her outside her home, she paid out-of-pocket for that support. The state compensated Jessica's PAs $13 an hour.

Perspectives on Wages and Workers' Rights

The 21 consumer interviewees generally decried low wages paid to PAs. Ariana was lobbying in her state to increase PA wages:

> We're going to the legislature and start fighting for a higher wage for attendants. When you're looking for someone and you tell them,

"You're going to get paid $8 an hour or $9 an hour," it's laughable. It's like, "Are you crazy? I'm not going to work for that." They're paying $12 at Burger King, so it's an insult. . . . We're really suffering right now. We're overworking the attendants because there's such a need. There are people who actually enjoy doing this as a job, and those are the ones that get overworked because everybody's just, "I need. I need. I need. I need." Then you have burnout. . . . It's become a real issue here, and it starts with the low wage.

However, giving PAs overtime pay generates diverse opinions. In debating the extension of federal labor protections to home-based PAS, some disability rights activists worried that overtime payments would topple fragile Medicaid funding or compromise consumer control (see Chapter 4). New Federal Labor Standards Act regulations for home care workers entitle PAs to overtime pay. Concerned about escalating Medicaid budgets, some states have tried to avoid paying overtime by limiting PAs' weekly work hours (e.g., to 35 hours). This has forced some PAs to take additional jobs.

Consumer interviewees had diverse attitudes about this. Sam saw cutting PAs' overtime pay and hours as a human rights issue and fought for his state to keep paying higher overtime rates. Tom lived in a different state that was debating the overtime issue, but he organized his PAs so each works for him only 20–25 hours per week. This removes the overtime question for Tom, although he professes support for workers' rights to overtime wages. Jessica views her state's overtime policy—which limits individual PAs to billing up to 45 hours weekly—as eliminating consumer control.

Perspectives of PAs

PAs' perspectives on money matters are clear, straightforward, and unequivocal: they earn too little for the work they do. Furthermore, rules that supposedly protect their rights, notably their recent inclusion under Fair Labor Standards Act provisions, have sometimes had the opposite effect—preventing PAs, willing to work, from increasing their incomes by overtime hours. Many patch together multiple jobs to work extra hours.

For example, Trina works 60 hours per week across two agencies. When she started providing home-based PAS, she was in severe financial straits. Having her agency, which paid $13 an hour, limit her to 40 hours a week prevented her from earning enough to pay her bills. She started working at a second agency to increase her hours and was thrilled that agency paid $16 an hour. However, Trina lived in a high-cost city, and even with those longer hours and higher wages, she still had trouble making ends meet. She therefore took every opportunity to boost her income:

> I like to go to church on Sundays. I'm praying that I don't have to accept any job on Sunday, but I need that money to pay my bills. And Sundays they pay the most money—on Saturdays and Sundays, you're paid $1.10 more. I need the money now. But I'm praying that I'm not going to love money more than I love my God.

Agency Versus Consumer Self-Directed PAS

PAs do not blame consumers for these low wages. They recognize that aspects of PAS—notably minimal job qualifications and training requirements—make low wages almost inevitable. Other attributes of PAS jobs, such as flexibility, compensate somewhat for low wages. Nonetheless, to increase their incomes, PAs often scramble, patching together hours from one agency with those from another. Wages vary somewhat across agencies, but agencies desperate for workers, especially people with certain language skills (e.g., ability to speak Spanish), offer higher hourly wages.

Self-directed PAS jobs do not pay more than agencies—these PAs earn what Medicaid or other state programs pay. PAs advocating with their union—such as 1199 SEIU in Massachusetts—can negotiate increases in Medicaid PAS wages. Some consumers may provide extra dollars on top of the paychecks, such as Natalie who tips her workers and submits 1099 tax forms for the amount. These extra amounts are idiosyncratic and arranged privately between individual consumers and PAs. Mona, who organizes PAS for brothers Bob and Dan (see Chapter 1), views low wages as a major barrier to PAS work. She has negotiated several payment arrangements with various consumers:

> Medicaid's only $12.50 an hour! That deters people from wanting to do this work. In my area, the rent has just skyrocketed. You can make more money going to work for Walgreens—some McDonalds now are paying $15 an hour, and that work's not as physically challenging. . . . So, with the brothers, I have value in what I do for them, and I do a lot. I talked with them, and I said, "Listen, I'm not minimizing what everyone else does, but I work a lot around here, and I organize things." I was really surprised that they were all for it. We came to an arrangement. They pay me $15 an hour. Everyone else gets paid $12.50. I don't disclose that with the other caregivers. That extra is private pay.
>
> I've got a private-pay client who pays me $20 an hour, for a very good reason. With higher pay, you tend to bring in more quality

people. When you pay less, you don't get the same quality. So, that's why she pays a little more. Then my other lady, she pays me $17 an hour. With one brother, the state gives me 20 hours per week, with the other brother, it's 22.5 hours per week, and with my private pay, it's about 18 hours per week.

Mona has figured out how to manage the multiple time sheets with her different clients as she seeks wages that reflect the value of her work.

PA interviewees viewed low wages as a substantial barrier to remaining in PAS jobs. "The absolutely number one thing is pay," said Sarah, when asked about job retention. "There's no doubt that we could keep people in the field with better pay." Other interviewees viewed PAS as a steppingstone to another job, such as nursing, which has higher salaries and respect. Nevertheless, for some PAs, human relationships offer a compensation for low-wage work. According to Abby,

What could make the job better? Increased pay for everybody, obviously. That is huge. It's been hard to find other people that want to do the work. I think people don't see the benefits of doing this kind of work. I've often thought, "Man, I wish I could tell people how much I love this job."

Electronic Visit Verification

PAs are generally paid according to how many hours they work during each pay period. Some PAs submit timesheets, on paper or electronically; others clock in and out at the beginning and end of their shift, using the consumer's telephone or some other device to prove they are on site. The process of accounting for work hours has implications for the sense of trust between consumers and PAs—or between PAs and the entity issuing their paychecks, such as agencies or Medicaid. Although fraudulent reporting of work hours does occur, no evidence exists that such abuse is widespread or adds substantially to Medicaid costs.[13] Some consumers worried that finding and retaining high-quality, reliable PAS workers is already hard enough—imposing burdensome requirements to verify hours could further impede PA recruitment.[14]

Section 12006 of the 21st Century Cures Act, signed by President Obama in December 2016, mandated that Medicaid programs implement electronic visit verification (EVV) to confirm the accuracy of work hours for home-based PAS and home health care services (HHCS). Unless states apply for and receive extensions, CMS required them to implement EVV for PAS by

January 2020 and for HHCS by January 2023.[15] States lose up to 1% of their Medicaid federal matching funds (i.e., federal payments to states to finance their Medicaid programs) if they do not institute EVV.

EVV involves real-time tracking of PAs' arrival and departure times, locations, and sometimes activities, and it also verifies the consumer's identity. No uniform standards exist for EVV, and states have flexibility in how they implement EVV. Some PA interviewees described calling in and out using the consumer's telephone (preferably a landline), and others reported having to download an EVV app, which included GPS tracking, onto their personal smartphones. One consumer described being given a small box that generates codes that PAs must enter into the EVV system after calling in. Two consumers described their PAs clocking in and out on a tablet computer that remains at the consumer's home and connects with the agency's data systems, including electronic health records.

Little is yet known about how consumers and PAs perceive the EVV mandated by the 21st Century Cures Act.[16] EVV arrives as the public grows increasingly wary about being tracked—by their smartphones, surveillance cameras, social network providers, and facial recognition technologies. Nevertheless, people willingly share intensely private images worldwide on readily available apps, and these technologies have clear public benefits (e.g., documenting criminal behaviors). Perceptions of EVV will therefore likely evolve.

Consumers' Views of EVV

Some consumer interviewees valued the ability of EVV to ensure accurate reporting of PAs' work hours. However, other consumers, primarily those with self-directed PAS, worried that EVV—particularly the timekeeping and GPS monitoring features—takes away their control and erodes their flexibility in organizing their PAS workflow. EVV assumes that PAs follow specified and consistent work hours. However, consumers described needing a little more PAS support on some days, whereas on others they need less. Fluctuating needs reflect natural differences in consumers' daily activities and health status. Although hours total out over the week, they vary from day to day. "My stuff's really complicated," said one self-directed consumer, "because there are days, with my autoimmune problems, I need people to stick around much longer. And then, there are days they can leave sooner."

Flexibility can be mutually beneficial, as consumers can accommodate PAs' scheduling preferences. "EVV takes away from the relational piece of it," Matt observed. "For somebody who is taking a bus and a train or two buses to get here, and they're getting here 15 minutes late, and they want to leave 10 minutes early, are you really going to have them check out? That's unethical. It's wrong." Matt felt that clocking in and out makes home-based PAS "a virtual nursing home." He also believed that EVV generates inefficiencies, forcing PAs to stay even if their work is done. "I don't want somebody to stay for the whole three hours," said Mark. "Let's get done and get out and start our days. With the EVV stuff, I have somebody sitting there killing time."

Consumers worried that EVV GPS tracking, which monitors PAs' locations during their work hours, violates their privacy—"like Big Brother watching." Tracking PAs' geographic locations also interferes with efficient performance of activities. For instance, suppose PAs must get groceries for consumers, and the supermarket is located along the PA's route to the consumer's home. Having PAs stop at the grocery on the way to work makes sense, rather than going first to the consumer's home to clock in and then backtracking to the supermarket. However, with EVV GPS monitoring PAs' locations, they must follow the rules. Backtracking to perform tasks like grocery shopping is especially inefficient in rural regions with long travel distances.

PAs' Views of EVV

Some PA interviewees liked EVV, primarily because of its convenience and the end of paper timesheets, which they frequently forget or misplace. Other PAs disliked having EVV apps on their own smartphones, much preferring having a tablet or device from the agency or payor to clock in and out. As did consumers, other PAs worried about the intrusiveness of EVV, its implications of distrust and disrespect, and its failure to understand the dynamics of PAS work. Like some consumers, PAs voiced concerns about the loss of flexibility from EVV, citing the common example of picking up groceries for consumers on the way to work, before clocking in.

Some PAs feared being tracked on their own devices outside working hours, although Medicaid programs deny that they would ever do this. "You're invading personal space," said one of Matt's PAs. "You're asking people to utilize their personal property to track where they are. . . . I'm afraid of what it does to the PCA and consumer relationship." Abby went further:

We're fighting EVV. Everybody's against it here. It basically assumes people are criminals. It's the government treating people with disabilities and their caregivers as if they're scapegoats [for high Medicaid costs] . . . They think these [PAs] are poor people, people of color, not native English speakers, and they aren't going to fight back. They're always the targets of the surveillance state. I see it as an extension of the prison industrial system where they're trying to ding people and say, "Aha, we caught you committing fraud."

Many PAs viewed EVV as an unnecessary impediment to serving their consumers in the most efficient and productive ways. As Sarah observed,

This is, in theory, to prevent fraud. However, they did studies, and the amount of waste and fraud in [my state's] Medicaid programs was so minor. Most of it was happening through the agency model, not in the consumer model where I work. So, to spend money to prevent fraud that there's so little of it, it's just absurd—to put us through these hoops. . . . For some workers who cook at home and then deliver food to different clients, that isn't going to work. Maybe technically, yeah, I'm not supposed to cook a bunch of food at home and then bring it to my clients so that they can have food to eat. But it actually saves a lot of time. They can pay me one hour of Medicaid for that instead of me having to shop and go to a client's house just for them and having to pay three hours from Medicaid for that. The EVV is going to be such a mess for so many of us who are working in a little more creative way.

V

MAKING PAS HAPPEN

P ART V examines practical aspects of obtaining in-home PAS support,
both today and in the future. The needs and concerns of Fred—a
20-year old college student with a severe congenital disability—frame
these discussions about PAS today and tomorrow. Both consumers and PAs
underscore the value of finding a good fit, a match between the goals, expectations, and preferences of consumers with the career objectives, aspirations,
and practical realities of PAs. Few structures exist to match consumers with
appropriate PAs and facilitate their professional—and perhaps eventually
personal—relationships. Chapter 13 describes the demands on Fred as he
seeks PAS supports and the choices and options his potential PAs confront.
Challenges in matching consumers and PAs will grow in the future, with
increasing demand for these services and a shrinking PAS workforce. Chapter 14 envisions what Fred and his PAs might face in coming decades, and it
suggests policy priorities for addressing the growing gap between consumers'
needs and the available PAS workforce. These issues are complicated and
seemingly intractable, and Chapter 14 offers no easy answers. Nevertheless,
to live the happy, productive, and full life he seeks, Fred must navigate these
complexities.

13

Finding a Good Fit

F red was baptized the day he was born because his parents weren't sure he would live. Born with severe physical impairments, Fred spent his first five months in the neonatal intensive care unit. He needed mechanical ventilation until the age of 2, and he still has a tracheotomy in his neck even though he doesn't use it. He had multiple surgeries in early childhood, and his doctors have left the tracheotomy in place in case he needs it for another operation. Although Fred has never walked, since infancy he has gotten around on his own.

> When I was less than a year old, my physical therapist and my dad, who is trained as an engineer, figured out this system. They put me in a laundry basket with a motor and a button. I pushed the button to go forward. And then they put in a backwards button. So, I tell people I've been driving since before I was a year old. . . . By preschool, I had a wheelchair, and I was decently adept at driving it for a three- or four-year-old.

Now 20 years old, Fred is a rising senior at a prestigious college majoring in physics. His parents both have professional degrees and value education, but they always encouraged Fred to follow his dreams. He thinks they would have supported him fully if he'd wanted to become a plumber. "That said," Fred acknowledged, "due to my physical disability, 99.99999% of the jobs that I could ever see myself doing happily and that would provide a decent lifestyle need a college education."

Progressing from elementary through high school, Fred didn't focus on how his day-to-day activities diverged from those of his peers: "I didn't know anything different!" Throughout his 12 years in public schools, Fred was "mainstreamed," placed in classes with other students his age. He did receive accommodations, such as being given extra time for taking tests, having materials on touch-screen computers, and having aides help with certain manual tasks. Looking back, though, he realizes he differed from other kids in important ways:

> I definitely was more lonely. I definitely suffered socially. When you're on the playground, everyone's on the slides. I was never on the slides. Even something as simple as playing tag, you're in a wheelchair. You could kill someone. . . . As I got older, I had trouble interacting with people. In middle school and high school, people would go to someone else's house and play video games or hang out. Before coming to college, I could count on one hand the number of people's houses I'd go into. . . . Don't get me wrong—I had friends, a couple of people I had playdates with. I wasn't alone. But there's definitely stuff I was missing.

Fred did recognize that the most significant and sometimes embarrassing way his daily existence differed from that of his peers was the 24/7 presence of an LPN—required by his state's Medicaid program funding HCBS for children with developmental disability. In his state, LPNs receive 12 months of training and therefore possess skills beyond those of standard PAs. Medicaid requires this skilled support because of Fred's severe disability and early history of breathing problems. For instance, Fred must keep an oximeter on his toe while he sleeps at night so that the LPN can monitor his oxygen level, administering supplemental oxygen if his oxygen falls below a certain value. Fred says this happens, on average, once a year. Fred reports that the LPN does not literally sit at his bedside staring at his toe oximeter: "That would be cruel and unusual punishment. Mostly, they're reading a book or playing video games on the computer or doing whatever. They just need to stay awake."

Although Medicaid requires Fred to receive 24/7 LPN coverage, most of Fred's needs do not demand special skills—he primarily requires standard ADL supports. Throughout elementary school and midway through high school, Fred's major need was managing urinary incontinence. During those years, Fred wore diapers, which the LPN changed periodically, typically in the school nurse's office. Fred didn't think much about explaining the LPN's constant presence to his schoolmates. Nevertheless,

Yeah, it can be embarrassing. When you're so young, you don't even know the difference of life with a nurse and life without a nurse. That's where it gets rough. Because I didn't know, "Oh, I should not be sitting with this 60-year-old grandmother at the lunch table in middle school." I did not know that was not a normal thing. When you're that young, you gravitate towards what's comfortable.

In high school Fred was fitted with an external urinary catheter with a leg bag—and a smartphone. Both "transformed my life." Nevertheless, Medicaid still required him to have 24/7 LPNs, who emptied his leg bag several times a day.

Fred got special accommodations to take the SAT—extended time at a separate testing facility and a large bubble scantron format (enlarged ovals for filling in answers). He did well and applied to several universities. He got into a prestigious college in his state, which meant he would retain his Medicaid HCBS coverage and 24/7 LPNs. Fred's college adapted his dormitory room: "Engineers came from the college to my home to look at my lift, and they hired the same people who put in my home lift to do the one in my dorm room. . . . That said, other kids had roommates. I did not. My nurses are my roommates!"

Fred does not mean this literally—he lives alone in his dormitory room. But Medicaid requires him to have 24/7 LPNs present, taking shifts, even while he attends classes. These LPNs provide basic ADL assistance, getting Fred up and dressed in the morning; then the LPN accompanies him to his classes. "My nurse will generally sit outside," said Fred. "If it's a giant lecture hall, they might sit in the back. It depends on the nurse. Different nurses do different things, and I just go, 'Okay.' Some nurses are like, 'I prefer to have eye contact at all times.' All right. Go and sit in the back or whatever. Or if it's a small classroom, they'll sit right outside so they can see me through the window."

Fred views this level of oversight as unnecessary: he does not need skilled services, just basic ADL support. "But tell that to Medicaid. This is what they think is safe for me. These are the rules I've had the most trouble with." The LPNs' presence especially hampers Fred's efforts to have privacy and a social life. "In high school, I didn't really know what a social life was. It's only since I came to college, really, that I would say I have an actual, normal, nonmedical social life." He joined a fraternity, which is admittedly "nerdy" but that he loves. He's frustrated, though, when he needs to leave a party because LPNs change shifts.

Although they do not think he needs 24/7 LPN coverage, Fred and his parents face a catch-22. Fred does need many hours of daily basic ADL supports, which the LPNs provide, and Medicaid is their only option for funding this costly PAS. Medicaid requires Fred to prove that he has LPNs 24/7—or a parent present when LPNs are absent. Otherwise, Medicaid will remove Fred from the program. However, Medicaid does not identify and hire these LPNs: that's a job for Fred and his parents. With Fred attending college in a small town, hiring and retaining LPNs has become a constant hassle. LPNs have left or quit for various reasons (e.g., pregnancy, family emergency, being fired by Fred and his parents for poor performance). The situation has devolved into constant anxiety for Fred and his parents, primarily his father, who has more flexibility with his job:

> I'll tell you all about the struggles that I've had with nursing since coming to college. According to Medicaid rules, my nurses have to sign off to another nurse or to my parents, who signed documents saying they will be the backup. If anything happens to me, they go to jail. My nurses can't leave me alone legally. . . . My prior authorization says 24 hours. Medicaid expects 24 hours. And so that's why my dad has to be there over 60 hours a week, plus two-hour drives both ways, to be my nurse, night and day.

At the moment, Fred and his parents have only found LPN coverage for 12 hours per day, so his father must fill in.

———————

Everyone who needs paid ADL support to live in their homes and communities has their own individual stories, personal preferences, values, and hopes for their daily lives. Consumers must find PAs with personal and professional qualities that are a good fit for achieving these individual needs and aspirations. As Fred's situation shows, outside factors influence the choice of PAs. At the age of 20, Fred's Medicaid program for people with developmental disability still considers him a juvenile. NPAs and other regulations require him to have LPN coverage 24/7, although he has rarely needed skilled interventions. He lives in a small college town, making it hard to recruit LPNs.

Nevertheless, Fred's story contrasts sharply with the experiences of Charlie Carr more than 50 years earlier. In his mid-teens, Carr was forced to live in a hospital school after his spinal cord injury in 1968, and in 1971 he moved into a county long-term care hospital, hoping to attend a nearby community college (see Chapter 2). A half-century later, despite his severe disability, Fred lives the college life, resides in an on-campus dormitory in a room outfitted with an automated lift, and proudly belongs to a fraternity. He is currently deciding where to attend graduate school. Despite its complexities and frustrations, paid PAS has made this life happen for Fred.

This chapter pulls together information from earlier chapters to explore both the challenges to and approaches for finding the right fit between consumers and PAs. It draws on comments from familiar consumer and PA interviewees and findings from studies about paid PAS. As Fred's situation exemplifies, consumers cannot always control key decisions about paid PAS. Even if consumers have choices, staff turnover and changing needs can force frequent searches for new workers who are good matches. For PAs, once they make the decision to provide PAS, whether they find a good fit with consumers is often an ongoing and continuing process.

What Is Unique about Home-Based Paid PAS

In important ways, home-based PAS is a unique job:

- The workplace is the consumer's home, especially the most private spaces (bedroom, bathroom). If the physical or emotional safety of either consumers or PAs is threatened for whatever reason, the hazards could be difficult for people outside the home (e.g., family members or friends) to detect and remedy—immediately or over time.
- ADL support tasks involve intensely intimate physical proximity between two people, often strangers—at least initially. With this intimacy, both consumers and PAs become physically and emotionally vulnerable, susceptible to complex interpersonal dynamics as well as tangible risks (e.g., of bodily injury, transmission of infectious diseases).
- PAs might have basic training about providing core activities, but individual consumers have their own specific requirements and preferences for performing ADL tasks. Therefore, although ADL support skills have common elements that apply across all people, providing this assistance is highly individualized and requires PAs to respect consumers' preferences and follow their instructions. No uniform, nationwide certification standards or core competency requirements exist for PAS providers.
- External rules and regulations, which vary widely across states, often regulate and delineate support activities that are critical to consumers' well-being.
- Consumers prefer to retain control over their PAS, but many factors threaten their control, including state regulations and the potentially complicated power dynamics between consumers and PAs, interference or involvement of family or other household members, and—in the context of agency PAS—rules and oversight from agency staff.

- Paid PAS happens in the context of disability or chronic disease, attributes that disadvantage and often stigmatize or marginalize people whom others might see as weak or not normal. In PAS, "when you ask for help," said one consumer, "it's because you really need the help." PAS consumers should not "internalize the shame of disability," which society sometimes imposes on them.

Finally, paid PAS has almost existential implications for people with disability requiring ADL supports. These services are literally life-sustaining. Using language introduced in the 2020–2021 COVID-19 pandemic, home-based PAs are essential workers. As Michael said,

> I absolutely need PAs to live. I can't function for much more than maybe 12 hours without them. The only other alternative is to be in a nursing home. My last confinement in a nursing home completely cemented for me that that's absolutely the line in the sand that I'm not going to cross. If it's a choice between living a happy life in my home and dying earlier or possibly living longer by being put in a nursing home—which I don't for a minute believe, nursing homes are dangerous places—I'm going to have a happy life in my home and die earlier. It's not even a choice for me.

Many of the unique qualities about PAS work have critical practical consequences, both for consumers and for PAs. These pragmatic implications raise questions about ways to ensure good matches between consumers and PAs when recruiting and hiring workers. Some practical concerns are foundational but hard to address—such as guaranteeing living wages and employment benefits for PAs, sufficient to entice them to want PAS jobs (see Chapter 14). Recognizing these realities, however, finding a good fit between a consumer and PA requires several key steps, beginning with examining personal priorities.

Perspectives of Paid PAS Consumers

Consumers vary in which traits and qualities they prioritize in their paid PAs. At a minimum, most consumers want PAs to recognize that providing PAS is a serious job that requires commitment and skill. "Sometimes I interview people who say, 'Oh, I help my grandmother, so therefore I know what this is like,'" said one self-directed PAS consumer, describing interviewing PA candidates. "And I would say, 'No, I'm not your grandma. This doesn't make you a personal assistant.'"

What Qualities Do Consumers Seek in Their PAs?

When asked what makes a good PA, the 21 consumers coalesced around five core attributes. Consumers differed somewhat in how they ordered the importance of these traits, but all viewed these five qualities as essential for their PAs:

1. Reliability (i.e., showing up)
2. Timeliness (i.e., arriving on time)
3. Ability to follow and remember specific instructions about consumers' particular ADL support preferences and approaches
4. Competence to perform required tasks safely and efficiently
5. Honesty and trustworthiness

These five core attributes appear to be employment basic minimums—applicable across most occupations. Such foundational requirements, however, confront challenges in the PAS context, because of complex interpersonal dynamics (Part IV) and characteristics of the workplace (consumers' homes).

Consumers also mentioned personal qualities they desire in PAs, including being friendly, patient, empathic, respectful, open to suggestions (i.e., not defensive), transparent, good communicators, good listeners, good cooks, calm in a crisis, industrious (e.g., keeping busy doing tasks around the home), proactive, self-motivated, flexible, independent, and having a genuine interest in helping people. For some consumers, physical strength is critical (e.g., if consumers require manual transfers because lift devices cannot accommodate their body's biomechanics). When workers are scarce, consumers might set aside these preferences, taking potential hiring risks—such as employing people with complex histories.

As described in Chapter 7, no national standards exist for training or the certification of PAS workers. To address this concern, the Centers for Medicare & Medicaid Services convened national stakeholders to develop a set of basic competencies for this field.[1] The competencies aim to apply not only to agency PAs but also to PAs employed directly by consumers, who might use the competencies as guidelines when training their own PAs. The 12 core competencies (Box 7.2) intersect to some degree with the five core attributes sought for by consumers:

- The core competency of **professionalism and ethics** encompasses the need to be on time, as well as to dress appropriately for the job and perform work tasks responsibly, although it does not specifically note showing up for work or being honest or trustworthy. (The competencies do mention building trust through respectful and clear communication—although that concept differs somewhat from being trustworthy.) Presumably, these latter concerns are subsumed within the rubric of professionalism and ethics

- The core competency of **person-centered practices** involves assisting consumers to set goals and requires PAs to provide services that assist people in attaining these goals. It also includes developing collaborative and professional relationships with the consumer and other PAS workers to make this happen. However, the competencies do not specifically address the ability to follow and remember instructions from consumers
- The core competency of **safety** requires workers to recognize and report various unsafe situations but does not explicitly state that they must provide ADL support services safely and efficiently
- **Cultural competency** requires workers to provide services that meet consumers' preferences

Other aspects of the 12 core competencies envision PAs training and guiding consumers, overseeing them in various ways while also recognizing their own biases that might contribute to conflicts. Another core role is following external rules and regulations and interacting productively with other members of the health care professional team supporting the consumer. While these 12 core competencies include language and key words recognizing the centrality of consumers' values and preferences, the competencies nonetheless contain hints of paternalism—that PAs are there to protect consumers with a medical model (Box 2.1) sensibility. Some consumers might view these 12 core competencies as reassuring, just as some consumers prefer agency PAS. Other consumers might desire taking more direct control.

What Is Known about Consumers' Preferences?

Over the last 50 years, numerous initiatives and demonstration programs have examined diverse models of home-based paid PAS, offering important insights into what consumers want from these services. Multiple societal factors have driven the development of new PAS programs, including the fallout from deinstitutionalization and impetus to shift long-term care from nursing homes into communities (see Chapter 2).[2] Different states and regions nationwide have implemented various publicly financed paid PAS innovations, many stopping when demonstration funding ended while others evolved into longer-lasting programs. Some demonstration projects strongly affected Medicaid and other public policies relating to paid PAS.

The Cash & Counseling demonstration—dubbed "an experiment in consumer-directed personal assistance services"[3]—was perhaps the most influential and informative study of various models of paid PAS. The vision statement of Cash & Counseling conveyed sweeping aspirations for its PAS approach:

> Cash & Counseling is a self-direction model that seeks to empower individuals by providing them maximum flexibility to choose and control their services and supports. Its goal is to enhance their ability to live the lives they wish to lead in their communities. . . . Cash & Counseling reflects a belief that individuals, when given the opportunity to choose the services they will receive and to direct some (or all) of them, will exercise their choice in ways that maximize their quality of life. . . . Because participation in Cash & Counseling is voluntary, there should be a seamless process for moving between this option and the traditional system.[4]

Box 13.1 summarizes activities of the Cash & Counseling demonstration, which spanned 1998–2002 and involved younger and older adult Medicaid beneficiaries with disability in Arkansas, Florida, and New Jersey.[5] Unlike most other demonstration projects, Cash & Counseling randomly assigned participants to receive either standard agency PAS or self-directed services, in which the involved consumers received a monthly budget to obtain PAS, as well as other items and services to support their ADLs and IADLs. It is important to note that Cash & Counseling participants could hire family members or friends as paid PAs. The experimental design of the Cash & Counseling demonstration, with its random assignment of consumers to either self-directed or agency PAS, permitted comparison of the experiences and attitudes of consumers across these two PAS models.

Box 13.1 highlights key takeaway findings from the Cash & Counseling demonstration, comparing results for self-directed participants with those receiving agency PAS. Overall, Cash & Counseling consumers reported better outcomes and experiences than those assigned to agency services. For example, Cash & Counseling participants indicated greater satisfaction (e.g., with assistance in performing ADLs, routine health care, and transportation) and fewer unmet needs—by 10% to 40%—than agency consumers in most state and age groups (i.e., older versus younger than age 65).[6] Consumers receiving Cash & Counseling were less likely to report interpersonal problems with their PAs, such as neglect, disrespect, and theft. They also reported choosing family members or friends to provide PAS, greatly preferring this familiar person to a stranger to assist with intimate activities, like bathing and dressing.[7] Among Cash & Counseling participants, those who used family members as PAs reported better outcomes on five indicators

Box 13.1 Cash & Counseling Demonstration

Goal: To provide consumers with disability more choice and control over their PAS. This experiment tested financing and delivering self-directed PAS on a large scale. It also aimed to improve workforce shortages and turnover without increasing Medicaid costs.

Funding: The Robert Wood Johnson Foundation; U.S. Department of Health and Human Services, Office of the Assistant Secretary for Planning and Evaluation

Dates: 1998–2002

Locations: Arkansas, Florida, New Jersey

Consumer participants:
- Arkansas: 2,008 total participants: persons ages 65+ or adults with physical or cognitive disability; all eligible for Medicaid.
- Florida: 2,820 total participants: persons ages 65+ or adults with physical disability ($n = 1,818$); and children with developmental disability who received HCBS waiver services ($n = 1,002$).
- New Jersey: 1,755 total participants: persons ages 65+ or adults with physical disability; all enrolled in New Jersey's Medicaid PAS program.

Program:
- Consumers given a capped monthly cash allowance to manage their own care plan
- Consumers recruited, hired, trained, supervised, and fired PAs providing in-home PAS
- Budgets flexible: could be used on services, hiring PAs, assistive technologies, home modifications, cab fare for doctor visits, and other supportive items and services
- All consumers worked with a counselor to develop their care plans; counselors educated consumers on hiring PAs and monitored monthly fund use and consumer satisfaction
- Consumers could (but were not required to) elect a representative to manage their care plan for them and a fiscal agent to manage finances. The representative and fiscal agent could not be the same person.

Personal assistance services: Paid PAs could include family members and friends. Florida and New Jersey authorized spouse and parent as paid PAs. Assisting with ADLs/IADLs and routine health care were the primary duties of PAs.

Evaluation design: Participants randomly assigned to either standard agency-provided services or Cash & Counseling self-directed services.

Randomized trial results:

- Cash & Counseling significantly reduced unmet PAS need (10% to 40% fewer Cash & Counseling participants reported unmet needs across states)
- Cash & Counseling participants more likely to report positive health outcomes (e.g., fewer falls, contractures, pressure ulcers, respiratory problems, and urinary tract infections)
- Quality of life significantly improved both for Cash & Counseling participants and for their informal, unpaid caregivers
- Medicaid costs increased slightly, primarily because Cash & Counseling participants received more of the care they were authorized to receive under Medicaid
- Decrease in institutional and other long-term care costs partially offset higher Medicaid PAS expenditures
- Cash & Counseling participants did not misuse their monthly budgets
- Among PAs hired by Cash & Counseling participants, 50% to 70% received formal training on how to perform their PAS jobs as compared with ≥ 95% of agency workers, but they felt equally prepared to handle their responsibilities

Data source: De Milto, L. Cash & Counseling. Program Results Report. Robert Wood Johnson Foundation; 2015. Accessed May 17, 2021. https://www.rwjf.org/en/library/research/2013/06 /cash---counseling.html

---

relating to safety and satisfaction than those who did not hire family members.[8] Furthermore, having family members as PAs was more convenient for consumers, allowing them to receive PAS at times they preferred, rather than when an agency allowed: for example, an early riser would not have to wait in bed until the agency PA arrived at their earliest permissible time. Cash & Counseling participants were more likely than those with agency PAS to report their PAs were punctual, reliable, and likely to complete tasks.[9] Among participants receiving agency supports, their most common complaint was that agency rules restricted the activities that PAs could perform, including tasks like shopping, picking up prescriptions, doing housework, and assisting with transportation.[10]

Questions had been raised about whether consumers could effectively manage their monthly budgets (i.e., budget authority) and obtain their required supports. Cash & Counseling participants included younger and older adults who had physical or intellectual disability or both. Nevertheless, most consumers were able to independently direct their own care and manage their cash plans.[11] Some consumers did receive assistance from family members (e.g., spouses, adult children, or extended family) in directing their care. In particular, family members helped with managing finances, coordinating services, making medical decisions, hiring and overseeing PAs, and purchasing assistive devices or personal care items. Another question had been whether younger and older participants would prefer different PAS models. Younger participants did prefer Cash & Counseling more than older recipients did, although age differences were small across most outcome measures.[12]

Other states replicated their own versions of Cash & Counseling, which have evolved over time and been branded with state-specific monikers—such as Home Help in Michigan, Mi Via in New Mexico, and the Independent Choices Program in Oregon. The phrase "cash and counseling" is now considered somewhat dated. Nonetheless, the core demonstration concepts of consumers having budget authority and the ability to hire family members are now key components of many Medicaid and other public PAS programs (see Chapter 3). Whether individual consumers prefer this approach to standard agency PAS is an intensely personal decision. Nonetheless, giving consumers options ensures people have flexibility in choosing the best fit to meet their PAS needs and personal preferences.

Finding the Right Fit with PAs

For consumers, finding the right PA or PAS support team to meet their preferences and needs starts with understanding what their needs and goals are. Indeed, perhaps the leading reason for PAs quitting their job is lack of clarity upfront about what the consumer needs and expects, as well as continually changing job descriptions (Box 13.2).[13] Certainly, consumers' needs do change over time, with alterations in their health, functional status, or personal circumstances. Nevertheless, when considering paid PAS, consumers should start by taking time to delineate the supports they need, their feelings about managing PAs themselves rather than hiring agency PAs, and deeply individual feelings about these intimate services and their comfort with different PAS options. This assessment process may benefit from involving family and friends and evaluations by various health care professionals, including physicians, nurses, and rehabilitation therapists. Understanding options could require additional investigation, such as assessing what is required for individual consumers to qualify for Medicaid or other public programs (e.g., for military veterans). Making informed decisions also necessitates accounting realistically for people's financial assets—the supports needed can make paid PAS very expensive.

As with Fred, how PAS is funded will largely determine the range of choices that consumers have in selecting their PAs. Payor policies generally set PAs wage levels and benefits, a critical factor in recruiting and retaining

---

Box 13.2 Top Ten Reasons Personal Assistants Quit Their Jobs

1. Wages are too low, and PAs do not get appropriate raises or paid sick time
2. Initial job description is unclear or incomplete and job description keeps changing
3. Consumer asks PAs to perform tasks in illogical or inefficient manner, which wastes time
4. Work environment is messy, unpleasant, unsafe, or otherwise unappealing
5. PAs feel their efforts are not appreciated or the consumer prefers another PA over them
6. PAs feel that consumers interact with them in a passive-aggressive style
7. PAs feel the consumer has inappropriate or dishonest views and expectations, such as about wages owed, hours worked, monetary loans, or sexual favors
8. PAs feel that the duties are inappropriate; for example, the consumer can actually perform the task themselves, the tasks cannot be performed in the time allotted, or the consumer supervises performance too tightly
9. PAs feel the consumer is intolerant of honest mistakes
10. Consumers do not appear to respect PA's personal life, expecting that their needs should take priority over all other aspects of the PA's life

Adapted from Craig Hospital, Spinal Cord Injury Resource Library. Personal care assistants: How to find, hire and keep. Accessed June 8, 2020. https://craighospital.org/resources/personal-care-assistants-how-to-find-hire-keep

---

PAs. Overall guidelines about hiring paid PAS providers, such as those offered by AARP[14] or the Family Caregiver Alliance,[15] give helpful advice. All recommendations, including those presented here, must consider the unique context of each consumer, payor, state, and locale.

Basic considerations cut across many situations. As described in Part III, perhaps the first choice is between the agency and self-directed models of PAS. Box 13.3 shows the pros and cons of each model. State Medicaid programs or other payors may require consumers to use one PAS model or—less often—a hybrid approach (e.g., agency with choice models, where consumers recruit, interview, and select workers while an agency serves as the employer, managing taxes and other payroll requirements). Each model has pluses and minuses. If consumers can make their own decisions, they should carefully examine their preferences and whether they feel comfortable fulfilling their roles required by the chosen model (e.g., in consumer self-direction).

Box 13.3 Pros and Cons of Agency Versus Consumer Self-Directed PAS

Agency PAS
- Pros
  - Agencies recruit, screen, hire, and fire PAs
  - No employment paperwork: agency submits payroll taxes, workers' compensation, unemployment insurance, and other employment taxes required by states
  - May have workers at different skill levels, facilitating a match of PA's skill level to consumer's needs. Will typically evaluate consumer (e.g., by a nurse) to determine tasks to be performed and necessary skill required
  - Generally conducts initial skill training and periodic additional or refresher training
  - Provides substitute if usual PA takes vacation or is sick (may depend on timeliness of notice and staff availability)
  - Agency supervisors assist in resolving conflicts with PA. If resolution not reached, send another PA who is better fit
  - Liability protection: agency handles situations when PA is injured on the job
- Cons
  - Limited in tasks that PA can perform because of state nurse practice act regulations, agency rules, or both
  - May have limitations in time availability (e.g., might not schedule PAs before 7:00 A.M.)
  - Because of staff working hours, schedules, and retention, may send different PAs for different days and shifts over time; new PAs need training about consumer's individual needs and preferences
  - Fees for agency PAs build in profit or other margins; PAs get only a portion of these hourly fees; agencies may require that PAs work a minimum number of hours per shift, even if consumers do not need all those hours

Consumer Self-Directed PAS
- Pros
  - Consumers recruit, screen, hire, and fire PAs; thus, consumers explicitly control choice of PAs
  - Training controlled and directed by consumer
  - Greater flexibility in tasks PAs can perform, including some tasks that agency PAs may not be allowed to perform
  - Greater flexibility in establishing work hours

- ○ Greater potential to develop long-term relationships with a single or team of PAs
- ○ In some circumstances, may cost less per hour than agency
- **Cons**
  - ○ Identifying job candidates and conducting screening is challenging and time consuming, and is not free (e.g., consumers must pay to post positions on many online job search sites and pay for background checks)
  - ○ Consumer is responsible for the payroll and tax obligations of an employer, as well as understanding labor laws (e.g., requirements for overtime pay); some PAs (and consumers) may prefer payment as an independent contractor (IRS Form 1099-MISC), but consumer needs to ensure they meet federal and state criteria for contractor status
  - ○ Training, supervising, assessing job performance, and firing PAs may feel uncomfortable to some consumers
  - ○ If consumer has more than one PA, consumer may need to manage interactions among PAs
  - ○ If PA takes vacation, is sick, or quits suddenly, consumer needs to find substitute
  - ○ Potential liability for on-the-job injury

Adapted from Family Caregiver Alliance. Hiring in-home help. Accessed June 12, 2020. https://www.caregiver.org/hiring-home-help; AARP. How to hire a caregiver. AARP; November 7, 2019. Accessed June 12, 2020. https://www.aarp.org/caregiving/home-care/info-2018/hiring-caregiver.html

The leading challenge with self-directed PAS is the difficulty in recruiting suitable PAs. Chapter 8 lists approaches consumers use to identify potential PAs, including word of mouth, asking friends, through social media, posting the position on online job sites, and public registries, when available. Once candidates respond, consumers must have clear strategies for assessing candidates' qualifications and suitability for the job. Box 13.4 lists suggestions for various steps of this process. Some consumers might benefit from involving family members or friends, but final decisions should rest with consumers—their level of comfort and trust in the PA candidate, even their gut instinct about the person. Certain aspects of vetting job candidates may feel awkward to consumers, such as confirming candidates' driving records or credit histories. As described in Chapter 8, some consumers do not believe criminal background checks are relevant or appropriate to their situation—they have hired people with histories of incarceration who were excellent PAs.

Box 13.4 Interviewing and Screening Candidates for Self-Directed PAs

Recruitment Basics
- First, prepare a detailed job description specifying tasks consumer needs PAs to perform
- Check local registries of persons interested in PAS employment to identify candidates; also network with friends, peers, use websites, advertise locally
- Perform initial screening by telephone to determine whether candidate is viable
- Mail or email job description to viable candidates
- Meet candidate in person, either at home or another comfortable setting where private conversations are possible
- If consumer brings a family member or friend to the interview and the candidate defers to that person rather than to the consumer, the candidate is likely not a good fit
- If candidate is viable, record full name and contact information, confirming information by reviewing a government-issued identification card or driver's license
- Ask for three references, including at least two from former PAS employers; check references
- Trust gut instinct about candidate; if family member or friend participates in interview, seek their honest views

Potential Interview Topics and Questions
- Organize questions around tasks in the job description, supplemented with consumer's preferences for performing tasks
- Understand consumer's preferences for interpersonal communication while performing tasks. For example, does the consumer prefer chatty interactions or not?
- General interview questions
  - Why does this position interest you?
  - Tell me something about yourself.
  - Where have you worked before?
  - Does anything in the job description make you uncomfortable?
  - What are your experiences transferring people, such as out of bed or into a wheelchair?
  - What types of situations or people push your buttons?
  - How do you handle people who are upset, anxious, or fearful?
  - What is your time availability? Are you a morning person or evening person?
- Relevant allergies, health problems that could affect ability to perform tasks, and, if pets are present, comfort with these animals

- Smoking; ensure consumer's preferences relating to smoking are acceptable
- Discuss and establish preferences for PA's meals, if work hours cross mealtimes (e.g., should PA provide own food or will consumer supply food?)

Performing Background Checks
- Confirm licenses or certification with appropriate licensing or certification authorities
- If driving is expected, confirm driving record with local department of motor vehicles or relevant authority
- Obtain waiver or authorization from candidate to perform a credit check; consider not hiring candidates who refuse to give authorization
- Use an online service to confirm information candidate has provided or perform a criminal history check (this process requires payment)

Adapted from Family Caregiver Alliance. Hiring in-home help. Accessed June 12, 2020. https://www.caregiver.org/hiring-home-help; Family Caregiver Alliance. Background checking: Resources that help. Accessed June 12, 2020. https://www.caregiver.org/background-checking-resources-help; AARP. How to hire a caregiver. November 7, 2019. Accessed June 12, 2020. https://www.aarp.org/caregiving/home-care/info-2018/hiring-caregiver.html

Every consumer must decide what they need to know about PA candidates before bringing them into their homes. Designating several weeks or a month as a trial period, for both the consumer and PA, offers an opportunity for a joint appraisal about whether they have the makings of a good fit.

As suggested throughout Part IV, home-based PAS is often a two-way street. Although meeting consumers' needs is, ultimately, the sole imperative of PAS—and thus takes clear precedence—consumers benefit from striving to do well by their PAs. Box 13.2 suggests leading reasons that PAs quit their jobs. While consumers may have little say or flexibility over some factors, like low wages, other issues fall squarely under their control. To maximize the likelihood of keeping good PAs, the bottom line is to treat them well, with honesty and respect.

Perspectives of Paid, Home-Based PAs

Now that some payors, notably certain Medicaid waiver programs in various states, allow relatives—including spouses and parents—to be paid for providing PAS, this work is not only a job but also often a labor of love for many people. However, for other PAs, PAS is solely their job, albeit one with unique, intimately personal attributes. Relatives generally have filial obligations to continue providing PAS, even when the effort is emotionally draining and physically demanding. Other paid PAs can simply quit when the job doesn't suit them, especially when the labor market is tight and other employment opportunities are plentiful. When unemployment rates are high, however, PAs might think twice before quitting. Nevertheless, with the ever-growing number of people needing paid PAS, they might be able to find a more palatable position in short order. Whether PAs can afford even a brief lapse in income is an individual calculus.

What Qualities Do PAs Seek in a PAS Job or Consumer?

PAs' views of their jobs are complex and multilayered. They deplore the low wages. But, for many, other considerations counterbalance practical concerns—especially their imperative to do good for other people.

Low wages are virtually universal and widely acknowledged. "People don't value this kind of work," said Abby. She linked the devaluation to sexism, with PAS being viewed as women's work and thus poorly compensated. Other practical concerns for PAs can include:

- Being required to buy their own hygiene supplies, such as soap, gloves, and hand sanitizer, to bring to the consumer's home; PAs from one agency reported being required to purchase their own facemasks during the COVID-19 pandemic
- Inadequate compensation for transportation
- Lacking health insurance as an employment benefit
- No paid time off for vacations, sick time, or family medical leave
- Paucity of meaningful training and skills development
- Absence of upward mobility and opportunities for advancement, as options to increase income

Furthermore, financial pressures often prompt PAs to work multiple jobs, setting them up for job burnout.

Many PAs, however, find intensely personal meaning in their jobs. "You can't come into this because it's a paycheck," said Isaiah. "You have to come in the job with the frame of mind that this person needs help. How can I help them?" Janice is in her forties and the single mother of an autistic son in his mid-twenties. She worked part-time in PAS and, despite concerns about low wages, Janice believed that

> PCAs should have more pride in their work. It is a very great job. PCAs should feel good about themselves because they are miracle

workers. Some go above and beyond what they are required to do. They do a tremendous service by allowing people to stay in their homes and out of impersonal, institutionalized care. It's an awesome job, and they should feel great about what they do.

PAs generally believe that their work requires empathy, understanding, and genuine concern for consumers. Many PA interviewees emphasized the importance of "having love" and being "people persons." They observed that certain personal qualities that bolster PAS job satisfaction cannot be learned—as Shauna said, "It has to come from the heart. . . . I feel like this is my passion."

PAs recognize that doing a good job requires professionalism, attention to consumers' priorities, such as showing up and timeliness. Janice has seen many other PAs who have not taken their jobs seriously. "They wouldn't be very professional," Janice commented. "They would do the minimum things required, like the light housekeeping. . . . But a lot of times, they would be late, or would call out at the last minute, or not call out at all and not show up." Janice viewed treating consumers with respect as central to professionalism. "You can't be rude to someone when you are inside their home," Janice observed, wondering how she would feel if she needed a stranger in her home to assist her.

Some workers commented on the importance of dressing appropriately, an element of professionalism and a sign of respect when entering another person's home. Rachel, who is in her mid-thirties, viewed the consumer's home as her professional workplace and stressed the importance of always looking respectable, with special attention to upper-body garments and not showing too much cleavage. Rachel therefore never wears tank tops or other revealing clothing to work but instead dons scrubs, with a tee-shirt underneath. Mona also raised the importance of proper attire, linking it not only to professionalism but also to risks of sexual harassment and thus safety (see Chapter 11). Mona recalled a male client making lewd remarks about her cleavage. "I'm more of a seasoned woman," said Mona, who is in her early fifties. "I'm more matronly dressed. I don't like V-necks, and if it's a V-neck, it can't be too low. I make sure that I stay appropriate because I don't want to be looked at in that manner. I want to be taken serious." How she presents herself translates into respect, which Mona sees as essential for strong relationships with consumers.

PAs are, however, realistic about difficulties dealing with some consumers, admitting that "feelings do get hurt" and "you've got to sometimes just swallow a lot of stuff." They underscore the need to remain patient and caution that people with impatient, inflexible, volatile, or angry personalities should not take PAS jobs. Having patience is critical to prevent conflicts with consumers, to deescalate disputes. "Sometimes you have to step outside yourself and say, 'I can make this work,'" said one PA. "You can't let certain things get to you. I know firsthand that your feelings are hurt. But you've got to go back. You've got to figure it out. And it's so rewarding in the end if you do."

Nevertheless, bad behavior by consumers can leave PAs unwilling to continue working for them—there are breaking points. Chenoa is in her mid-forties and works in self-directed PAS. She described a situation that irrevocably severed her relationship with a long-term consumer:

> It was a good relationship. But in 2016 my son was murdered. Because PCAs don't have grievance time, I still had to work for her—I didn't have any time off. She actually came to my son's memorial service, and she wanted me to make her a plate of food at the repast! I was so frustrated. I'm here, mourning my son, and you want a plate of food? That put a lot of friction in our relationship. I only cared for her for maybe about a week after.

Chenoa wondered whether, if the Medicaid-funded PCA program had given her grievance time, the outcome might have been different: "If I would've had time to bury my son and be able to grieve, then I would've been able to go back and take care of her."

In positive relationships with consumers, however, many PAs go above and beyond what their agency or payor rulebook states. For example, Janice reported working night shifts for a consumer but always making the woman coffee and a small breakfast before leaving in the morning, even though Janice's care plan did not include her making breakfast. Janice felt that the two hours that elapsed before the consumer's next PA arrived were too long for the consumer to wait unfed by herself, and Janice wanted to make sure the consumer was comfortable in the meantime. Shauna also described making extra efforts for her consumer:

> I try to make her as comfortable as possible. She's like, "Can you just do this or that?" I say, "You know what? You don't have to ask me that. Anything to make you feel comfortable is what I'm here for." She'll take a shower. I'll color her hair, then I'll blow-dry it, and I'll curl it for her. Her daughter was like, "Shauna, my mother hasn't smiled in a long time. She barely talked!" She does now. When I'm doing her hair, I'll play some Elvis for her. Then she has her tea, and we just sit and talk about everything.

What Is Known about PAs' Preferences?

As described earlier for consumers, various governmental demonstration programs and initiatives around the country have targeted direct care workers, including people employed in nursing homes and assisted living settings. These programs have primarily offered additional training, higher wages and benefits, improvements in the work environment, and opportunities for career advancement.[16] However, most of these initiatives have included relatively few home-based PAs and were not designed to compare different models of PAS. Furthermore, they generally stop when the funding stream ends. However, studies of PAs in two initiatives give helpful insight into their perspectives about their jobs.

First, in the Cash & Counseling demonstration summarized in Box 13.1, some evaluations addressed the views and experiences of the PAs who supported the participating consumers. One important question involved the impact on family members who, through Cash & Counseling, could now be paid for providing PAS. "As intended, Cash and Counseling favorably affected consumers," wrote researchers. "It could be, however, that the model's effects on consumers came at the expense of those who helped them."[17] In contrast to this concern, the study largely found that Cash & Counseling PAs (i.e., consumer self-directed PAs, some of whom were related to the consumer) were more satisfied with their working conditions, their wages, and the quality of the care consumers received than PAs working for agencies; they also experienced less physical and financial strain. PAs directly related to consumers did report more emotional stress than agency PAs. Nonetheless, "consumers and the family members they hired both reported getting along very well with each other, and program counselors did not report observing frayed family relationships under Cash and Counseling."[18]

Second, In-Home Supportive Services (IHSS) in California preceded Cash & Counseling but is similar in giving consumers the choice to self-direct their PAS—although the state determines the hours of PAS support consumers can receive and the wages they pay PAs. One study randomly selected IHSS-funded PAs to interview, including 365 workers employed by agencies and 253 hired and self-directed by consumers.[19] Consumer self-directed PAs reported better satisfaction, less stress, and better work-life balance than agency PAs. In addition, PA-consumer relationships were better under the self-directed PAS model than under agency services. Hiring family members as PAs was associated with getting along better and experiencing fewer interpersonal problems than hiring nonfamily members. However, within the self-directed model, family members working as PAs were more likely to provide unpaid help than nonfamily workers; furthermore, the responsibilities of paid family members encompassed a wider range and were more demanding than those of nonfamily workers. Family-member PAs were also more emotionally involved in the care of consumers.

Another survey found that, for PAs employed in consumer self-directed PAS, job satisfaction relates to the physical demands at work, emotional suppression (i.e., need to hide feelings at work), social support, and perception of being supported by the workers' union.[20] In contrast, job dissatisfaction is associated with abuse from consumers, working unpaid overtime, caring for multiple consumers, and job insecurity. In another survey, two-thirds of PAs reported that they chose to provide self-directed PAS because of prior commitments to their consumer and flexibility of the job, regardless of wages and benefits.[21] Health insurance was the most important reason for job retention; higher wages bolstered job recruitment and retention.

Finding the Right Fit with Consumers

Opportunities for PAS work are highly local. Statewide policies determine some options, such as whether Medicaid programs cover home-based PAS (see Chapter 3). Some allow relatives to become paid PAS providers, including spouse and parents. The marketplace for agencies is also highly local, with some including new franchise operations and others relying more heavily on standard legacy home health agencies, which have expanded to also offer supportive care (see Chapter 7). Different states have different certification and training standards for home-based PAs (see Chapter 7). Therefore, for people wanting to enter the PAS workforce, figuring out their employment options and deciding which they prefer are initial steps, before addressing the more personal questions about finding a good match with specific consumers.

Although PAS employment has unique qualities, it is nevertheless a job. People contemplating providing paid PAS should consider not only their personalities and value systems but also their physical strength and comfort in being alone with consumers who might—albeit rarely—have urgent or emergency needs. The National Institute for Occupational Safety and Health in the U.S. Department of Health and Human Services, Centers for Disease Control and Prevention, reviewed hazards that workers might confront in home-based care, including home health care and home-based PAS (see Chapter 11).[22] Table 11.1 provides a checklist for potential home care workers from this review. For agency PAs, their employer might offer some of this training or oversight, whereas people employed directly by consumers will be largely on their own—in consultation with the consumer—in considering any concerns.

As described in Part III, agency and self-directed PAs have different job dynamics. Agency PAs' bosses are technically agency supervisors, although in the home they are expected to follow consumers' directions and preferences. Agencies typically assess consumers' specific needs through evaluations by a nurse, who then prepares a formal care plan in consultation with the consumer. Agencies assign PAs to consumers on the basis of their understanding of the workers' personality, skills, time availability, and transportation access—with sensitivity to other attributes, such as allergies or fear of certain animals (e.g., if consumers have pets). Agency PAs generally have relatively little choice about initial assignments to individual consumers, although agencies typically reassign PAs to consumers where they establish good working relationships. If safety threats or irremediable personality conflicts arise, supervisors would likely remove PAs. Agencies perform all payroll functions, including setting wages and meeting federal and state tax obligations.

In contrast, in self-directed PAS, PAs work directly for consumers, who provide their training, supervision, and organize payments (either directly or through some financial management intermediary, e.g., provided by Medicaid). People who seek to provide consumer self-directed PAS can find these jobs through the same sources consumers use to find candidates—such as word of mouth, joining a public registry, through social media or online job sites, seeing a posting on a local bulletin board, or through a union. Candidates have the choice about whether to apply for—or take the job—on the basis of the job description and the interview with the consumer (taking the PA's perspective on items in Box 13.4).

Just as consumers interview PA candidates, potential workers should also assess whether the employment situation suits their preferences and needs. Standard considerations include wages and benefits (if any), overtime and vacation policies, work hours, job description (including physical demands), and workplace safety (location and nature of the home environment, including other household members, humans and animals). In addition, PA candidates should evaluate how well their personality and interaction style fits with the consumer's and how comfortable they would feel in intimate proximity with that person. PAs may have specific preferences, for example, relating to the nature of the consumer's disability, such as working with younger people with developmental disability or with older people with Alzheimer's disease.

In self-directed employment, PAs should be clear about whether they want to be treated as an employee or as an independent contractor (see Chapter 12). For employees, consumers must withhold state and federal taxes and pay other costs (e.g., for unemployment benefits, worker's compensation). Since PAs perform their duties under direct supervision and control of the consumer, being an employee is most consistent with U.S. Internal Revenue Service guidelines about that relationship. However, consumers and PAs may have personal reasons for paying a PA as an independent contractor (IRS

Form 1099-MISC). Independent contractors are not eligible for unemployment benefits or worker's compensation, and they must pay their own Social Security, Medicare, and other taxes.

Just as consumers assess the performance of PAs, so too—inevitably, given human nature—do PAs assess their consumers. PAs who appreciate the ethos of the self-directed model of PAS generally want to support consumers in preserving their control. However, PAs also emphasize the importance of personal boundaries and needing to retain appropriate control when consumers appear to take advantage of their kindness. Sarah has always viewed herself as the "client's employee" in the almost 40 years she has provided PAS. After all, she started working in an independent living program assisting students wanting to live on their own and participate actively in their university communities. She fully endorses the independent living, self-directed model. Nevertheless, Sarah has confronted situations with young people transitioning from living with their parents to residing on the university campus where the student—the consumer—had inflexible preferences about performing basic tasks:

> We've had a lot of students who've had difficult transitions. They've done things one way their whole life with their parents helping them, and then they don't realize, "No. We can't lift you up off the floor. That's not realistic. You're never going to find anybody to work for you if you want to sleep on the floor. I know it's nice because you can roll onto the floor and crawl around and do things. But you're going to have to get a bed." . . . I had somebody who's used a toilet on the floor, a little potty chair. I was like, "Uh-uh. This is what you had in your home? But we're going to fix you up with something else here." I realize now as I'm saying it, it really sounds condescending, but . . .
>
> The students who come to school and their parents, they're amazing people. These parents have raised their kids, and taken care of them, and helped them grow up emotionally, able to go to college. But some of the ways that they provided care was not good for the kids as they become adults and now need to find their own assistants. I tell them, "You want to bring your routine daily needs down to the lowest common denominator so that you have the most options of people to help you. If you keep doing things the way you've done them as a kid, you're going to have very few people that are going to be able to do your transfer. You're going to have a lot smaller choice of who works for you." Thinking this through, that's one of the things that we would help students with.

14

PAS in the Future

Fred is a college senior studying physics. Two major aspects of his life are about to change dramatically. First, when he turns 21—as will happen shortly—Medicaid, which because of his developmental disability covers his LPNs 24/7, will no longer consider him a juvenile (i.e., pediatric case). Medicaid will treat him as an adult. Second, Fred needs to decide where to go and what to do after graduating from college, his initial steps toward his future life and career.

The Medicaid transition from juvenile to adult will significantly affect Fred's ability to recruit his required LPNs. "Here's how my nurse's salary is calculated," said Fred. "They get paid $21 an hour, plus a 30% bonus because I'm a pediatric case. That pediatric status ends at 21. Without that 30% bonus, I'm going to have an even harder time finding nurses."

Even with the relatively high pediatric wage, Fred has had difficulty in his small college town recruiting LPNs. Medicaid requires Fred to prove 24/7 LPN—or parental—coverage, but currently he only has two reliable LPNs. Fred's father therefore must leave work and drive two hours to fill in the coverage gaps. Fred hopes that he can convince his two reliable LPNs to continue covering him after he turns 21 and their hourly wages drop by 30%. He has alerted them to the coming wage cuts and senses they might be willing to stay, perhaps picking up extra shifts alongside other work. Being realistic, however, Fred realizes that the LPNs may be unable to sustain 30% pay cuts.

Fred is tired of Medicaid demanding that he hire LPNs when his primary needs are ADL supports, not skilled services. He has lived with disability his entire life and believes he can manage his needs by closely supervising his own chosen assistants—even maintaining his tracheotomy, which he has not needed for ventilation since early childhood. Fred acknowledges that selling his argument to eliminate LPNs to his mother will be tough, but he is prepared to make the case.

> For my care, there's no middle ground. I either need someone at the doctor level or my care could be done by someone like my fraternity brother. . . . I can change my own trach. I need help with setup, but I can definitely teach somebody that. Other things don't need a nurse. The suppository for my bowels, I know that's gross, but that doesn't need a nurse. Emptying my leg bag—that doesn't need a nurse. Basic skin checking—I could have a nurse visit once a week. . . . Yeah, I know. I'm 20, I think I'm immortal. . . . I don't think of disability in my life as what I can't do. What hurts me emotionally is what I have to do because of my disability. I'm told I have to have nurses 24/7. . . . I feel really guilty because my dad has to be here to fill in hours without a nurse. I'm very lucky he is, but he shouldn't be doing this.

Fred has begun exploring his Medicaid options after he turns 21, including a program for community-based living where he can hire whomever he wants. He has a fraternity brother in mind, a recent graduate, to provide paid PAS support under Fred's direction.

These thoughts lead Fred to the second question—his life. "I'm hoping to pursue a Ph.D. in theoretical physics and become a professor," Fred laughs. "I've been looking at graduate schools outside my state, but I don't know if that will be logistically possible." Despite his complaints about his Medicaid rules, he realizes his state is more generous than many other states, and he is already entrenched in the system. If he moves to another state, he might take months to qualify for their Medicaid program, and he would need assurance he could get at least equal benefits—not a sure bet.

Medicaid coverage of community-based PAS—and Fred's eligibility for such programs—thus limits his choices about graduate school. Although Fred no longer wants his parents to feel or be responsible for his support, he still wishes to live nearby. Fred therefore has more on his mind than most college seniors contemplating graduate education:

> I spoke with my financial planner who specializes in disability. He's on statewide committees about this stuff, so he knows his thing. I mentioned I was going to graduate school, and he was like, "Oh, cool, cool." And then I mentioned I might be going out of state, and he said, "Don't do this to me!" My best chance is to get into my college's

grad school and just stay here. I've had a lot of anxieties, honestly, about how to make graduate school work. The easiest path I see is to use my computer science minor, go to a startup, become a multibil-lionaire, and then be, like, I don't need Medicaid anymore! But that's not likely to happen. And so we're just going to have to figure it out as it comes.

F red, who will always need ADL supports, confronts a daunting future on many levels—beyond the universal existential questions about finding purpose, happiness, and fulfillment in life. To recruit PAs over the coming decades, he will compete with aging baby boomers who also need ADL and IADL supports and with other employment opportunities that offer better wages and benefits than PAS. For the first time in U.S. history, by 2034, when Fred turns 34 years old, older Americans will outnumber children—with a projected 77.0 million people 65 years old and older and 76.5 million 18 years old and younger.[1] Births will no longer be sufficient to increase the total popu-lation (i.e., births will not keep pace with mounting numbers of deaths among baby boomers). Thus, in the 2030s, net international immigration will out-strip birth-driven growth of the U.S. population. Fewer younger people, ex-cept for immigrants, may therefore be available to take PAS jobs. By the time Fred turns 60 in 2060, population growth will have slowed considerably, with proportionally fewer younger people. In 2020 there were roughly 3.5 working-age adults for every older person; by 2060, that ratio will fall to 2.5.[2]

To attract PAs from this decreasing pool of potential workers will there-fore require making PAS jobs considerably more attractive, starting with bet-ter wages. However, if Fred does become a physics professor at a college or university, he will not earn enough to pay substantially higher wages to PAs that he may eventually need nearly 24/7. Thus far, he has benefited from his state's Medicaid program that provides LTSS to people with significant developmental disability. Medicaid pays more than half of LTSS costs in the United States, including both community-based and institutional services. In 2018 national spending on LTSS totaled $379 billion, with Medicaid ac-counting for 52%, other public and private payors 20%, consumers' out-of-pocket payments 16%, and private insurance only 11% of spending.[3] Of the Medicaid spending, 57% overall was on HCBS, the percentage varying wide-ly across states. However, with the aging population and increasing demand for HCBS, state Medicaid programs—and federal matching funds—will face substantial budgetary pressures. How these public programs will respond to these future demands is unclear, but dramatically increasing Medicaid wages for PAs seems unlikely.

To consider the future of paid PAS, this final chapter examines important questions that Fred will face about his paid PAS. Fred has lots of company in these dilemmas. Today, roughly 15 million Americans living at home require some personal assistance—about 7.6 million need ADL supports like Fred, and 13.8 million require IADL assistance.[4] By 2060, an estimated 94.7 million Americans will be age 65 and older, with 19 million age 85 and above.[5] Today, 50% of Americans turning 65 years old are expected to need LTSS at some point during their remaining years. However, increasing rates of chronic health conditions among older Americans suggest that the percentage requiring LTSS will grow in the future.

This chapter raises more questions than it answers. For half a century, various strategies have tried, generally without lasting success, to find ways to ensure affordable and sustainable paid PAS to Americans who need it. Reports from PHI, formerly known as the Paraprofessional Healthcare Institute, an organization founded to improve the quality of direct care jobs, including home-based PAS, examine the current landscape, future trends, and make recommendations for bolstering the PAS workforce.[6,7,8,9,10] Table 14.1 draws from PHI and other recommendations to suggest strategies to address various challenges. However, Chapter 14 offers no tidy ending. To support Fred as he lives into middle and later ages, much remains to be done across various sectors of the United States.

TABLE 14.1 RECOMMENDATIONS FOR STRENGTHENING HOME-BASED PAS AND THE PAS WORKFORCE

Reforming LTSS funding in the United States	
Reform long-term care financing in the United States	For nearly a century, policy makers have repeatedly tried and failed to develop a financially sustainable and politically feasible approach to funding long-term care, including home-based LTSS. The aging population and growing need heighten the urgency of finding a solution for millions of Americans.
Increase Medicaid incentives for community-based supports	Medicaid policies vary considerably across states. States have diverse policies about what PAS support they allow and who can provide paid assistance (e.g., paying relatives of the consumer). Medicaid has strict eligibility criteria and therefore is not the solution to broad national need for home-based PAS supports.
Rethinking models of PAS	
Expand and test strategies for sustainable PAS models	For the last 50 years, many demonstration projects have tested new ways to provide and fund PAS. Few evaluations have studied these efforts or devised ways to support good approaches long-term. New efforts must test different strategies, identify best approaches, and develop supports to sustain and fund them over time.

Widely disseminate information about PAS "best practices"	Best practice information should emphasize recruiting and retaining PAS workers and maximizing the quality of PAS. Dissemination efforts should reach individual consumers self-directing PAS, PAS agencies, and other entities involved in supporting home-based PAS.
Amend nurse practice acts to allow greater nurse delegation to home-based PAS workers	Amending nurse practice acts is challenging and requires careful thought. Nurse delegation to allow PAS workers to administer medications and perform other health-related tasks can help address consumers' unmet needs and enhance skills of PAS workers. Studies should evaluate the effects of any nurse practice act changes to ensure safety.
Building the PAS workforce	
Increase wages	Raising wages is the leading way to increase recruitment and retention of PAS workers. Increasing minimum wages in states can help. As the major public payor, Medicaid funding policies should support wage increases.
Increase job benefits	Job benefits should include paid sick leave, health insurance, paid vacation time, and eligibility for workers' compensation for workplace injuries.
Building the pipeline for PAS workers	High school training programs could attract young people into the field. Older workers might also be good PAS candidates for certain consumers. Conducting a special outreach to men could expand the pool of potential workers.
Support immigration policies that bolster the PAS workforce	Immigrants provide large proportions of home-based PAS, especially in certain communities. Immigrants thus benefit consumers; PAS jobs also benefit immigrants. Policies addressing immigration should support potential PAS workers and thus the consumers requiring their assistance.
Training and credentialing	
Focus training on core competencies	Stakeholders nationwide have specified sets of core competencies for PAS training. Simply recommending this approach has not led to widespread adoption. National and state officials should develop national standards for training PAS workers in core competencies. For consumers with self-directed PAS, maintaining control over training and competencies will be critical.
Credential workers based on core competencies	Credentialing PAS workers provides documentation they can use to gain job opportunities and career advancement. States should develop credentials linked directly to core competency training standards.
Develop upskilling opportunities	Minimum training standards may not be adequate for home-based PAS for consumers with complex health needs. Upskilling involves additional training on specific topics relating to these complex patients, enhancing workers' skills and potentially their job opportunities.

(continued)

TABLE 14.1 RECOMMENDATIONS FOR STRENGTHENING HOME-BASED PAS AND THE PAS WORKFORCE *(continued)*

Underscoring safety	
Supporting consumers in unsafe settings	Some consumers live in dangerous neighborhoods, in substandard housing that poses hazards to both consumers and PAS workers. States must develop policies and procedures to ensure these consumers receive the PAS supports they need, while minimizing risks to PAS workers. Greater attention to safe and accessible housing is essential.
Reduce lifting tasks	To the extent possible, assistive technologies should be used to lift and move patients within the home. Funding these technologies could prevent injuries among PAS workers and future expenditures on workplace injury compensation.
Train PAS workers to reduce physical risks	PAS workers require training on ergonomics, body mechanics, and safe techniques for performing ADL and IADL support tasks.
Develop policies for emergency protections	Both consumers and PAs require protections during emergencies, including natural disasters and pandemics. Policies for distributing emergency supports, restoring electricity and other utilities, testing during pandemics, and provision of personal protective equipment within homes are essential.

Who Will Fred Live With?

This book is about paid PAS. However, as noted in Chapter 1, more than three-quarters of Americans who need in-home ADL supports receive this assistance from the vast unpaid workforce of family members or friends.[11] In addition to providing ADL and IADL supports, this informal workforce also performs nursing-type tasks, such as giving medications, tube feedings, wound care, monitoring blood pressure or blood sugar, and managing incontinence. In 2020, 58% of the 53 million Americans serving as informal caregivers provided these types of assistance.[12] Participants in the 2014 Future of Home Health project observed, "Without caregivers in the home, health care at home is simply impossible for those with functional limitations."[13] Even models of care that provide extensive in-home ADL supports, such as PACE, generally expect that participants live with someone, not alone. The present chapter ends by describing how these expectations affected Michael's PACE participation and the broader implications for people like Fred.

As he enters adulthood, Fred doesn't want to return to his childhood home or depend on his parents for ADL supports or other assistance. He feels it isn't fair to them or to him, although, in 2020, 6% of Americans serving as informal caregivers provided supports for an adult child.[14] However, Fred hasn't yet had an intimate personal relationship (in any case, with LPNs constantly present, finding private moments for intimacy would require subterfuge or explicit negotiation). Fred is only 20 years old and clearly has plenty of time to find a partner. Nevertheless, in 2019, 28% of Americans lived alone.[15] As shown in Table 3.1, people with any type of disability are somewhat more likely than nondisabled people to have never married (30% in comparison with 26%) and more likely to be divorced (18% versus 11%).

Even if Fred finds a spouse or partner, he cannot assume that person could or would support his ADL needs. Among the consumer interviewees, for example, several had partners who themselves were disabled and needed ADL supports; others had spouses (now ex-spouses) who refused to help; and Natalie felt that having her boyfriend assist would intrude on time he needs to work and earn critical income (Chapter 5). Thus, even people who live with others receive paid PAS, although patterns vary by age, as follows:

- Among adults under age 65 living in the community and needing LTSS, only 5% of those who live with family receive paid PAS, as compared with 24% of those living alone or with roommates
- Among adults 65 years old and older living in the community and needing LTSS, 16% of those who live with family receive paid PAS, as compared with 36% of those living alone or with roommates[16]

In 2020, 31% of informal caregivers of adult recipients who live in the community received assistance from paid PAS providers.[17] This assistance from paid caregivers—in addition to informal supports—was more common among recipients who were 65 years old and older than among recipients 18–64 years old (38% versus 16%). Women informal caregivers reported greater use of paid assistance than men caregivers (34% versus 26%). Adding paid PAS to supplement informal caregiving increased as the complexity of the recipient's support needs rose.

For Fred, looking forward, his complex needs make it unlikely that he could get by with only informal supports from a future spouse, partner, or friends. If he lives alone, he will have no choice but to receive paid PAS. Nonetheless, the program paying for his PAS might confront Fred with expectations—as happened to Michael with his PACE plan (explored later)—that he not live alone (i.e., have a family member or friend present at night to handle urgent needs). Despite the growing number of Americans living alone, the assumption remains that people with disability do not or should not live alone.

What Home Will Fred Choose?

The possibility of residing in a nursing home is anathema to Fred. Unlike Charlie Carr, who 50 years earlier had no choice but to live in a chronic disease hospital while attending college (see Chapter 2), Fred plans, without question, to live in the community like others his age. Nevertheless, although numerous private and public community-based residential options now exist, finding accessible housing is very challenging for people with disability. With aging baby boomers, developing accessible and affordable housing—increasingly integrated with supportive services—is a policy priority that will grow in coming decades.

All consumer interviewees rented (some with public subsidies) or owned their own homes or apartments (i.e., none lived in assisted living facilities). Except for two women with live-in PAs, including Ariana who parked an RV in her backyard for her PA, all consumers had agency- or self-directed PAs who came into their homes—the consumer's home is the PA's workplace. For both consumers and PAs, home accessibility has crucial implications for safety and ADL performance. For example, Natalie's bathroom is too small for a shower chair; she therefore gets sponge baths and washes her long hair in a pail of water, a technique she has perfected over years.

Some aspects of existing housing can be adapted to improve accessibility, such as installing stair lifts, grab bars, and raised toilets. However, major renovations, such as widening doorways, expanding bathrooms, and altering weight-bearing walls, are not only expensive but also sometimes structurally infeasible. Before moving in, Michael spent most of his retirement savings making his modest home accessible, including widening certain doorways, enlarging his bathroom, and installing two ceiling-mounted automated lift devices. Widening one of the hallways was not practical, and its walls now bear numerous scrape marks from threading wheelchairs through the narrow passage. Medicaid sometimes pays for certain home accessibility features, such as installing grab bars in bathrooms or ramps at entryways. As for other supportive services, Medicaid policies about funding home accessibility modifications vary substantially from state to state.

Over time, American housing stock is becoming somewhat more accessible, at least in multiunit buildings that since 1990 must meet Fair Housing Act accessibility requirements. (FHA accessibility regulations do not cover single-family, two-family, or three-family homes.)[18] Since 1973, the U.S. Department of Housing and Urban Development has conducted the biennial American Housing Survey, which asks about the physical condition of the nation's housing stock, among other questions. The 2011 American Housing Survey added detailed questions about the accessibility of housing across the United States. As shown in Table 14.2, certain accessibility features, such as entryways without steps and accessible bathrooms, are more common in

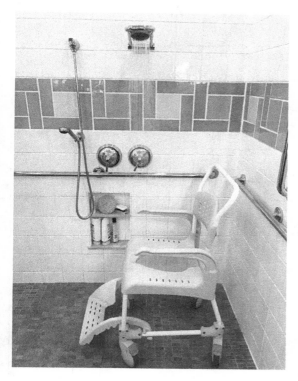

Renovations—expensive and time-consuming—turned this space into the perfect accessible bathroom, recognizing that what constitutes perfect for one consumer might have flaws for another. In this 1911 house, the renovations involved sacrificing a closet in a guest bedroom and moving back a wall, behind which was empty space. The faucet to the left operates a handheld showerhead; the faucet to the right operates two showerheads affixed to a frame, which pulls up from the wall on hinges over the shower chair. Grab bars surround the space. The footrest of the shower chair pushes under the seat to facilitate safe transfers. (Photo credit: Reed Drews)

With recent engineering advances, custom-built stairlifts can fit even narrow and winding staircases, such as from the second to third floor in this 1911 house. Almost hidden, at the top and bottom of the stairlift are the scooters the homeowner uses to get around on each floor after transferring from the stairlift. However, this technology is expensive and requires the ability to transfer safely. More than 10 years ago, the homeowner was told that putting in an elevator—which would be more functional but structurally complicated—would cost more than $250,000. (Photo credit: Reed Drews)

TABLE 14.2 HOUSING ACCESSIBILITY FEATURES: FINDINGS FROM THE 2011 AMERICAN HOUSING SURVEY

Accessibility feature	All owner-occupied units	All renter-occupied units	Multifamily dwellings (4+ units)		
			All	Built before 1990	Built 1990 or later
(%)					
Can enter unit without steps	44.4	38.6	38.8	36.1	49.3
Elevator in home	0.4	0.4	0.6	0.6	0.6
Extra-wide doorways, hallways	8.8	6.5	8.0	5.5	17.4
No steps between rooms	61.5	72.1	77.3	77.0	78.6
Bedroom on entry level	73.5	78.8	77.9	77.5	79.4
Full bathroom on entry level	88.8	85.0	82.8	82.3	84.8
Handrails, grab bars in bathroom	19.4	15.9	17.8	16.0	24.5
Door handles instead of knobs	12.7	8.4	11.1	7.4	25.4
Sink handles, levers	33.0	20.6	21.5	17.9	35.2
Built-in shower seats	11.0	4.0	4.1	3.3	7.0
Raised toilets	8.6	3.7	4.1	3.4	6.8
Wheelchair-accessible					
Bathroom	42.5	37.3	37.8	34.5	50.3
Kitchen cabinets	17.1	15.0	14.5	14.0	16.4
Kitchen countertops	54.9	47.9	46.8	44.7	55.0
Electrical switches	68.3	60.3	59.6	57.2	68.7
Electrical outlets	66.6	59.5	58.8	56.4	68.4
Climate controls	50.2	44.0	43.8	40.6	56.1
Estimated number of units (in millions)	76.09	38.82	25.90	20.53	5.37

Source: Adapted from Bo'sher L, Chan S, Ellen IG, Karfunkel B, Liao HL. Accessibility of America's housing stock: Analysis of the 2011 American Housing Survey. Multi-disciplinary Research Team Report. U.S. Department of Housing and Urban Development; 2015:17–18.

multiunit buildings constructed since 1990 than in older buildings, and while almost one-third of housing is potentially modifiable for accessibility, just 0.15% of housing is fully wheelchair accessible.[19] Even among units occupied by wheelchair users, only 0.73% are fully wheelchair accessible.[20] Lacking full accessibility complicates daily living for consumers, impedes

PAs in performing certain tasks, and poses potential safety risks for both consumers and PAs.

Accessible housing units combined with supportive services do exist. But today they are often either in short supply or available only in settings that are generally expensive, such as private assisted living facilities or independent living communities. With the aging population, private developments are springing up nationwide that offer packages of accessible housing and supportive services, from daily PAS to health care available 24/7. Today, more than 800,000 primarily older and frail Americans live in assisted living facilities,[21] which provide private rooms or small apartments for residents, as well as communal spaces for meals, recreation, and wellness activities. States license, register, or certify assisted living facilities, but regulations vary across states. Independent living communities typically include communal spaces and accessible housing but expect residents to have fewer ADL or IADL support needs; people requiring assistance generally hire it privately, such as through outside agencies or the gray market.

In coming years, innovation in combining housing with supportive services will continue, producing niche options to meet specific needs (e.g., settings designed explicitly for people with Alzheimer's disease or other cognitive deficits, so-called memory care facilities). As shown during the COVID-19 pandemic, however, assisted living situations—where people reside in close proximity, some receiving PAS from staff living in nearby communities—carry significant risks, allowing rampant spread of infectious diseases. In October 2020, COVID-19 case fatality rates were 21% for assisted living facility residents, as compared with 2.5% for the general population.[22] States varied widely in their regulations for preventing infectious disease transmission at assisted living facilities. A June 2020 study found that only 16 states and the District of Columbia required that assisted living facility staff use personal protective equipment.[23]

For low-income Americans, federal housing programs across six decades have aimed to combine affordable, accessible housing with supportive services. Prominent examples include the following:

- **Section 202.** In the 1950s, the decade before enactment of Medicare and Medicaid, the precarious lives of older Americans with health problems but few resources attracted public attention. In response, Section 202 of the Housing Act of 1959 "enables elderly persons to live with dignity and independence by providing supportive housing that accommodates special needs and provides services tailored to the needs of such elderly persons."[24] Section 202 links affordable housing directly to supportive services for low-income older people with health and functional needs. Nonhousing sources, currently Medicaid, fund most supportive services in Section 202 housing.

- **Section 811.** As part of the 1990 Cranston-Gonzalez National Affordable Housing Act, Section 811 funded supportive services and rent subsidies for very low-income, younger people with disability, including individuals with developmental disability, serious mental illness, and significant physical disability. Section 811 also funds certain group homes and independent living settings.

- **Melville Act.** In 2010 Congress enacted the Frank Melville Supportive Housing Investment Act, which amended the Section 811 program to make it more consistent with ADA mandates for community integration and best-practice models of supportive services for younger people with disability. Melville Act provisions also incentivize state housing agencies to collaborate with state health and human services agencies to comprehensively address the needs of their residents with disability.

- **Money Follows the Person.** The MFP demonstration (Box 14.1), authorized by the Deficit Reduction Act of 2005, aimed to address a major barrier for people transitioning out of nursing homes—the lack of affordable housing. MFP involved (1) identifying Medicaid beneficiaries living in nursing homes who wanted to transition into the community and, to make that happen, (2) assisting with finding housing and other services, including PAS, homemaker services, and adult day care. The demonstration, which lasted from 2007 to 2019, operated in 43 states and the District of Columbia, and assisted 91,540 Medicaid beneficiaries—16% with intellectual or developmental disability and 84% with physical, mental health, or adult-onset cognitive disability—to move into communities.[25]

From the start, demand for Section 202 and Section 811 programs far outpaced availability. Eligible applicants can linger on waiting lists for many months. Cancellation of the MFP demonstration program defied its positive performance. As the 2017 *Report to the President and Congress* on MFP outcomes concluded:

> After transitioning to the community, participants experience increases across all seven quality-of-life domains measured, and the improvements are largely sustained two years post-transition. The changes in the quality of life that occur when participants move to the community are remarkable and important indicators that this demonstration has had positive impacts on participants' lives. . . . [A]ny

Box 14.1 Money Follows the Person Demonstration

Goal: To give states incentives to move Medicaid consumers from institutional to community-based settings. Participating states received one year of extra funding for HCBS supports for every Medicaid beneficiary who transitioned from an institution to community-based setting.

Funding: Centers for Medicare & Medicaid Services. Authorized by Section 6071 of the Deficit Reduction Act of 2005; extended by 2010 Patient Protection and Affordable Care Act

Dates: 2007–2019

Locations: 43 states and the District of Columbia

Consumer participants:[1]

- 76,684 (84%) persons with physical, mental health, or adult-onset cognitive disability
- 14,856 (16%) persons with intellectual or developmental disability
- 91,540 total Medicaid beneficiaries with disability

Program:

- States received 75% to 90% higher federal matching funds for first year that participant lived in community
- HCBS typically included PAS, adult day health, case management, homemaker, habilitative services, and respite
- During first year in community, participants could receive more PAS or transition coordination hours than ordinarily allowed
- Participants received assistance in finding accessible and affordable housing, as well as funds for security and utility deposits and costs for setting up their households
- Program also included training for direct care workers, evaluations of participants' needs, and instituting data gathering

Personal assistance services: Forty states offered self-directed PAS. In 2015 an estimated 16% of MFP participants chose this option, with rates varying widely across states.[2]

Evaluation results: Quality of life increased significantly after transitioning back to the community and very few consumers reported unmet needs with bathing, meal preparation, medication administration, and toileting.[3] Participants who transitioned out of nursing homes with the highest-care needs reported the fewest unmet needs after transitioning. MFP participants also reported increased satisfaction with life, the quality of care they received, their living arrangement, and community integration. Depression rates significantly decreased.

[1] Musumeci M, Chidambaram P, Watts MO. Medicaid's Money Follows the Person program: State progress and uncertainty pending federal funding reauthorization. Issue Brief. Henry J. Kaiser Family Foundation; November 2019:2.

[2] Watts MO, Reaves EL, Musumeci M. Money Follows the Person: A 2015 state survey of transitions, services, and costs. Henry J. Kaiser Family Foundation; October 2015:1.

[3] Irvin C, Denny-Brown N, Bohl A, et al. Money Follows the Person 2015 Annual Evaluation Report. Mathematica Policy Research; 2017.

dollar value placed on these improvements would not adequately reflect what it means for people with significant disabilities when they can live in and contribute to their local communities.[26]

Federal dollars have not kept pace with demand for public affordable housing, combined with supportive services like PAS, for people with disability. In any case, Fred might not qualify for these programs because eligibility criteria require low incomes. Unless Fred becomes sufficiently wealthy to build or substantially renovate his own home, finding accessible housing will likely remain challenging for the foreseeable future. The accessibility of Fred's housing will substantially affect not only his safety and quality of life but also, potentially, his ability to recruit paid PAs who feel safe within their workplace.

Who Will Pay for Fred's PAS, and Should Fred Change States?

In the near future, no public program will universally pay for LTSS, including PAS, in the United States. Medicaid has become a last resort for thousands of people needing LTSS who cannot afford it.[27] Because of his developmental disability, Fred will be able to stay on Medicaid in his state for the time being. Medicaid eligibility rules are complex, and Fred's near-term eligibility depends on whether his parents receive Social Security and other factors.[28] Later, if he does become a college physics professor, Fred's income could put his Medicaid eligibility at risk, despite being inadequate to cover his PAS costs:

> The population with functional impairments due to intellectual and developmental disabilities are most dependent on Medicaid funding—77 percent of the funding for I/DD services and supports comes from the Medicaid program, compared to 61 percent of the LTSS funding for the total non-elderly adult population and 22 percent of the LTSS funding for the elderly population. . . . But Medicaid is a means-tested program and is available only to those with very limited income and assets. Those receiving Medicaid benefits face a dilemma in considering work: if they work successfully, their income would likely disqualify them from receiving Medicaid coverage of the LTSS they need to work, yet they may not earn enough to pay for the services on their own. The implicit tax on working overwhelms earned income, even from high-paying jobs.[29]

Therefore, Fred might face a Hobson's choice between continuing to work and leaving the workforce but gaining PAS coverage through resuming Medicaid eligibility (i.e., his severe disability will almost certainly meet Social Security Administration disability standards).

As noted earlier, little is known about people living in communities who need paid PAS supports but cannot afford it. Many people or their families make private and undocumented arrangements with workers to provide this assistance. "This segment, known as the gray market, is difficult to characterize and impossible to quantify—but certainly sizable, given the large proportion of consumers who do not qualify for public funding but cannot afford to pay out-of-pocket for agency services."[30] Some people with ADL impairments lack Medicaid, resources to enter the gray market, and informal PAS supports. No one knows their numbers or how they live their daily lives.

Returning to Medicaid as the last resort for covering PAS, another question is where to live. In the absence of a universal federal requirement for specific LTSS, Medicaid programs will continue to vary substantially across the states in their PAS options and details of coverage, such as the number of PAS hours allowed and whether beneficiaries can pay certain relatives to provide their PAS (see Chapter 3). "The optional nature of most [Medicaid] HCBS results in substantial variation across states in enrollment and spending, reflecting states' different choices about optional authorities, benefit package contents, and scope of covered services."[31] In 2016, for example, Mississippi spent 27% of its Medicaid LTSS dollars on HCBS rather than institutional services, while Oregon allocated 81% of its Medicaid LTSS spending to HCBS.[32] In 29 states and the District of Columbia, HCBS spending exceeded 50% of Medicaid LTSS expenditures.

Some people decide where to live on the basis of what a state's Medicaid program offers. Several years after his spinal cord injury, Matt ended up in the Midwest, living in what had been advertised as a forward-thinking transitional learning center but turned out to be a nursing home. "You didn't have control over your care," said Matt. "There was this Nurse Ratched situation"—alluding to the domineering nurse in *One Flew Over the Cuckoo's Nest*—"and she tried to hold things over me. We had huge disagreements." Matt needed to escape. He had learned about independent living centers, and "I contacted the one in Boston and did my due diligence." He found out that Massachusetts Medicaid, in collaboration with the Boston Center for Independent Living and the advocacy of Charlie Carr, had begun the first-in-the-nation consumer self-directed PCA program (see Chapter 3). In that program, Matt could control his PAS and thus his daily life. Matt relocated to Boston.

However, moving in search of desirable Medicaid policies carries substantial risks. Medicaid program eligibility requirements vary across states, and people are not assured of gaining immediate access to the program or its services. In addition, Medicaid options change with state priorities, fluctuating budgets, and political winds. Furthermore, federal policies considerably shape state Medicaid programs, such as by trying to incentivize HCBS. Since Fred has a long history with his state's Medicaid program—and if his new PAS program works out well—he might want to stay put.

How Should Fred Recruit, Train, and Retain His Paid PAS Workers?

Fred anticipates difficulties recruiting PAs when Medicaid stops treating him as a pediatric case and eliminates the 30% bonus for his LPNs. He lives in a small city, where he has trouble finding LPNs, even with the extra pay. Once he turns 21, Fred hopes to start recruiting less costly PAS providers. Nonetheless, offering a competitive wage will remain essential to his ability to hire and retain these workers.

PHI, which advocates for improving the quality of direct care jobs, notes that the roles of these workers, including PAs, will evolve in coming years to meet the changing needs of the populations they serve. The changes include not only the increasing clinical complexity of people with multiple chronic health conditions but also shifts in basic demographic characteristics: 23% of older Americans today are people of color, but that percentage will rise to 45% by 2060; furthermore, a growing number will openly identify as lesbian, gay, bisexual, or transgender.[33] These factors increase the need for wide-ranging training across essential competencies (see Box 7.2) and upskilling (training in specific skill sets, e.g., supporting people with diabetes, autism, or Alzheimer's disease) for direct care workers to better perform their jobs:

> Direct care workers are supporting individuals with more complex needs in every setting, particularly in private homes and communities, and these workers require more technical, interpersonal, and linguistic and cultural competencies than ever before.
>
> Despite the changes in their roles and responsibilities, compensation for direct care workers—who are primarily women, particularly women of color and immigrant women—remains notoriously low, leading to high rates of poverty in the workforce. And the data reveal further disparities in wages and annual earnings within the direct workforce, according to gender, race and ethnicity, and other demographic characteristics.
>
> This paradox—between the changing profile of direct care and the persistent marginalization of direct care workers—cannot be sustained in the face of growing demand. . . . From 2018 to 2028, the workforce is expected to add 1.3 million jobs, and an additional

6.9 million jobs will become vacant as existing workers leave the field or exit the labor force. These figures indicate the pressing need to improve direct care jobs—because without broad and targeted efforts, we will experience an escalating national crisis of unmet need for long-term services and supports.[34]

To bolster the PAS workforce in coming decades will be challenging. Unlike consolidated industries, with central decision makers, Fred represents the millions of individual employers who largely, within the privacy of their homes, set the daily terms of work for what will likely be dozens of PAs over his lifetime. Thousands of home care agencies and private home care franchises nationwide have their own rules, within each state's regulatory environments (e.g., NPA rules). Furthermore, as noted, although Medicaid is the single largest payor for PAS, each state has its own approach to LTSS and HCBS. Within this fragmented context, as described briefly in what follows, three core factors will drive efforts to build and sustain the PAS workforce: increasing wages, improving training and opportunities for career advancement, and maximizing the safety of the job and workplace.[35]

Increasing Wages

Increasing the incomes of paid PAS workers is essential: "the bottom line is that workers must be better compensated, in line with the value of their contribution. Otherwise, the LTSS sector will continue struggling to recruit and retain a strong workforce, especially given the fierce competition for entry-level workers across the labor market."[36] How this will happen—either now or across Fred's lifetime—is unclear.

Neither private insurance nor Medicare covers paid PAS (see Chapter 3), and only those who meet strict low-income and other eligibility criteria qualify for Medicaid. Otherwise, consumers generally pay for PAS themselves, through agencies or the gray market. Few Americans have adequate incomes to pay for extensive home-based PAS, let alone provide living wages to their PAs. If Fred wants to pay his PAs living wages in the small city where he currently lives, the amount per hour is $13.74 for someone living alone; for single parents with dependent children, like many PAs, a living wage is $28.33 per hour for someone with one child, $38.38 with two children, and $50.81 hourly with three children.[37] Fred would ideally like 18 hours per day of PA support: if each of his PAs is a single parent with one child, that would translate into annual costs of $186,128 ($28.33/hour × 18 hours/day × 365 days/year), before paying overtime for holidays, Social Security, and other employer costs (see Table 12.1).

Few Americans could afford this amount. In 2018 the median household income in the United States overall was $61,937—$67,937 for White, not Hispanic, $41,511 for Black, $87,243 for Asian, and $51,404 for Hispanic (any race) households.[38] Postsecondary physics teachers, like Fred hopes to become, earn more than these median incomes: in 2019, their median salary was $89,590.[39] If he pays his PAs a living wage, Fred's annual PA costs of roughly $186,128 would total more than twice this salary.

For most Americans, resources become even more strained after retirement. Nearly half of families across all ages have $0 in retirement savings, with median retirement savings in 2016 ranging from $1,000 for families headed by persons in their mid-thirties to $21,000 for people approaching retirement age.[40] Many factors contribute to these numbers, including movement in recent years from traditional retirement pensions to account-type savings plans or 401(k)s. Certain segments of the U.S. population are especially hard hit: "The shift from pensions to account-type savings plans has been a disaster for lower-income, black, Hispanic, non-college-educated, and single workers, who together add up to a majority of the American population."[41] In 2016 only 41% of Black and 35% of Hispanic families had any retirement savings.[42]

For people who do gain Medicaid PAS coverage, this public program—which chronically faces budgetary stresses and shortfalls—is unlikely to pay PAs a living wage. Increasing minimum-wage levels within states can help; raising state minimum wages is politically easier than boosting the federal minimum wage. Facing chronic worker shortages, some states have implemented "wage pass-through" programs, allowing home care agencies, for which Medicaid strictly constrains total budgets, to pay their PAS workers higher wages. Wage pass-throughs involve allocating Medicaid funds specifically to increase payments to direct care workers. One study found that this approach increased wages for direct care workers by 12%, roughly $1.18 per hour; Hispanic workers and those without a high school diploma received lower increases.[43] Twenty-four states implemented wage pass-through programs for direct care workers in 2019.[44] What remains unclear is whether the hard-won gains through the Fair Labor Standards Act (see Chapter 4) have raised incomes for home-based PAS workers, especially with employers trying to limit overtime hours and thus hours spent earning time-and-a-half wages.

Improving Training and Career Advancement Opportunities

No uniform standards exist for PA training or certification (see Chapter 7). According to a report on building the direct care workforce, without training standards and certification, these workers find it impossible to be recognized for their skills.[45] This substantially limits potential career advancements that might help recruit and retain workers within the PAS field, as well as possibly raise their incomes. Different training options—optimally organized around core competencies—should be available to fit career goals of individual workers:

> By repositioning direct care jobs as a stepping stone to a career in the "caring professions," industry can appeal to untapped labor pools and broaden the universe of job seekers who consider this work. Further, incumbent workers are likely to be retained longer as they complete training and advance up the career ladder. . . . Career lattices should be available for direct care workers who want to continue providing direct care and can increase their skill and possible pay. It is important to note that many direct care workers are committed to their jobs as a career and are not interested in a career ladder. For these workers, developing a career lattice would be more appropriate, along with providing a respectful work environment with better pay for all workers.[46]

Changing NPA regulations to allow home-based PAs, with demonstrated competencies, to perform health-related tasks under nurse delegation offers important advantages. With the growing clinical complexity of consumers, these changes would allow PAs to expand their skills (upskilling) and thus potentially their job opportunities: "allowing direct care workers greater flexibility, respect, and responsibility has been shown to increase job satisfaction, which could have positive effects on retention of the workforce."[47] However, changing NPA regulations is difficult, with nurses concerned about reducing their own roles and possible worsening care quality. Few studies have examined outcomes of NPA changes. Research from New Jersey found that training and delegating home health aides to provide medications had positive effects for both consumers and workers.[48]

Organizing competency-based training and enhancing skills development face many challenges, however, because PAs often work alone, employed by consumers like Fred, or have fluid relationships with various agencies. One option, which has worked well in California, Oregon, Washington state, and elsewhere, is the "public authority"—a registry of available PAS workers, including people seeking additional hours, which provides referrals to consumers and offers training for both consumers and PAs. Public authorities can improve the efficiency of self-directed care without diluting its essential elements, "such as the ability of consumers to choose their own worker and determine how and when care will be provided. . . . [P]ublic authorities have been able to raise wages and improve the quality of the workforce, giving consumers confidence in the home care program and workers a renewed interest in the field."[49]

Ensuring Safety in the Work Environment

Their workplaces raise wide-ranging safety concerns for PAs, from threats in neighborhoods where consumers live to dangers in consumers' homes (e.g., from pets or other human household members) to ergonomic stresses from performing ADL support tasks. Fulfilling all safety guidelines, as recommended by the National Institute for Occupational Safety and Health (see Table 11.1), is unlikely. Therefore, PAs will continue to venture into unsafe neighborhoods and hazardous homes to support consumers. Ensuring that they have paid sick leave and workers' compensation to cover costs should they be injured or disabled at work is essential but not yet routinely available for all PAs. With the goal of keeping PAs safe and preventing injuries, two approaches predominate:[50]

- **Fit the worker to the task**, for example, by training on ergonomics, body mechanics, and safe techniques for performing ADL and IADL support tasks
- **Fit the task to the worker**, by modifying ADL support tasks, for example, using assistive technologies (e.g., lift devices) to reduce injury threats

Approaches for training PAS workers are more advanced—and accessible—than technological interventions. Over the course of PAS careers, however, relying only on training in safe body mechanics, even if intensive, may not ensure worker safety. Indeed, the National Institute for Occupational Safety and Health recommends that all programs on safe patient handling should aim to eliminate manual lifting whenever possible.[51] Aspects of the home environment can impede efforts to implement safe handling techniques. For example, small bathrooms—as in Natalie's home—can prevent PAs from using optimal body mechanics to assist consumers on and off a shower chair, if the bathroom has enough room for that equipment. Natalie's bathroom does not, and she makes do with sponge baths.

Many consumers do not have resources to purchase assistive technology, such as lift devices, and for Medicaid beneficiaries, states vary in whether they cover such equipment. Some assistive equipment may be relatively inexpensive. For instance, one study examined the effects of using a transfer board to assist consumers in moving from one surface to another (e.g., from chair to bed), rather than being manually lifted by their PAs. A simple device, a transfer board offers important benefits, improving PAs' postural dynamics and reducing hand force.[52] Product liability risks and the long U.S. regulatory approval process required for health-related devices impede development of assistive technologies for use in homes.

In the future, the critical question is whether assistive technologies will someday safely replace human ADL supports. If so—and these technologies became affordable—concerns about the PAS workforce, safety, and costs could substantially recede. However, this holy grail of home-based, technology-driven PAS remains a distant goal. Technologies currently exist to remind people about taking medications, monitor certain vital signs, identify falls, and track other outcomes, as well as perform certain household tasks (e.g., vacuuming). But providing ADL supports, such as assisting in toileting, bathing, dressing, and feeding, are not easily performed by robots or other devices. Most likely, future technologies will augment rather than replace human ADL supports:

> A vision of the future in which robots fully substitute for personal support remains distant. Instead, technology is likely to remain supplementary to paid personal assistance services. . . . The relational and reciprocal nature of home care cannot be replaced by robotics. Although technology may support independence and improve quality of life in some cases or for some consumers, for others the substitution of technological for human support may exacerbate social isolation, loneliness, and unmet needs. As the developer of Stevie, [a] socially assistive robot prototype, stated: "None of this will mean we won't need human carers anymore. . . . Instead, we're trying to develop technology that helps and complements human care. We want to combine human empathy, compassion and decision-making with the efficiency, reliability and continuous operation of robotics."[53]

Other Uncertainties About Paid
PAS Awaiting Fred

As recounted earlier, if Fred wants to pay living wages to his PAs for 18 hours of daily PAS, annual costs would total more than $186,128. If he stays on Medicaid and the minimum wage in his state rises to $15 per hour (less than the living wage for a worker who is a single parent but what Medicaid would likely pay), his annual costs for his desired PAS would exceed $98,550. Fred's PAS expense for remaining in the community might therefore surpass annual nursing home costs, making it cheaper for Medicaid to institutionalize Fred.

The U.S. Supreme Court's 1999 *Olmstead* decision clearly asserts Fred's civil right to live in the community if he wishes (see Chapter 2). The court does not have authority, however, to tell states how to spend their Medicaid dollars. *Olmstead* could prohibit substantial cuts to Medicaid community-support budgets that would increase the risks of institutionalizing beneficiaries.[54] But the court cannot compel states to spend specified amounts on HCBS. In its *Olmstead* decision, the court instead provided guidance for states on making measured but steady progress from institutionalization toward community-based supports. Their opinion suggests that putting people on waiting lists to move from institutions into communities is acceptable, as long as those waiting lists move along at a reasonable pace. In 2016, 75% of states reported a total of 656,195 people on waiting lists for HCBS programs, with average wait times of 23 months—48 months for programs specifically for people with developmental disability.[55]

Payment Policies for Long-Term Community-Based Supports

For nearly two centuries, Americans have wrestled with how to provide daily supports and basic care at home for people with chronic health conditions and disability. As yet, "no agreement has been reached concerning the proper balance between governmental resources and the private resources of family, friends, and insurance."[56] These debates build on often unspoken assumptions that family members—primarily women as informal caregivers (acknowledging that Fred's dad is the parent on call when LPNs fall through)—are the ubiquitous backstop when formal care systems break down or become too expensive. In policy deliberations about home-based care, there are "unavoidable tensions between fiscal reality and legitimate need. Tough political and societal questions are inescapable: Who should get care? For how long should it be provided? Under what circumstances should public funds pay for care?"[57]

Repeatedly, since the mid-20th century, public consternation about finding ways to better provide home-based supportive services has periodically flared. Governmental commissions have taken up the issue, ultimately failing to reach practical solutions. For instance, Section 643 of the American Taxpayer Relief Act of 2012 empaneled the 15-member bipartisan Commission on Long-Term Care to consider the issue and report back to Congress in short order. The panel started its work in June 2013 and delivered its final report in September 2013, painting a bleak but realistic picture of upcoming challenges: "Governments are facing serious budget constraints that threaten funding for existing health care, disability, and retirement programs. We cannot assure the safety net will hold for the most vulnerable who must rely on public programs if we also publicly finance care for millions of Americans who could prepare now for their needs in future years."[58]

The commission agreed on the urgent need for strong community-based LTSS but then stalled: "The Commission considered very different approaches regarding the mechanisms needed to make this vision possible. The Commission did not agree on a financing approach, and, therefore, makes no recommendation."[59] Instead, the commission offered two competing possibilities: (1) strengthening LTSS financing through private means, such as long-term care insurance products that are affordable and attractive to consumers; and (2) strengthening social insurance to finance LTSS through public mechanisms that spread costs across the government and participants and possibly employers and employees. Absent recommendations on this driving but divisive issue, the commission's report faded rapidly from public consciousness.

The commission first recommended expanding private long-term care insurance coverage among Americans. Although most working-age Americans and their families receive health insurance as an employment benefit, relatively few employers today offer long-term care insurance. As the commission observed,

> While private long-term care insurance products have been sold for more than 30 years, any potential for them to serve a large percentage of the population has not been realized. Private long-term care insurance policies currently play a minor role in financing LTSS—only 10 percent of the potential market of Americans age 50 and above is currently insured. New issuance of policies has declined in recent years, and a significant number of insurers have left the private LTCI market. . . . Features of the products, the insurance market, and some regulatory requirements limit the value and attractiveness of private LTCI, including: underwriting standards that prevent many individuals from qualifying, high monthly premiums, policy forfeiture rules, limits on benefits, and a lack of public understanding and confidence in the private LTCI products.[60]

Fred's future employer is unlikely to offer private long-term care insurance. Even if it does, Fred may not qualify for long-term care insurance because his preexisting disability would make him a bad insurance risk (i.e., insurers would face 100% certainty that Fred would require substantial resources). Even if Fred could obtain long-term care insurance, private insurance is highly unlikely to cover 18 hours of daily PAS support across years, let alone across his lifetime. Therefore, private long-term care insurance will not cover the costs of Fred's in-home PAS.

Fred's only option—unless, as he puts it, he uses "my computer science minor, go to a startup, become a multibillionaire"—will therefore remain public programs, notably Medicaid. Despite *Olmstead*, the major question is whether Medicaid, across Fred's lifetime, will finance the many hours of in-home PAS he needs, possibly eventually expanding to 24/7 coverage. If Medicaid limits his in-home PAS support, Fred could be forced into the previously unthinkable, entering a nursing home. Such a move would clearly violate Fred's civil rights under *Olmstead* and the ADA. But to circumvent his *Olmstead* rights, could Medicaid impose this decision by asserting that Fred is unsafe in his own home, even with PAS support?

Concerns About Safety and Who Decides

In *Olmstead*, the U.S. Supreme Court deferred to medical professionals in deciding whether an institutionalized person could live in the community with appropriate supports. Giving doctors this authority, however, runs counter to independent living principles—that consumers have the right to make decisions about their lives. Disability advocates raised concerns about deference to physicians in the *Olmstead* opinion, noting that doctors often know little about the daily lives of people with disability in their homes and communities. The vast majority of practicing U.S. physicians (82% in a 2019–2020 national survey) believe that the quality of life of people with significant disability is worse than that of nondisabled people.[61]

To clarify the intent of *Olmstead*, in 2011 the U.S. Department of Justice Office of Civil Rights issued technical guidance about various issues. Among multiple questions addressed was the evidence required to demonstrate that people can appropriately live in communities or integrated settings:

> An individual may rely on a variety of forms of evidence. . . . A reasonable, objective assessment by a public entity's treating professional is one, but only one, such avenue. Such assessments must identify individuals' needs and the services and supports necessary for them to succeed in an integrated setting. . . . People with disabilities can also present their own independent evidence of the appropriateness of an integrated setting, including, for example, that individuals with similar needs are living, working and receiving services in integrated settings with appropriate supports. This evidence may come from their own treatment providers, from community-based organizations that provide services to people with disabilities outside of institutional settings, or from any other relevant source.[62]

For doctors—guided by their ethical imperative of *primum non nocere* (first, do no harm)—concerns about safety generally drive their perceptions about whether specific people with disability can live in the community with appropriate supports rather than in an institution. Facilities presumably provide round-the-clock access to care. However, safety is not an absolute. No setting is 100% safe. Each environment poses its own hazards, which everyone—regardless of disability—must weigh in accord with their personal preferences and life goals.

Fred anticipates problems convincing his parents that he doesn't need 24/7 LPN coverage and that he could instead train a willing fraternity brother to provide his supports: "My parents would be like, 'Fred, that's not safe!'" Nevertheless, down the road, Fred is likely to confront skepticism from health care professionals about his safety living in the community, especially if he lives alone. What happened to Michael in 2017 exemplifies this concern.

In 2012, paying out-of-pocket, Michael could no longer afford enough PAS hours through his commercial franchise agency to meet his growing needs (see Chapter 7). Unable to reliably get water from his sink or food from his refrigerator, he sometimes did not eat or drink between his brief early morning and late evening PA visits. I suggested that he explore joining the Program of All-Inclusive Care for the Elderly (PACE; see Chapter 3). PACE plans are generally small, roughly 300 members, and they receive monthly, preset payments from Medicare and Medicaid to cover all costs for each member. PACE aims to support Medicare and/or Medicaid beneficiaries 55 years old and older with extensive chronic health problems or severe disability to remain in their homes and communities. PACE transports typical participants to adult day care each weekday, returning them home in the evening to their families, with in-home PAS supports as needed. Here, Michael broke the mold: he lived alone and refused adult day care. He preferred auditing courses at the local university or pursuing community-based activities, such as visiting museums or attending afternoon concerts.

"I later heard whispers," Michael wrote, "that some [PACE providers] felt that, especially since I lived alone, I was too disabled for [them] and belonged in a nursing home."[63] Nevertheless, PACE initially worked well for Michael. With 10 hours of PAS daily—70 hours per week—home health aides (HHAs, local terminology for PAs) showered and shaved him every morning, provided food and fluids throughout the day, and performed IADL tasks (e.g., positioning and charging his tablet computer, which he had programmed to operate functions throughout his home). PACE purchased Michael's power wheelchair, which he maneuvers using a chin-operated miniature trackball joystick. To prevent pressure injuries, the wheelchair has a high-tech, alternating air pressure seat cushion. After about 30 months of active use, his wheelchair odometer read 2,563 miles. Hints of potential trouble with PACE surfaced, as suggested by his need to jerry-rig a mechanism to self-administer his second daily medication dose (see Chapter 5). But for four years, Michael, living a full life, was happy overall with PACE PAS supports.

In June 2017 Michael's high-tech seat cushion malfunctioned, and during the three days it was away for repair, he sat on a seat cushion without adequate pressure relief and developed a single pressure injury (i.e., pressure ulcer). For the next month, PACE home care nurses visited him daily, tending his wound and reporting it was steadily healing, albeit slowly. Finally, after a month, Michael's PACE primary care physician had him transported to their health center so that she could examine him. Several days later, without consulting Michael, the physician sent an ambulance to his home to take him to a nursing home, prescribing complete bed rest and turning every several hours to treat the pressure injury.

Michael's nursing home experiences were deplorable, reinforcing his desire to remain in his accessible home. Nonetheless, after several weeks, the pressure injury showed improvement. An expert wound-care nurse told Michael the injury had healed sufficiently that he could return home with daily nursing support to complete his recovery.

However, almost a month after he entered the nursing home, Michael's primary care physician came to his bedside and announced that she would not allow him to go home, at that time or any future point. Without providing any evidence, she asserted he was not safe living at home alone. If Michael left the nursing home on his own, PACE would not restart his HHAs or home nursing visits. He could file an appeal to contest the doctor's decision. But while that appeal process played out, PACE would keep Michael against his will in the nursing home, ostensibly to keep him safe.

Unlike a nondisabled person, Michael could not simply leave the nursing home and return home. His physician withheld his home-based PAS, which he needed to live at home as he had done successfully for nearly four years. While awaiting the decision on his appeal, Michael therefore remained trapped in the nursing home, which—because his pressure injury had theoretically healed—left him largely untended. Michael "grew increasingly despondent, losing hope. With a patient to certified nursing assistant ratio of 10 to 1 and my complete quadriplegia, nursing home staff neglected my most basic needs. I was hungry, thirsty, unwashed, unshaven, untoileted, and despairing. I lost all dignity and self-respect, except when Nelita"—Michael's original HHA from years earlier, visited the nursing home and "washed my hair and gave me a shave."[64] I spoke daily with Michael and visited several times, witnessing his decline with alarm and fearing he could not survive much longer.

Ironically, I was able to spring Michael from the nursing home only because its poor-quality care threatened his immediate safety.[65] Michael won his appeal: Medicare's adjudicating agency ruled that PACE must restore his HHAs and send him home. But one day later, Michael developed a fever. PACE had decided to appeal the ruling against them and to keep Michael in the nursing home for the three to four months required to process their appeal. Nursing home staff neglected his infection, and eight days later, Michael's blood tests showed extreme dehydration, severe enough that he risked acute kidney failure.

This threat was Michael's ticket out of the nursing home. An ambulance took him to a community teaching hospital, which successfully treated his infection. Unfortunately, hospital staff found multiple pressure injuries and macerated skin across Michael's backside: once his original pressure injury had healed, the nursing home had failed to turn him to prevent additional wounds. To avoid being forced back into the nursing home, Michael left PACE. Three months later he learned that PACE lost its appeal of the original judgment. The adjudicating agency once again ordered PACE to return Michael home with full PAS support.

Who Decides: Dignity of Risk

Michael's story is not unique. Despite the protections of *Olmstead*, questions about whether people with significant disability can remain at home or require institutionalization to supposedly ensure their safety arise every day. Legal cases over several decades have confirmed that people with decision-making capacity (i.e., the mental ability to understand and balance the risks confronting them), such as Michael, have the right to make their own health care decisions. Michael therefore had the legal right to decline nursing home care and return home. Under *Olmstead*, it was Michael's civil right to live at home, if he wished.

Although Michael had strong legal grounds to return home from the nursing home, how could he achieve these rights? His primary care physician, with her power to authorize or withhold his PAS, controlled his essential home-based supports. Since she refused to restore his HHAs, under the guise of protecting his safety, Michael's legal rights seemed like a mirage. As the maxim goes, justice delayed is justice denied.[66]

Michael's situation highlights questions that arise when a third party or public payor is covering PAS supports—concerns that will increase with tightening fiscal constraints and a growing number of people requesting public PAS support. These questions include:

- How are decisions made about where people with disability live and what PAS supports they receive?
- What parameters or considerations drive these decisions?
- Who is the ultimate arbiter?

From his physician's perspective, Michael was unsafe living at home, and institutionalizing him in the nursing home would maximize his safety. From Michael's perspective, neither his health nor functional status had substantively changed, and he had done well with PACE's HHAs for several years. Furthermore, the nursing home harmed him, threatened his well-being, and ruined his quality of life. He felt hopeless. The physician held the power to make this decision about sending Michael home with PAS, and she said no: it was unsafe.

Michael's story highlights a central tenet of the disability civil rights movement, the principle of "dignity of risk." The principle holds that individuals with decision-making capacity have a right to make decisions for their lives, even if others perceive those decisions as risky:

> "Dignity of risk" . . . involves respect for persons, self-determination, and attempts to minimize paternalism or parentalism. If you combine common dictionary definitions of "dignity" and "risk" . . . they help you to understand the term as conveying that individuals are "worthy of honor and respect" even when they make decisions that may increase "the possibility that something bad or unpleasant . . . will happen."[67]

Under the dignity of risk principle, Michael has the moral right to decide where he prefers to live. Certainly, many people have cognitive declines or serious mental health conditions that compromise their decision-making capacity. It is unrealistic to expect that people with substantial cognitive deficits and memory difficulties, as well as significant ADL impairments, could live alone in the community, even with paid PAS. These concerns raise questions about who makes decisions for their care if trusted family members or friends are not available to faithfully represent and carry out their wishes, including balancing the risks against benefits of different housing options (e.g., assisted living facility versus nursing home). But Michael clearly understood the risks of living alone in his home, which he had done for several years. Nonetheless, he lacked the authority to reinstate his PACE HHA services, and his physician failed to recognize Michael's dignity to make this decision for himself.

Although Michael's physician's stated rationale for denying his home-based PAS was concern for his safety, was more going on? Was his physician concerned about possible legal liability—that if something went wrong for Michael at home, she could be blamed? With the rampant litigiousness in U.S. health care, are liability concerns justified? Instead, perhaps the cost of Michael's home-based PAS fell into a gray zone, where expenses for his daily HHA hours and skilled nursing visits exceeded nursing home costs. Maybe PACE felt financial pressures to rein in expenditures for his care, although that rationale does not appear to be considered legally defensible under *Olmstead*.

Finally, stigmatization of people with disability remains widespread, and many physicians share these societal attitudes.[68] Could his physician have devalued Michael's quality of life, seen only his disability and not the joy and happiness he finds in his life? "Given what the alternatives are," said Michael, "it's still roughly a million times better losing my life inside my own house— if that happened—than being somewhere where I don't want to be. Anyway, there's literally a risk of dying in other places." He wants to live at home.

Looking Ahead

As acknowledged at the outset, this chapter raises more questions than it answers. Across nearly two centuries, the United States has periodically tried but failed to create lasting and sustainable solutions to supporting people with chronic disease or disability—specifically those who lack the dedication of persistent and capable informal caregivers—in their homes.

> Given the public's desire for a uniquely American health care system with expanded coverage and considerable choice, along with minimal increases in out-of-pocket expenses, it is difficult to envision an approach to care at home that would create an universally acceptable balance of self-sacrifice, personal responsibility, and expanded financial resources, both public and private.[69]

These failures do not augur well for Fred's future ability to pursue his dream career of teaching physics while living in his own home in the community. However, several factors suggest that hope is not lost (see Table 14.1). First is the impending wave of millions of Americans needing home-based PAS and the decreasing ability of informal caregivers to meet the demands of their care. Since these millions are baby boomers—and in just over two decades will also include millennials—they will raise their voices, articulate their needs. They will vote. Intergenerational concerns will inevitably arise. Expending public resources on parents, leaving children and grandchildren in debt, could derail potential options. However, finding some hybrid system, like Social Security, where people contribute resources in earlier life anticipating later need, could over time evolve. Actuaries will sharpen their pencils, needing to ensure that contributions will in fact cover future costs. Nevertheless, the public clamor for a solution to this problem can only grow with the increasing need.

If sustainable financing mechanisms are ultimately developed, that will be the springboard for further professionalizing and bolstering the PAS workforce. Paying living wages and meeting protections of the Fair Labor Standards Act are minimal requirements, but this change could also catalyze broader opportunities. Establishing certification and training standards for PAs would advance skill development and build ladders for advancement. Creating registries or other ways for consumers and PAs to find each other and make workable matches would benefit both. Developing systems to protect PAs in situations such as natural disasters or the COVID-19 pandemic (e.g., distribution channels for personal protective equipment, testing as appropriate, additional training) would enhance safety for consumers and PAs. Finally, whatever systems are instituted will need to respect the goals and preferences of each worker. People become PAs for different reasons; these diverse motivations have consequences for the training and supports they would value.

Second, people with severe disability—like Fred and Michael—are often intensely practical people. They live in environments that were not necessarily designed for them, and they figure things out. Technologies assist that process in numerous ways, such as Michael's tablet computer that he programmed to operate functions throughout his home and his ceiling-mounted lift. Although technologies are unlikely to replace human assistance in the most intimate tasks, like toileting and bathing, innovation could make many activities easier for both consumers and PAs. The efficiency of performing basic tasks might therefore improve, reducing the hours required for PAs to assist consumers.

Finally, failing to assist millions of people needing ADL supports to continue living in their homes will lead, inevitably, to human suffering. It will also prevent people like Fred, who could contribute to his community, from adding to the common good. Over the last half-century, the broad sweep of disability-related policy changes, big and small—such as deinstitutionalization, civil rights protections for people with disability, and trends toward consumer direction of PAS—have pushed forward efforts that improve quality of life for people with disability.

This goal is not explicit. The language laying out these policies and regulations avoids phrases like "improving quality of life." Nonetheless, this intent is clear in other language choices. Echoing our nation's founding documents, permutations of the word *independence* appear in critical laws and regulations, as do concepts reprising "life, liberty, and the pursuit of happiness." For example, the opening of the ADA, Section 12101(a)(1), states, "physical or mental disabilities in no way diminish a person's right to fully participate in all aspects of society." Several points later, Section 12101(a)(7) observes, "the Nation's proper goals regarding individuals with disabilities are to assure equality of opportunity, full participation, independent living, and economic self-sufficiency for such individuals." For people like Fred, paid PAS is essential to making this happen.

COVID-19 Postscript from Fred

On December 12, 2020, Fred emailed me. He wrote that COVID-19 had upended his thinking and might scuttle his life's plans, at least in the short term. At the time, about 3,000 Americans were dying daily from COVID-19, and finding people to provide his PAS was even more difficult than before. For the first time ever, circumstances forced Fred to consider the unthinkable—that he might need to enter a nursing home. With his usual levity, Fred assured me he had no intention of doing so, but fear broke through his brave words. If he could not find community-based PAS, Fred might have to attend graduate school from a nursing home. He would have no choice.

Epilogue

In the last week of February 2020, the U.S. Centers for Disease Control and Prevention announced the first known U.S. case of community spread of the novel coronavirus—a person in California with no relevant travel history.[1] At the time, the United States had 15 total documented COVID-19 cases. But, of course, by that point, the virus had already established invisible beachheads on the East and West Coasts and was off to the races. As the pandemic emerged into public view in the United States, Michael and I tracked its spread with alarm. Because of our disabilities and older ages, we knew the virus posed lethal threats to us. I could easily lock down at home, secure from exposure. However, with his essential contingent of home health aides—HHAs, their New Jersey professional title—circulating into and out of his home from their own homes and communities, Michael faced substantial risks. An HHA could bring the novel coronavirus to his bedside.

Michael and I discussed this situation with our usual combination of candor, reality, and practicality. I had been Michael's health care proxy since 2010, when I saw him through surgery for a stage 4 pressure injury.[2] Over subsequent years, I tracked him in and out of the hospital multiple times, most notably for major cancer surgery in 2015 (he remains cancer-free).[3] In between and since 2015, I've sat at Michael's hospital bedside multiple times and have worn a path between Philadelphia's Thirtieth Street Station, where Amtrak deposits passengers, and the Hospital of the University of Pennsylvania. We have talked openly and honestly about death and his preferences for care, since I am the one whom doctors will turn to if he cannot express his own wishes. Michael had so many near misses across the decade that he feels—embracing the cat metaphor—that he is counting down his allotment of nine lives. We agreed that, if he contracted COVID-19, he would likely die. So Michael needed to figure out how to stay safe while receiving 18 hours of PAS daily—15 hours from five self-directed HHAs who provided his tube feeds and other supports and three overlapping hours every morning from a commercial franchise agency HHA, to help with showering and getting Michael set for the day.

In those early weeks, public health messages about preventing the pandemic's spread were confusing and some eventually proved false. For instance, U.S. officials initially urged Americans to eschew masks. They ultimately reversed that advice but left a contrail of confusion and resistance. However, in four of his five self-directed HHAs (Nickie, Shelly, Tasonia, and Nelita)—each with primary jobs in health-related fields—Michael had reasonably well-informed allies in fortifying him against COVID-19. The pandemic hit New Jersey hard in early March, closing its schools and economy by mid-March, and requiring those workers who could to shelter at home. As essential workers, however, HHAs didn't have the luxury of staying home. For his four HHAs who also have health-related primary jobs, those workplaces provided training about the novel coronavirus, preventing its spread, and some PPE.

Nickie trained as a phlebotomist, and her primary job is with a commercial, nationwide diagnostic testing laboratory. When New Jersey shut down, the commercial laboratory cut Nickie's work hours. Nevertheless, while she was at the lab, the company gave Nickie the gold standard N95 mask, a plastic face shield, gowns, gloves, and training about safely putting on and off this PPE—PPE that even doctors and nurses at many hospitals lacked.

Michael had always provided nonlatex gloves for HHAs to use while performing his PAS. By early March, Nickie took it on herself to ensure that HHAs who entered Michael's home also followed additional coronavirus safety precautions, including wearing paper or cloth masks (she would reuse her N95 mask). Nickie convinced the franchise agency HHAs to wear masks, which they had to buy themselves. Michael underscored the need for HHAs to take their temperatures daily before coming, stay away if they had any symptoms suggestive of COVID-19, and reduce their community exposures if they could (challenging, since some have school-age or young adult children or live in multigenerational households). Despite repeated efforts, however, Nickie could never convince Michael's fifth self-directed HHA—whom I'll call "P"—to wear a mask.

We can never be 100% sure that P gave Michael COVID-19, but the circumstantial evidence is strong. Since his other four self-directed HHAs have primary jobs, largely during weekday business hours, P provided most of

Michael's daytime PAS Mondays through Fridays. She was unreliable, however, sometimes absent without warning, leaving Michael stranded for hours without support. P had a chaotic family life and understandable competing priorities, with teenage and young adult children whose serious troubles demanded P's immediate presence at a moment's notice. Nonetheless, P's erratic communication often left Michael unsure whether he would have PAS on some days.

I called Michael immediately after getting his morning text on Wednesday, April 15. P's teenage daughter had texted Michael around 1:00 A.M. that her mother would not be coming that day; P had just gone to the emergency room. Michael told me that P had worked for him about 10 hours on Tuesday, April 14, not wearing a mask and performing routine tasks—such as turning him in bed—in close physical proximity. Over the ensuing several days, P's health situation remained confusing, communication sporadic. Sometime that weekend, Michael heard that P was hospitalized with pneumonia and the following Monday that she tested positive for COVID-19. During her final telephone call with Michael some weeks later, P denied the COVID-19 diagnosis. By that point, it no longer mattered—Michael had let P go.

Over the weekend, my FaceTime calls found Michael either asleep or exhausted—barely able to keep his eyes open. His morning temperature, which his HHAs had taken daily for several weeks and had been solidly normal, was up slightly. Our conversations were short, as he nodded off midsentence. Nelita had a full workload with a local home care agency and spent only two to three hours weekly with Michael, providing his Sunday evening feed—keeping their long-term relationship going and giving his other HHAs welcome time off. Nelita told me later that Michael's appearance worried her that Sunday night. He did not look well.

COVID-19

At 9:00 A.M., Monday, April 20, 2020, Tasonia called, sounding concerned: Michael's morning temperature was 101.8°. He was neither coughing nor short of breath, but he looked sick. I remember my brain going blank for a moment, not wanting to fully absorb this news. Then it kicked into its Michael-serious-health-crisis mode—I had work to do.

I contacted Michael's primary care physician, a young doctor who provides extraordinary care with inexhaustible empathy. We spoke briefly, I told her about P, and we agreed that Michael's fever and exhaustion were presumptive early signs of COVID-19. The question then became Michael's preferences for care. I told her what I believed Michael would wish, but she appropriately wanted to hear directly from him. During the pandemic, face-to-face group communication migrated to Zoom videoconferencing; I scheduled a Zoom meeting for Michael, his primary care physician, and me for 11:00 A.M.

Before our Zoom meeting, I called Michael to confirm I understood his wishes correctly in the context of COVID-19. Michael has long been "DNR"—"do not resuscitate"—status, indicating that if his heart or breathing stops, he does not want emergency steps to save his life; he wants to be allowed to die. Severe COVID-19 damages the lungs, progressing sometimes to respiratory distress necessitating mechanical ventilation. By April, hospitals had begun reporting discouragingly high death rates among COVID-19 patients placed on ventilators. Michael and I had talked this over and agreed that his chances of surviving mechanical ventilation with COVID-19 were slim. In addition to DNR status, Michael therefore desired "DNI"—"do not intubate"—status, no mechanical ventilation. Michael also confirmed my final expectation: he did not want hospital admission for any reason, even supportive care. Pre-COVID-19, hospitals—including the very best—did not have staffing, equipment, or knowledge to care comfortably and safely for people with Michael's level of disability. With COVID-19 stretching local hospitals nearly to the breaking point, Michael stated, "I would certainly die if I went to the hospital. I want to stay home, no matter what."

During our Zoom call, Michael's physician probed for other symptoms and watched him breathe, counting his respiratory rate. She then explored his preferences for care, pushing to see his boundaries. For example, with fever he could benefit from intravenous fluids for hydration; he could be closely monitored for bacterial infections, which antibiotics might treat; methods short of ventilators, such as CPAP (continuous positive airway pressure, often used in sleep apnea), might help with lung problems. But Michael never wavered in wanting to remain home. Understanding that, over subsequent weeks, Michael's physician did everything she could to respect his wishes. First off, she arranged for a home care nurse, outfitted in full PPE regalia, including a powered air-purifying respirator, to visit Michael that afternoon to swab his nose and throat for coronavirus. (The test came back positive on Wednesday.)

Sending Michael to the hospital would have been easy. From that point forward, the hospital would bear all responsibility for his care. Michael's wish to stay home seemed simple, rational, and justifiable. Making it happen, however, was hard. Finding home-based PAS supports is difficult in the best of times. In a pandemic, supports melt away.

Home-Based PAS with COVID-19

Tuesday morning, I began in earnest, from my 250-mile distance, to inventory what was needed to keep Michael home. The franchise agency pulled its HHAs, who had helped with his morning ADLs: their policy prohibited staff from working in homes with COVID-19 patients. Michael's Medicaid managed LTSS program had implemented an emergency provision during the pandemic, giving COVID-19 patients 10 hours daily of in-home private duty nursing. His case manager contacted a half-dozen local home care agencies and failed to find any nurse willing to cover a COVID-19 patient. Michael's few local family members did not step forward, for various reasons. After consulting with Michael, I told Nelita she should stay away for the time being: with her age and other personal factors, COVID-19 posed too many risks to her health. After thinking it over, she agreed and stopped her Sunday evening hours.

Before COVID-19, Michael had been alone from 10:00 P.M. to 7:00 A.M.—he had weighed the risks and felt comfortable with his trade-off, the dignity of risk (see Chapter 14). With COVID-19, however, he clearly needed someone with him 24/7. But there were only three HHAs left—Nickie, Tasonia, and Shelly—and they all had other primary jobs. Because of the pandemic, these jobs had cut work hours somewhat, but not entirely. Covering Michael round-the-clock would require stitching together their remaining free hours, recognizing they needed some time to sleep. Nickie took the lead in putting these puzzle pieces in place, 24/7. As she told me later, "I had to do whatever it took for us to get through with Michael."

Things did not start well. Sisters of one of the other HHAs worried she was putting her life at risk caring for someone who was not family and pressured her to quit. These arguments were reasonable—she *was* putting her life at risk. Nevertheless, patching together coverage for Michael required that third person. Under her sisters' exhortations, she missed one shift. But Nickie talked with her, convincing her to return—which she did, with the same level of commitment and willingness to do whatever was needed to keep Michael home.

Michael had a benefactor—known to us but wanting her identity kept anonymous—who a day after his COVID-19 diagnosis dropped off two cartons of N95 masks, 10 masks per carton. N95 masks were scarce, and health care providers nationwide had likely died lacking this critical protection. These N95 masks were game changers for protecting Michael's HHAs. Nickie had her plastic face shield from work, and the others fashioned eye protection of some sort; all had the gloves Michael provided; and they established routines for hand cleaning, wiping surfaces, and maintaining hygiene. At the end of her shift, each woman removed her clothes, showered in Michael's guest bathroom, and donned clean clothes, never taking home potentially contaminated garments. One HHA followed the other, covering Michael round the clock, day after day.

During those weeks with COVID-19, Michael became very sick. He asked me to stay on FaceTime with him for hours, to be there as he struggled to breathe. COVID-19 delirium disoriented and entangled his mind—sometimes he couldn't tell day from night. For so many people during COVID-19, smartphones became lifelines of communication with patients, allowing us to be present while miles apart. Although Michael had chosen DNR and DNI status, he didn't want to die. He was scared—repeatedly pleading with me, through his delirium, to reassure him he would live—and I kept telling him to breathe in and breathe out, so that he would. We had arranged for an oxygen concentrator machine to be delivered; it was fortunately in place when his pulse oximeter showed dangerously low oxygen levels, remedied by breathing the essential gas through nasal prongs. We had also ensured he had liquid morphine with a dropper, in case he had trouble breathing and grew terrified from air hunger.

Although his breathing was arduous, Michael kept pushing, complaining how horrible he felt—the worst illness he had ever had—as I watched on FaceTime, hour after hour. I saw Michael wretchedly and repeatedly vomit up his feed and his HHAs wipe and clean away the sticky, pale-yellow mess. COVID-19 delirium gave him terrors, vivid dreams of violent threats, set in exotic locations and populated by swarms of vicious villains, intent on harm. By 10:00 P.M., I was usually exhausted, and I would tell Michael's evening HHA that I was signing off, that she knew where to reach me. Several nights, I was certain the 2:00 or 3:00 A.M. call would come. I did not think Michael would live through the night—but he did.

Heroes Work Here

Michael turned the corner on Saturday, May 2, when—during a 6:20 A.M. call—he told me he planned to survive. COVID-19 delirium still commandeered his mind and speech; he remained dehydrated and needed supplemental oxygen. But, seen over FaceTime, Michael's face glowed, suffused by a wide smile. I heard birds chirping outside his window, and Michael proudly announced that a crimson male cardinal bird had just swooped by. A little while later, Michael again appeared ill and exhausted. Nevertheless, the seed of life was planted, and he seemed determined to nurture it. Over ensuing days, his mental fog lifted gradually. On Friday, May 8, a home care nurse administered another coronavirus test; this test was negative. Michael has recovered completely from COVID-19.

During Michael's illness, I was in touch daily with his HHAs, by text or telephone call, checking in, making sure coverage was in place. I repeatedly was astonished by the women's generosity and professionalism, their dedication

July 21, 2020, Michael, with the three HHAs who saved his life from COVID-19—left to right, Nickie, Shelly, and Tasonia. His friend Debbie had made the sign, planting the second copy in his front yard. His franchise PAS agency staff had made him his T-shirt, which says, "I SURVIVED COVID-19." (Photo credit: Paul Connelly)

to his care. One evening, I told Nickie that her words made me want to cry, and she replied sharply, "No tears! No tears here." I immediately shook myself into shape.

Nickie told me during those weeks that she was sure Michael would live—they just needed to do their jobs. Since then, Michael tells me that his HHAs have confided to him that they had not expected him to live. He was so sick, they thought he would die—nevertheless, they just needed to do their jobs.

Early in his illness, Michael told me that he viewed his HHAs as heroes—they were keeping him alive. At the time, residents in cities with surging COVID-19 infections applauded nightly as evening nursing shifts changed, giving communal shout-outs to those essential workers treating patients and putting their own lives at risk. Signs and banners began festooning hospitals with the message "Heroes work here." I mentioned this to Michael's friend Debbie, and she had two signs made lauding Michael's HHAs and Michael. Debbie planted one in Michael's front yard and gave the other to his HHAs to keep indoors for him to see.

Nickie, Tasonia, and Shelly allowed Michael to remain at home, keeping him out of the hospital where he would likely have died. He views their services as acts of "outstanding bravery and professionalism—they let me stay at home and saved my life." That service will be a forever bond linking Michael with Nickie, Tasonia, and Shelly.

Notes

CHAPTER 1

1. Henry J. Kaiser Family Foundation. Update on the public's views of nursing homes and long-term care services. Toplines. Henry J. Kaiser Family Foundation; 2007:3. https://www.kff.org/wp-content/uploads/2013/01/7719.pdf

2. SCAN Foundation. Who provides long-term care in the U.S.? (Updated). SCAN Foundation; October 2013:1. https://www.thescanfoundation.org/sites/default/files/us_who_provides_ltc_us_oct_12_fsrevised-10-10-13.pdf

3. National Academies of Sciences, Engineering and Medicine. *Families Caring for an Aging America*. National Academies Press; 2016:21. doi:10.17226/23606.

4. AARP and National Alliance for Family Caregiving. *Caregiving in the United States 2020*. AARP; 2020:4. doi:10.26419/ppi.00103.001.

5. Ibid., 10.

6. Ibid., 16.

7. Ibid., 6.

8. Ibid., 20.

9. Ibid., 50.

10. Ibid., 52.

11. Ibid., 53.

12. Ibid., 57.

13. Kaye HS, Chapman S, Newcomer RJ, Harrington C. The personal assistance workforce: Trends in supply and demand. *Health Aff (Millwood)*. 2006; 25(4):1113–1120. doi:10.1377/hlthaff.25.4.1113.

14. Scales K. It's time to care: A detailed profile of America's direct care workforce. PHI, 2020:4. https://phinational.org/resource/its-time-to-care-a-detailed-profile-of-americas-direct-care-workforce/0

15. National Academies of Sciences, Engineering and Medicine, *Families Caring*, 2.

16. Division of Occupational Employment Statistics, U.S. Bureau of Labor Statistics. May 2008 to May 2018 National Industry-Specific Occupational Employment and Wage Estimates. OES; July 2, 2019. Accessed February 4, 2020. https://www.bls.gov/oes/current/oessrci.htm

17. PHI. The direct care workforce: Year in review (2018). PHI; 2018:2–3. https://phinational.org/resource/the-direct-care-workforce-year-in-review-2018/

18. AARP and National Alliance for Caregiving, *Caregiving in the United States 2020*, 44.

19. U.S. Bureau of Labor Statistics, May 2008 to May 2018.

20. PHI, Direct care workforce, 3.

21. U.S. Bureau of Labor Statistics, U.S. Department of Labor. *Home Health Aides and Personal Care Aides*. Occupational Outlook Handbook. Updated September 2019. Accessed February 3, 2020. https://www.bls.gov/ooh/healthcare/home-health-aides-and-personal-care-aides.htm

22. U.S. Bureau of Labor Statistics, U.S. Department of Labor. *Most New Jobs*. Occupational Outlook Handbook. Updated September 2019. Accessed February 3, 2020. https://www.bls.gov/ooh/most-new-jobs.htm

23. Institute of Medicine (US) Committee on the Future Health Care Workforce for Older Americans. *Retooling for an Aging America: Building the Health Care Workforce*. National Academies Press; 2008.

24. Espinoza R. 8 signs the shortage in paid caregivers is getting worse. PHI; 2017:2. https://phinational.org/wp-content/uploads/2017/11/workforce-shortages-phi60issues01.pdf

25. Spetz J, Trupin L, Bates T, Coffman J. *How Will Long-Term Care Workforce Demand Be Impacted by Changes in Demographics and Utilization Patterns?* University of California–San Francisco; 2015.

26. Espinoza, 8 Signs, 3.

27. PHI. Direct care workers in the United States: Key facts. September 8, 2020. https://phinational.org/resource/direct-care-workers-in-the-united-states-key-facts/

28. Institute of Medicine, *Retooling*, 209.

29. Hondagneu-Sotelo P. Families on the frontier: From braceros in the fields to braceras in the home. In: Suarez-Orozco M, Paez M, eds. *Latinos: Remaking America*. Psychology Press; 2009: Chapter 12.

30. Institute of Medicine, *Retooling*, 4.

31. Iezzoni LI. *When Walking Fails: Mobility Problems of Adults with Chronic Conditions*. University of California Press; 2003:270.

32. Institute of Medicine, *Retooling*, 4.

33. Espinoza R. *Would You Stay? Rethinking Direct Care Job Quality*. PHI; 2020:2.

34. Institute of Medicine, *Retooling*, 201–203.

CHAPTER 2

1. Carr C. Oral history conducted by Fred Pelka in 2001. In: *Massachusetts Activists and Leaders in the Disability Rights and Independent Living Movement*. Vol. 1, *Regional Oral History Office*. Bancroft Library, University of California–Berkeley; 2004.

2. Dreier P. Redlining cities: How banks color community development. *Challenge*. 1991;34(6):15–23. doi:10.1080/05775132.1991.11471545.

3. Occupational Safety and Health Administration, U.S. Department of Labor. *Home Healthcare*. Accessed February 7, 2020. https://www.osha.gov/SLTC/home_health care/index.html

4. Nielsen KE. *A Disability History of the United States*. Beacon Free Press; 2012:6.

5. Ibid., 11.

6. Steckel RH, Rose JC, eds. *The Backbone of History: Health and Nutrition in the Western Hemisphere*. Cambridge University Press; 2002.

7. Shapiro JP. *No Pity: People with Disabilities Forging a New Civil Rights Movement*. Times Books; 1993.

8. Nielsen, *Disability History*, 27.

9. Baynton DC. Disability and the justification of inequality in American history. In: Longmore PK, Umansky L, eds. *The New Disability History: American Perspectives*. New York University; 2001:35–57.

10. Nielsen, *Disability History*, 21.

11. Ibid., 26.

12. Katz M. *In the Shadow of the Poorhouse: A Social History of Welfare in America*. Basic Books; 1996.

13. Braddock DL, Parish S. An institutional history of disability. In: Albrecht G, Seelman K, Bury M, eds. *Handbook of Disability Studies*. Sage Publications; 2001:31.

14. Jefferson T. Notes on the state of Virginia. In: *Thomas Jefferson: Writings*. Library of America; 1984:259.

15. Buhler-Wilkerson K. *No Place Like Home: A History of Nursing and Home Care in the United States*. John Hopkins University Press; 2001.

16. Foundation Aiding the Elderly. The history of nursing homes. Foundation Aiding the Elderly. Accessed May 17, 2021. http://www.4fate.org/history.pdf.

17. Ibid.

18. Katz, *Shadow of the Poorhouse*, 19.

19. Trattner WI. *From Poor Law to Welfare State: The History of Social Welfare in America*. 6th ed. Free Press; 1999:59.

20. Nielsen, *Disability History*, 42.

21. Baynton, *Disability*, 35–37.

22. Nielsen, *Disability History*, 57.

23. Nielsen, *Disability History*.

24. Ibid., 45.

25. Ibid., 63.

26. Ibid.

27. Stone D. *The Disabled State*. Temple University Press; 1984.

28. Braddock, Institutional history, 31.

29. Linton S. *Claiming Disability: Knowledge and Identity*. New York University Press; 1998.

30. Katz, *Shadow of the Poorhouse*, 11.

31. Ibid., 11–12.

32. Nielsen, *Disability History*, 67.

33. Ibid., 67–68.

34. Ibid., 71.

35. Ibid.

36. Ibid.

37. Pelka F. *The ABC-CLIO Companion to the Disability Rights Movement*. ABC-CLIO, Inc, 1997:106–108.

38. Ibid., 107.

39. Ibid., 108.

40. Braddock, Institutional history, 38.

41. Katz, *Shadow of the Poorhouse*, 188.

42. National Council on Disability. Rocking the cradle: Ensuring the rights of parents with disabilities and their children. National Council on Disability; 2012. https://www.ncd.gov/sites/default/files/Documents/NCD_Parenting_508_0.pdf

43. Nielsen, *Disability History*, 117.

44. Koyanagi C. Learning from history: Deinstitutionalization of people with mental illness as a precursor to long-term care reform. Henry J. Kaiser Family Foundation; 2007:1. https://www.kff.org/wp-content/uploads/2013/01/7684.pdf

45. Shapiro, *No Pity*, 241.

46. Pappas Rehabilitation Hospital for Children. *About: History*. Accessed October 20, 2019. http://www.prhc.us/about/

47. Linton, *Claiming Disability*.

48. Litvak S, Enders A. Support systems: The interface between individuals and environments. In: Albrecht G, Seelman K, Bury M, eds. *Handbook of Disability Studies*. Sage Publications; 2001:711–733.

49. Litvak and Enders, *Support Systems*, 715.

50. Olkin R. *What Psychotherapists Should Know About Disability*. Guildford Press; 1999:26.

51. Oliver M. *Understanding Disability: From Theory to Practice*. St. Martin's Press; 1996:22.

52. Pelka, *ABC-CLIO Companion*, 266–267.

53. Ibid., 266.

54. Ibid.

55. Ibid.

56. Ibid.

57. Ibid.

58. Ibid.

59. Ibid., 267.

60. Ibid.

61. Ibid., 262.

62. Ibid.

63. Shapiro, *No Pity*, 65.

64. Pelka, *ABC-CLIO Companion*, 120.

65. Shapiro, *No Pity*.

66. 29 U.S.C. 705 and 706; 42 U.S.C. 12101, 12102, 12103, 12111, 12112, 12113, 12114, 12201, 12205a, 12206-12211, 12210, 12211, 12212 and 12213 (2008).

67. Ibid.

68. Musumeci M, Claypool H. Olmstead's role in community integration for people with disabilities under Medicaid 15 years after the Supreme Court's Olmstead decision. Henry J. Kaiser Family Foundation; 2014:2. http://files.kff.org/attachment/issue-brief -olmsteads-role-in-community-integration-for-people-with-disabilities-under-medic aid-15-years-after-the-supreme-courts-olmstead-decision

69. Rosenbaum S. The Olmstead decision: Implications for state health policy. *Health Aff (Millwood)*. 2000;19(5):228–232. doi:10.1377/hlthaff.19.5.228.

70. Olmstead, Commissioner, Georgia Department of Human Resources, et al. v L.C. 527 U.S. 581 (1999).

CHAPTER 3

1. Carr C. Oral history conducted by Fred Pelka in 2001. In: *Massachusetts Activists and Leaders in the Disability Rights and Independent Living Movement.* Vol. 1, *Regional Oral History Office.* Bancroft Library, University of California–Berkeley; 2004.

2. Ujvari K. Disrupting the marketplace: The state of private long-term care insurance, 2018 Update. AARP Public Policy Institute; 2018. https://www.aarp.org/content /dam/aarp/ppi/2018/08/disrupting-the-marketplace-the-state-of-private-long-term -care-insurance.pdf

3. Hado E, Komisar H. Long-term services and supports. Fact Sheet. AARP Public Policy Institute; 2018: 2. https://www.aarp.org/content/dam/aarp/ppi/2019/08/long -term-services-and-supports.doi.10.26419-2Fppi.00079.001.pdf

4. Ujvari, Disrupting the marketplace.

5. Robison J, Shugrue N, Fortinsky RH, Gruman C. Long-term supports and services planning for the future: Implications from a statewide survey of baby boomers and older adults. *Gerontologist.* 2014; 54(2):304. doi:10.1093/geront/gnt094.

6. Hado and Komisar, Long-term services, 3.

7. Eiken S, Sredl K, Burwell B, Amos A. Medicaid expenditures for long-term services and supports in FY 2016. Medicaid Innovation Accelerator Program; 2018:6. https://www.medicaid.gov/sites/default/files/2019-12/ltssexpenditures2016.pdf

8. Fox-Grage W. Medicaid: A last resort for people needing long-term services and supports. AARP Public Policy Institute; 2017. https://www.aarp.org/content/dam/aarp /ppi/2017-01/Medicaid-A-Last-Resort-for-People-Needing-Long-Term-Services-and -Supports.pdf

9. Martin P, Weaver D. Social Security: A program and policy history. *Soc Secur Bull.* 2005;66(1):1–15.

10. Ibid., 2.

11. Ibid.

12. Foundation Aiding the Elderly. The history of nursing homes. Foundation Aiding the Elderly. Accessed June 12, 2021. http://www.4fate.org/history.pdf

13. Reno VP, Grad S. Economic security 1935–85. *Soc Secur Bull.* 1985;48(12):5–20.

14. Henry J. Kaiser Family Foundation. Long term care in the United States: A timeline. Henry J. Kaiser Family Foundation; 2015. https://www.kff.org/wp-content /uploads/2015/08/8773-long-term-care-in-the-united-states-a-timeline1.pdf

15. Bernstein J, Stevens RA. Public opinion, knowledge, and Medicare reform. *Health Aff (Millwood).* 1999;18(1):180–193. doi:10.1377/hlthaff.18.1.180.

16. Cubanski J, Neuman T, Damico A. Medicare's role for people under age 65 with disabilities. Henry J. Kaiser Family Foundation; 2016. http://files.kff.org/attach ment/issue-brief-Medicares-Role-for-People-Under-Age-65-with-Disabilities

17. Centers for Medicare & Medicaid Services. NHE fact sheet. Accessed November 5, 2019. https://www.cms.gov/research-statistics-data-and-systems/statistics-trends -and-reports/nationalhealthexpenddata/nhe-fact-sheet.html

18. Centers for Medicare & Medicaid Services. CMS fast facts. Centers for Medicare & Medicaid Services; 2019. https://www.cms.gov/Research-Statistics-Data-and -Systems/Statistics-Trends-and-Reports/CMS-Fast-Facts/index.html

19. Marmor T. *The Politics of Medicare.* 2nd ed. Aldine de Gruyter; 2000: 6.

20. Lyndon B. Johnson: Remarks with President Truman at the Signing in Independence of the Medicare Bill, July 30, 1965. LBJ Presidential Library; June 6, 2007. Accessed May 6, 2018.http://www.lbjlibrary.net/collections/selected-speeches/1965/07 -30-1965.html

21. 42 U.S.C. 1395y.

22. Fox D. *Power and Illness. The Failure and Future of American Health Policy.* University of California Press; 1993:74–75.

23. 42 C.F.R. Ch. IV Section 409.45.

24. Newcomer R, Harrington C, Friedlob A. Social health maintenance organizations: Assessing their initial experience. *Health Serv Res.* 1990;25(3):425–454.

25. Jacobson G, Casillas G, Damico A, Neuman T, Gold M. Medicare advantage 2016 spotlight: Enrollment market update. Henry J. Kaiser Family Foundation; 2016. http://files.kff.org/attachment/Issue-Brief-Medicare-Advantage-2016-Spotlight -Enrollment-Market-Update

26. Sung J, Noel-Miller, C. Supplemental benefits in Medicare Advantage: Recent public policy changes and what they mean for consumers. AARP Public Policy Institute; 2019. https://www.aarp.org/content/dam/aarp/ppi/2019/07/medicare-supplement -series-two.doi.10.26419-2Fppi.00075.002.pdf

27. Ibid., 3.

28. Tanenbaum S. Medicaid and disability: The unlikely entitlement. *Milbank Q* 1989; 67(Suppl 2 Pt 2): 288–310.

29. Thompson FJ, Cantor JC, Farnham J. Medicaid Long-Term Care: State variation and the intergovernmental lobby. *J Health Polit Policy Law.* 2016;41(4):763– 780.

30. Thach NT, Wiener JM. An overview of long-term services and supports and Medicaid: Final report. Department of Health and Human Services, Office of Disability, Aging, and Long-Term Care Policy; 2018: 4. https://aspe.hhs.gov/system/files /pdf/259521/LTSSMedicaid.pdf

31. Ibid.

32. Centers for Medicare & Medicaid Services, CMS fast facts.

33. Centers for Medicare & Medicaid Services, NHE fact sheet.

34. Ibid.

35. Kaiser Family Foundation. Status of state Medicaid expansion decisions: Interactive map. November 2, 2020. https://www.kff.org/medicaid/issue-brief/status-of -state-medicaid-expansion-decisions-interactive-map/

36. Starr P. *The Social Transformation of American Medicine*. Basic Books, Inc; 1982:370.

37. Paradise J, Lyons B, Rowland D. Medicaid at 50. Henry J. Kaiser Family Foundation; 2015. http://files.kff.org/attachment/report-medicaid-at-50

38. Tanenbaum, Medicaid and disability, 303.

39. Paradise, Lyons, and Rowland, Medicaid at 50, 2.

40. O'Keeffe J, Saucier P, Jackson B, Cooper R, McKenney E, Crisp S, Moseley C. Understanding Medicaid home and community services: A primer. Department of Health and Human Services, Office of the Assistant Secretary for Planning and Evaluation; 2010. https://aspe.hhs.gov/system/files/pdf/76201/primer10.pdf

41. Ibid., 25.

42. Ibid.

43. Centers for Medicare & Medicaid Services. Community First Choice (CFC) state plan option technical guide. Centers for Medicare & Medicaid Services; 2012:12. https://www.medicaid.gov/sites/default/files/2019-12/cfc-technical-guide_0.pdf

44. Thach and Wiener, Overview, 15.

45. Ibid.

46. Crisp S, Doty P, Flanagan S, Smith G. Developing and implementing self-direction programs and policies: A handbook. Robert Wood Johnson Foundation and National Resource Center for Participant-Directed Services; 2009. https://www.bc .edu/content/dam/files/schools/gssw_sites/nrcpds/cc-full.pdf

47. Ibid.

48. Ibid., 1–7.

49. Ibid., 1–6.

50. Pelka F. *The ABC-CLIO Companion to the Disability Rights Movement*. ABC-CLIO, Inc; 1997:46.

51. O'Keeffe et al., Understanding Medicaid home and community services, 26.

CHAPTER 4

1. Martin D. Evelyn Coke, home care aide who fought pay rule, is dead at 74. *New York Times*. August 9, 2009. Accessed November 14, 2019. https://www.nytimes.com /2009/08/10/nyregion/10coke.html

2. Ibid.

3. Iezzoni LI, Gallopyn N, Scales K. Historical mismatch between home-based care policies and laws governing home care workers. *Health Aff (Millwood)*. 2019;38(6):973–980. doi:10.1377/hlthaff.2018.05494.

4. U.S. Department of Labor Bureau of Labor Statistics. Table 1.7. Occupational projections, 2018–2028, and worker characteristics, 2018. Accessed November 24, 2019. https://www.bls.gov/emp/tables/occupational-projections-and-characteristics.htm

5. Iezzoni et al., Historical mismatch.

6. Boris E, Klein J. Caring for America: Home health workers in the shadow of the welfare state. Oxford Scholarship Online; 2012:8. https://oxford.universitypressschol arship.com/view/10.1093/acprof:oso/9780195329117.001.0001/acprof-9780195329117

7. Ibid., 11.

8. Ibid., 19.

9. Ibid., 23.

10. Ibid.

11. Ibid., 25.

12. Grossman J. Fair Labor Standards Act of 1938: Maximum struggle for a minimum wage. U.S. Department of Labor; 1978. Accessed April 5, 2020. https://www.dol.gov/general/aboutdol/history/flsa1938.

13. Ibid.

14. Ibid.

15. Goldberg H. The long journey home: The contested exclusion and inclusion of domestic workers from federal wage and hour protections in the United States. International Labour Office; 2015. http://www.ilo.org/wcmsp5/groups/public/---ed_protect/---protrav/---travail/documents/publication/wcms_396235.pdf

16. Katznelson I. *When Affirmative Action Was White: An Untold History of Racial Inequality in Twentieth-Century America.* W. W. Norton & Co; 2005:22.

17. Ibid., 27.

18. Goldberg, Long journey home, 7.

19. Wage and Hour Division, U.S. Department of Labor. Private homes and domestic service employment under the Fair Labor Standards Act. Fact Sheet #79. U.S. Department of Labor; 2013. https://www.dol.gov/whd/regs/compliance/whdfs79.pdf

20. Ibid.

21. Goldberg, Long journey home.

22. Ibid.

23. Ibid.

24. 29 U.S.C. § 213(a)(15).

25. Goldberg, Long journey home, 15.

26. Ibid., 16.

27. Ibid., 17.

28. Martin, Evelyn Coke.

29. Ibid.

30. Ibid.

31. Marinucci C. Sen. Barack Obama on job with Alameda County home health worker. *SFGate.* August 9, 2007. Accessed April 24, 2018. https://www.sfgate.com/politics/article/Sen-Barack-Obama-on-job-with-Alameda-County-home-3049743.php

32. Ibid., 22.

33. Ibid.

34. Wage and Hour Division, U.S. Department of Labor. Companionship services under the Fair Labor Standards Act (FLSA). Fact Sheet #79A. U.S. Department of Labor; 2013. https://www.dol.gov/whd/regs/compliance/whdfs79a.pdf

35. Espinoza R. Remembering Evelyn Coke, 9 years after the Supreme Court's Coke decision. Accessed November 17, 2019. https://phinational.org/remembering-evelyn-coke-9-years-after-the-supreme-courts-coke-decision/

36. Ibid.

37. Harris v. Quinn, 573 U.S. 616 (2014). Accessed November 25, 2019. https://www.law.cornell.edu/supct/pdf/11-681.pdf

38. Crisp S, Doty P, Flanagan S, Smith G. Developing and implementing self-direction programs and policies: A handbook. Section 9. Robert Wood Johnson Foundation and National Resource Center for Participant-Directed Services; 2010:4. https://www.bc.edu/content/dam/files/schools/gssw_sites/nrcpds/cc-full.pdf

39. Ibid., 5.

40. Ibid., 6.

41. Reinhard SC. Consumer directed care and nurse practice acts. U.S. Department of Health and Human Services; 2001. https://aspe.hhs.gov/system/files/pdf/72896/nursprac.pdf

42. Ibid., 15.

43. Ibid., 16.

44. Reinhard S, Accius J, Houser A, Ujvari K, Alexis J, Fox-Grage W. Picking up the pace of change. AARP Foundation, Commonwealth Fund, SCAN Foundation; 2017. http://www.longtermscorecard.org/~/media/Microsite/Files/2017/Web%20Version%20LongTerm%20Services%20and%20Supports%20State%20Scorecard%202017.pdf

45. Ibid., 29.

46. Zallman L, Finnegan KE, Himmelstein DU, Touw S, Woolhandler S. Care for America's elderly and disabled people relies on immigrant labor. *Health Aff (Millwood)*. 2019;38(6):919–926. doi:10.1377/hlthaff.2018.05514.

47. Stone RI. The migrant direct care workforce: An international perspective. *Generations*. 2016;40(1):99–105.

48. Spetz J, Stone RI, Chapman SA, Bryant N. Home and community-based workforce for patients with serious illness requires support to meet growing needs. *Health Aff (Millwood)*. 2019;38(6):902–909. doi:10.1377/hlthaff.2019.00021.

49. Zallman et al., Care for America's elderly and disabled.

50. Ibid., 924.

51. Ibid., 925.

52. Espinoza R. Immigrants and the direct care workforce. PHI; 2017. https://phinational.org/wp-content/uploads/2017/06/Immigrants-and-the-Direct-Care-Workforce-PHI-June-2017.pdf

53. Ibid.

54. Zallman et al., Care for America's elderly and disabled.

55. Espinoza, Immigrants, 9.

56. Parmet WE, Ryan E. New dangers for immigrants and the health care system. *Health Aff Blog*. October 20, 2018. Accessed November 24, 2019. https://www.healthaffairs.org/do/10.1377/hblog20180419.892713/full/

57. Ibid.

58. Department of Homeland Security. DHS secretary statement on the 2019 public charge rule. March 9, 2021. https://www.dhs.gov/news/2021/03/09/dhs-secretary-statement-2019-public-charge-rule

59. Stone, Migrant direct care workforce, 103.

CHAPTER 5

1. Üstün TB, Chatterji S, Kostansjek N, Bickenbach J. WHO's ICF and functional status information in health records. *Health Care Financing Rev.* 2003;24(3):77–82.

2. Institute of Medicine Committee on Disability in America, Board on Health Sciences Policy. Summary. In: Field M, Jette A, eds. *The Future of Disability in America*. National Academies Press; 2007:1.

3. World Health Organization. International classification of functioning, disability and health. World Health Organization; 2001. https://apps.who.int/iris/bitstream/handle/10665/42407/9241545429.pdf;jsessionid=06AC184A5091CAEA56A26FC05A445D12?sequence=1

4. Centers for Disease Control and Prevention. Disability and health related conditions. Last reviewed September 16, 2020. Accessed December 7, 2019. https://www.cdc.gov/ncbddd/disabilityandhealth/relatedconditions.html

5. Froehlich-Grobe K, Lee J, Washburn RA. Disparities in obesity and related conditions among Americans with disabilities. *Am J Prev Med*. 2013;45(1):83–90. doi:10.1016/j.amepre.2013.02.021.

6. Sturm R, Ringel JS, Andreyeva T. Increasing obesity rates and disability trends. *Health Aff (Millwood)*. 2004; 23(2):199–205. doi:10.1377/hlthaff.23.2.199.

7. Reichard A, Stolzle H, Fox MH. Health disparities among adults with physical disabilities or cognitive limitations compared to individuals with no disabilities in the United States. *Disabil Health J*. 2011;4(2):59–67. doi:10.1016/j.dhjo.2010.05.003.

8. Altman B, Bernstein A. Disability and health in the United States, 2001–2005. National Center for Health Statistics; 2008. https://www.cdc.gov/nchs/data/misc/disability2001-2005.pdf

9. Reichard et al., Health disparities.

10. Reinhard SC, Given B, Petlick NH, Bernis, A. Supporting family caregivers in providing care. In: Hughes RG, ed. *Patient Safety and Quality: An Evidence-Based Handbook for Nurses*. U.S. Agency for Healthcare Research and Quality; 2008.

11. Wage and Hour Division, U.S. Department of Labor. Need time? The employee's guide to the Family and Medical Leave Act (WH1513). U.S. Department of Labor; 2015. https://www.dol.gov/whd/fmla/employeeguide.pdf

12. Centers for Disease Control and Prevention, National Center on Birth Defects and Developmental Disabilities, Division of Human Development and Disability. 2018 behavioral risk factor surveillance system survey. Disability and Health Data System (DHDS) Data [online]. Accessed August 19, 2020. https://dhds.cdc.gov

13. Ibid.

14. Ogg, M. Remaining at home with severe disability. *Health Aff (Millwood)*. 2019;38(6):1046–1049. doi:10.1377/hlthaff.2018.05532.

15. Yi SH, See I, Kent AG, et al. Characterization of COVID-19 in assisted living facilities—39 states, October 2020. *MMWR*. 2020;69:1730.

CHAPTER 6

1. U.S. Department of Labor Bureau of Labor Statistics. Table 1.7. Occupational projections, 2018–2028, and worker characteristics, 2018. Accessed November 24, 2019. https://www.bls.gov/emp/tables/occupational-projections-and-characteristics.htm

2. Ibid.

3. PHI. U.S. home care workers: Key facts. PHI; 2019:5. https://phinational.org/resource/u-s-home care-workers-key-facts-2019/

4. Ibid., 6.

5. Ibid., 2.

6. Scales K. It's time to care: A detailed profile of America's direct care workforce. PHI, 2020:15. https://phinational.org/resource/its-time-to-care-a-detailed-profile-of-americas-direct-care-workforce/

7. Boris E, Klein J. Caring for America: Home health workers in the shadow of the welfare state. Oxford Scholarship Online; 2012:8. https://oxford.universitypressscholarship.com/view/10.1093/acprof:oso/9780195329117.001.0001/acprof-9780195329117

8. Boris E, Klein J. We were the invisible workforce: Unionizing home care. In: Cobble DS, ed. *The Sex of Class.* Cornell University Press; 2017:178.

9. Ibid.

10. Marquand A, Chapman SA. The national landscape of personal care aide training standards. U.S. Health Workforce Research Center on Long Term Care, University of California–San Francisco; 2014:9. https://healthworkforce.ucsf.edu/sites/healthworkforce.ucsf.edu/files/Report-The_National_Landscape_of_Personal_Care_Aide_Training_Standards.pdf

11. Ibid., 5.

12. Ibid., 8.

13. Scales, It's time to care, 7.

14. PHI, U.S. home care workers, 2.

15. Khatutsky G, Wiener J, Anderson W, Akhmerova V, Jessup A. Understanding direct care workers: A snapshot of two of America's most important jobs. Department of Health and Human Services, 2011:11. https://aspe.hhs.gov/system/files/pdf/76186/CNAchart.pdf

16. Ibid., 12.

17. PHI, U.S. home care workers, 5.

18. Espinoza R. 8 signs the shortage in paid caregivers is getting worse. PHI; 2017. https://phinational.org/wp-content/uploads/2017/11/workforce-shortages-phi60issues01.pdf

19. Espinoza R. *Would You Stay? Rethinking Direct Care Job Quality.* PHI; 2020.

20. Khatutsky et al., Understanding direct care workers, 44.

21. Ibid., 27.

22. Scales, It's time to care, 15.

23. Khatutsky et al., Understanding direct care workers, 16.

24. Ibid., 14.

25. Ibid., 38.

26. Ibid.

27. Skillman SM, Patterson DG, Coulthard C, Mroz TM. Access to rural home health services: Views from the field. Final Report #152. WWAMI Rural Health Research Center, University of Washington; 2016. https://depts.washington.edu/edic/rhrc/wp-content/uploads/sites/4/2016/02/RHRC_FR152_Skillman.pdf

28. Ibid., 13.

29. Ibid., 10.

30. Boris and Klein. We were the invisible workforce, 181.

31. Spetz J, Stone RI, Chapman SA, Bryant N. Home and community-based workforce for patients with serious illness requires support to meet growing needs. *Health Aff (Millwood).* 2019;38(6):902–909. doi:10.1377/hlthaff.2019.00021.

32. Ibid., 904.

33. Khatutsky et al., Understanding direct care workers, 43.
34. Ibid., 49.
35. Ibid.
36. Ibid., 52.
37. Ibid., 54.

CHAPTER 7

1. Espinoza R. Creating a strong direct support workforce. PHI; 2018:16. https://phinational.org/resource/creating-a-strong-direct-support-workforce-policy-barriers-and-opportunities/
2. O'Malley Watts M, Musumeci M. Medicaid home and community-based services: Results from a 50-state survey of enrollment, spending, and program policies. Henry J. Kaiser Family Foundation; 2018:15. http://files.kff.org/attachment/Report-Medicaid-Home-and-Community-Based-Services
3. Marquand A, Chapman SA. *The National Landscape of Personal Care Aide Training Standards.* University of California–San Francisco; 2014:7.
4. Sung J, Noel-Miller C. *Supplemental Benefits in Medicare Advantage: Recent Public Policy Changes and What They Mean for Consumers.* AARP Public Policy Institute; 2019.
5. Buhler-Wilkerson K. Care of the chronically ill at home: An unresolved dilemma in health policy for the United States. *Milbank Q.* 2007;85(4):611–639. doi:10.1111/j.1468-0009.2007.00503.x.
6. Murkofsky R, Alston K. The past, present, and future of skilled home health agency care. *Clin Geriatr Med.* 2009;25(1):1–17. doi:10.1016/j.cger.2008.11.006.
7. Buhler-Wilkerson, Care of the chronically ill, 625.
8. Ibid., 626.
9. Ibid., 627.
10. Murkofsky and Alston, Past, present, and future, 5.
11. Cabin W, Himmelstein DU, Siman ML, Woolhandler S. For-profit Medicare home health agencies' costs appear higher and quality appears lower compared to non-profit agencies. *Health Aff (Millwood).* 2014;33(8):1460–1465. doi:10.1377/hlthaff.2014.0307.
12. Buhler-Wilkerson, Care of the chronically ill, 628.
13. Ibid., 629.
14. Rural Health Research Center. Access to rural home health services: Views from the field. Rural Health Research & Policy Centers; 2016:2. https://depts.washington.edu/edic/rhrc/wp-content/uploads/sites/4/2016/02/RHRC_FR152_Skillman.pdf
15. Ibid., 10.
16. Khatutsky G, Wiener J, Anderson W, Akhmerova V, Jessup A. Understanding direct care workers: A snapshot of two of America's most important jobs. Department of Health and Human Services; 2011:17. https://aspe.hhs.gov/system/files/pdf/76186/CNAchart.pdf
17. O'Malley Watts and Musumeci. Medicaid home and community-based services.
18. Khatutsky et al., Understanding direct care workers, 29.
19. Ibid., 31.
20. Ibid., 33.
21. Ibid., 39.

22. Ibid.

23. Ibid., 40.

24. Boris E, Klein J. Caring for America: Home health workers in the shadow of the welfare state. Oxford Scholarship Online; 2012:180. https://oxford.universitypress scholarship.com/view/10.1093/acprof:oso/9780195329117.001.0001/acprof-97801953 29117

25. Department of Health and Human Services Office of Inspector General. States' requirements for Medicaid-funded personal care service attendants. Department of Health and Human Services Office of Inspector General; 2006:5. https://oig.hhs.gov /oei/reports/oei-07-05-00250.pdf

26. Ibid., 7.

27. Ibid., 8.

28. Ibid.

29. PHI. Personal care aide training requirements by state. Accessed January 26, 2020. https://phinational.org/advocacy/personal care-aide-training-requirements/

30. Campbell S. Training standards for personal care aides: Spotlight on Iowa. PHI; 2017. https://phinational.org/resource/training-standards-for-personal care-aides-spot light-on-iowa/

31. Ibid., 3.

32. Spetz J, Stone RI, Chapman SA, Bryant N. Home and community-based workforce for patients with serious illness requires support to meet growing needs. *Health Aff (Millwood)*. 2019;38(6):904. doi:10.1377/hlthaff.2019.00021.

33. Ibid.

34. Ibid.

35. Ibid., 905.

36. AARP Foundation, The Commonwealth Fund, The SCAN Foundation. Long-term services and supports state scorecard 2020 edition. Appendices. AARP; 2020:66–67. http://www.longtermscorecard.org/-/media/Microsite/Files/2020/Full%20Appen dices.pdf

37. Reinhard S, Houser A, Ujvari K, Gualtieri C, Harrell R, Lingamfelter P, Alexis J. Advancing action. A state scorecard on long-term services and supports for older adults, people with physical disabilities, and family caregivers, 2020 edition. AARP, Commonwealth Fund, and SCAN Foundation; 2020:35. http://longtermscorecard .org/-/media/Microsite/Files/2020/LTSS%202020%20Short%20Report%20 PDF%20923.pdf

38. Ibid.

39. Spetz et al., Home and community-based workforce, 905.

40. Yoon S, Probst J, DiStefano C. Factors affecting job satisfaction among agency-employed home health aides. *Home Health Care Manage & Prac*. 2016;28(1):57–69.

CHAPTER 8

1. Edwards-Orr M, Ujvari K. Taking it to the next level: Using innovative strategies to expand options for self-direction. Long-Term Services and Supports Scorecard: Innovative and promising practices series. AARP Public Policy Institute, Commonwealth Fund, SCAN Foundation; 2018:3. https://www.aarp.org/content/dam/aarp /ppi/2018/04/taking-it-to-the-next-level.pdf

2. Crisp S, Doty P, Flanagan S, Smith G. Developing and implementing self-direction programs and policies: A handbook. Robert Wood Johnson Foundation and National Resource Center for Participant-Directed Services; 2010. https://folio.iupui.edu/bitstream/handle/10244/657/cchandbook090316.pdf?sequence=2

3. Edwards-Orr and Ujvari, Taking it to the next level, 1.

4. Ibid.

5. Crisp et al., Developing and implementing, 2–18.

6. Redfoot D, Fox-Grage W. Medicaid: A program of last resort for people who need long-term services and supports. AARP Public Policy Institute; 2013:2. https://www.aarp.org/content/dam/aarp/research/public_policy_institute/health/2013/medicaid-last-resort-insight-AARP-ppi-health.pdf

7. Doty P, Benjamin A, Matthias R, Franke T. In-home supportive services for the elderly and disabled: A comparison of client-directed and professional management models of service delivery. Non-technical Summary Report. U.S. Department of Health and Human Services, Office of Disability, Aging, and Long-Term Care Policy; 1999. https://aspe.hhs.gov/system/files/pdf/73871/ihss.pdf

8. O'Malley Watts M, Musumeci M. Medicaid home and community-based services: Results from a 50-state survey of enrollment, spending, and program policies. Henry J. Kaiser Family Foundation; 2018:2. http://files.kff.org/attachment/Report-Medicaid-Home-and-Community-Based-Services

9. Centers for Medicare & Medicaid Services. Self-directed services. Accessed July 7, 2020. https://www.medicaid.gov/medicaid/ltss/self-directed/index.html

10. Ibid.

11. Ibid.

12. Ibid.

13. Crisp et al., Developing and implementing.

14. Ibid.

15. O'Malley Watts and Musumeci, Medicaid home and community-based services, 16.

16. Newcomer RJ, Kang T, Doty P. Allowing spouses to be paid personal care providers: Spouse availability and effects on Medicaid-funded service use and expenditures. *Gerontologist*. 2012;52(4):517–530. doi:10.1093/geront/gnr102.

17. Ogg M. Remaining at home with severe disability. *Health Aff (Millwood)*. 2019; 38(6):1046–1049.

18. Crisp et al., Developing and implementing.

19. Ibid.

20. Ibid.

CHAPTER 9

1. Austin W, Bergum V, Nuttgens S, Peternelj-Taylor C. A re-visioning of boundaries in professional helping relationships: Exploring other metaphors. *Ethics & Behav.* 2006;16(2):78. doi:10.1207/s15327019eb1602_1.

2. Shakespeare T, Porter T, Stöckl A. Personal assistance relationships—power, ethics and emotions. University of East Anglia; 2017:2. https://www.thekkingarmidstod.is/media/frettir/PA-Report-final-copy.pdf

3. Ibid., 4.

4. Ibid., 5.

5. Byon HD, Zhu S, Unick GJ, Storr CL, Lipscomb J. Language barrier as a risk factor for injuries from patient violence among direct care workers in home settings: Findings from a U.S. national sample. *Violence and Victims*. 2017;32(5):858–868. doi:10.1891/0886-6708.VV-D-16-00021.

6. Shakespeare et al., Personal assistance relationships, 7.

7. Ibid., 20–21.

8. Saxton M, Curry MA, Powers LE, Maley S, Eckels K, Gross J. "Bring my scooter so I can leave you": A study of disabled women handling abuse by personal assistance providers. *Violence Against Women*. 2001;7(4):393–417. doi:10.1177/10778010122182523.

9. Byon HD, Storr CL, Lipscomb J. Latent classes of caregiver relationships with patients: Workplace violence implications. *Geriatr Nurs*. 2017;38(4):291–295. doi:10.1016/j.gerinurse.2016.11.009.

10. Ibid., 292–293.

11. Porter T, Shakespeare T, Stöckl A. Performance management: A qualitative study of relational boundaries in personal assistance. *Sociol Health & Illn*. 2020;42(1): 191–206. doi:10.1111/1467-9566.12996.

12. Shakespeare et al., Personal assistance relationships, 6.

13. Ibid., 24.

CHAPTER 10

1. Kohl T. Watching out for grandma: Video cameras in nursing homes may help to eliminate abuse. *Fordham Urban Law J*. 2003;30(6):2083–2106. https://ir.lawnet.ford ham.edu/cgi/viewcontent.cgi?article=2219&context=ulj

2. Niemeijer AR, Frederiks BJM, Riphagen II, Legemaate J, Eefsting JA, Hertogh CMPM. Ethical and practical concerns of surveillance technologies in residential care for people with dementia or intellectual disabilities: An overview of the literature. *International Psychogeriatrics*. 2010;22(7):1129–1142. doi:10.1017/S1041610210000037.

3. Center for Technology and Aging. Technology for remote patient monitoring for older adults. Center for Technology and Aging; 2010. http://www.phi.org/uploads /application/files/mjr85izva3yk7v3ah3yqtf5bt1phgzywg67a7zlsv7xcy9h85w.pdf

4. Austin W, Bergum V, Nuttgens S, Peternelj-Taylor C. A re-visioning of boundaries in professional helping relationships: Exploring other metaphors. *Ethics & Behav*. 2006;16(2):77–94. doi:10.1207/s15327019eb1602_1.

5. Shakespeare T, Porter T, Stöckl A. Personal assistance relationships—power, ethics, and emotions. University of East Anglia; 2017:9. https://www.thekkingarmid stod.is/media/frettir/PA-Report-final-copy.pdf

CHAPTER 11

1. National Council on Aging. Elder abuse facts. Accessed March 7, 2020. https:// www.ncoa.org/article/get-the-facts-on-elder-abuse

2. Ibid.

3. Ibid.

4. Oktay JS, Tompkins CJ. Personal assistance providers' mistreatment of disabled adults. *Health & Soc Work*. 2004;29(3):177–188. doi:10.1093/hsw/29.3.177.

5. National Council on Aging, Elder abuse facts.

6. Mitra M, Mouradian VE. Intimate partner violence in the relationships of men with disabilities in the United States: Relative prevalence and health correlates. *J Interpers Violence*. 2014;29(17):3150–3166. doi:10.1177/0886260514534526.

7. Mitra M, Mouradian VE, Fox MH, Pratt C. Prevalence and characteristics of sexual violence against men with disability. *Am J Prev Med*. 2016;50(3):311–317. doi:10.1016/j.amepre.2015.07.030.

8. Ibid.

9. Salwen JK, Gray A, Mona LR. Personal assistance, disability, and intimate partner violence: A guide for healthcare providers. *Rehabil Psychol*. 2016;61(4):417–429. doi:10.1037/rep0000111.

10. Ibid., 419–420.

11. Saxton M, Curry MA, Powers LE, Maley S, Eckels K, Gross J. "Bring my scooter so I can leave you": A study of disabled women handling abuse by personal assistance providers. *Violence Against Women*. 2001;7(4):393–417. doi:10.1177/10778010122182523.

12. Ibid., 404.

13. Ibid.

14. Ibid., 404–405.

15. Saxton M, Curry MA, McNeff E, Limont M, Powers L, Benson J. We're all little John Waynes: A study of disabled men's experience of abuse by personal assistants. *J Rehabil*. 2006;72(4):3–13.

16. Ibid., 7.

17. Ibid, 6.

18. Ibid.

19. Ibid., 8.

20. Disabled Persons Protection Commission, Executive Office of Health and Human Services, Commonwealth of Massachusetts. About DPPC. Accessed March 25, 2020. https://www.mass.gov/about-dppc

21. Schoenberg S. Baker signs law creating caregiver abuse registry. *CommonWealth*. February 13, 2020. Accessed March 25, 2020. https://commonwealthmagazine.org/state-government/baker-signs-law-creating-caregiver-abuse-registry/

22. Rosenbaum L, Lamas D. Residents' duty hours—toward an empirical narrative. *N Engl J Med*. 2012;367(21):2044–2049. doi:10.1056/NEJMsr1210160.

23. Ibid.

24. National Institute for Occupational Safety and Health, Centers for Disease Control and Prevention, U.S. Department of Health and Human Services. Occupational hazards in home healthcare. NIOSH Hazard Review. DHHS (NIOSH) Publication No. 2010–125. U.S. Department of Health and Human Services; 2010:49–51. Accessed March 9, 2020. https://www.cdc.gov/niosh/docs/2010-125/pdfs/2010-125.pdf?id=10.26616/NIOSHPUB2010125

25. U.S. Bureau of Labor Statistics, U.S. Department of Labor. Table SNR05. Injury cases—rates, counts, and percent relative standard errors—detailed industry—2018. Accessed March 9, 2020. https://www.bls.gov/iif/oshsum.htm#18Summary_Tables

26. Gershon RRM, Pogorzelska M, Qureshi KA, et al. Home health care patients and safety hazards in the home: Preliminary findings. In: Henriksen K, Battles JB, Keyes MA, et al., eds. *Advances in Patient Safety: New Directions and Alternative Approaches.* Vol. 1, *Assessment.* Agency for Healthcare Research and Quality; 2008:10.

27. Ibid., 9.

28. National Institute for Occupational Safety and Health, Occupational hazards.

29. Ibid., 4.

30. Ibid., 5.

31. Ibid., 29.

32. Ibid.

33. Ibid., 33.

34. Ibid.

35. Gershon et al., Home health care patients, 10.

36. Hanson GC, Perrin NA, Moss H, Laharnar N, Glass N. Workplace violence against homecare workers and its relationship with workers health outcomes: A cross-sectional study. *BMC Public Health.* 2015;15(11):7. doi:10.1186/s12889-014-1340-7.

37. Galinsky T, Feng HA, Streit J, et al. Risk factors associated with patient assaults of home healthcare workers. *Rehabil Nurs.* 2010;35(5):206–215. doi:10.1002/j .2048-7940.2010.tb00049.x.

38. Byon HD, Zhu S, Unick GJ, Storr CL, Lipscomb J. Language barrier as a risk factor for injuries from patient violence among direct care workers in home settings: Findings from a U.S. national sample. *Violence Vict.* 2017;32(5):858–868. doi:10.1891 /0886-6708.VV-D-16-00021.

39. Karlsson ND, Markkanen PK, Kriebel D, et al. Home care aides' experiences of verbal abuse: A survey of characteristics and risk factors. *Occup Environ Med.* 2019;76(7):448–454. doi:10.1136/oemed-2018-105604.

40. Ibid.

41. Ibid., 451.

42. Ibid., 450.

43. Hanson et al., Workplace violence, 8.

44. Ibid., 10.

CHAPTER 12

1. Shakespeare T, Porter T, Stöckl A. Personal assistance relationships—power, ethics, and emotions. University of East Anglia; 2017:2. https://www.thekkingarmidstod .is/media/frettir/PA-Report-final-copy.pdf

2. PHI. U.S. home care workers: Key facts. PHI; 2019:2. https://phinational.org /resource/u-s-home care-workers-key-facts-2019/

3. Ibid.

4. Espinoza R. Would you stay? Rethinking direct care job quality. PHI; 2020.

5. PHI. Paying the price: How poverty wages undermine home care in America. PHI; February 2015. https://phinational.org/wp-content/uploads/legacy/research-report/pay ing-the-price.pdf

6. Internal Revenue Service, Department of the Treasury. Household employer's tax guide. For use in 2020. Publication 926, Cat. No. 64286A. Internal Revenue Service; 2019:3. https://www.irs.gov/pub/irs-pdf/p926.pdf

7. Ibid.

8. Ibid., 5.

9. Internal Revenue Service, Department of the Treasury. About form 1099-MISC, miscellaneous income. Published March 11, 2020. Accessed May 27, 2020. https://www.irs.gov/forms-pubs/about-form-1099-misc

10. Internal Revenue Service, Department of the Treasury, Household employer's tax guide, 4.

11. Ogg M. Running out of time, money, and independence? *Health Aff (Millwood)* 2011;30(1):173–176. doi:10.1377/hlthaff.2010.0857.

12. Ibid., 176.

13. Hopkins A. How this "anti-fraud" device violates the rights of people with disabilities. *The Mighty*; March 4, 2018. Accessed June 1, 2020. https://themighty.com/2018/03/electronic-visit-verification-violates-rights-people-disabilities/

14. Espinoza R. 8 signs the shortage in paid caregivers is getting worse. PHI; 2017. https://phinational.org/wp-content/uploads/2017/11/workforce-shortages-phi60issues01.pdf

15. Centers for Medicare & Medicaid Services. Electronic visit verification (EVV). Medicaid.gov. Accessed May 25, 2020. https://www.medicaid.gov/medicaid/home-community-based-services/guidance/electronic-visit-verification-evv/index.html

16. Gallopyn N, Iezzoni LI. Views of electronic visit verification (EVV) among home-based personal assistance services consumers and workers. *Disabil Health J.* 2020;13(4):100938. doi:10.1016/j.dhjo.2020.100938.

CHAPTER 13

1. National Direct Service Workforce Resource Center. Final competency set. Centers for Medicare & Medicaid Services; 2014. Accessed June 12, 2020. https://www.medicaid.gov/sites/default/files/2019-12/dsw-core-competencies-final-set-2014.pdf

2. Doty P, Benjamin AE, Matthias RE, Franke TM. *In-Home Supportive Services for the Elderly and Disabled: A Comparison of Client-Directed and Professional Management Models of Service Delivery.* University of California–Los Angeles; 1999.

3. Doty PJ. *The Cash and Counseling Demonstration: An Experiment in Consumer-Directed Personal Assistance Services.* Department of Health and Human Services; 1998.

4. Crisp S, Doty P, Flanagan S, Smith G. Developing and implementing self-direction programs and policies: A handbook. Robert Wood Johnson Foundation and National Resource Center for Participant-Directed Services; 2010:1–13. (Section 1, p. 13). https://www.bc.edu/content/dam/files/schools/gssw_sites/nrcpds/cc-full.pdf

5. Doty P, Mahoney KJ, Simon-Rusinowitz L. Designing the cash and counseling demonstration and evaluation. *Health Serv Res.* 2007;42(1 Pt 2):378–396. doi:10.1111/j.1475-6773.2006.00678.x.

6. Carlson BL, Foster L, Dale SB, Brown R. Effects of cash and counseling on personal care and well-being. *Health Serv Res.* 2007;42(1 Pt 2):467–487. doi:10.1111/j.1475-6773.2006.00673.x.

7. Foster L, Brown R, Phillips B, Schore J, Carlson BL. Improving the quality of Medicaid personal assistance through consumer direction. *Health Aff (Millwood)* 2003;Suppl Web:W3-162–175. doi:10.1377/hlthaff.w3.162.

8. Benjamin AE, Matthias R, Franke TM. Comparing consumer-directed and agency models for providing supportive services at home. *Health Serv Res* 2000;35(1 Pt 2):351–366.

9. Foster et al., Improving the quality.

10. San Antonio P, Simon-Rusinowitz L, Loughlin D, Eckert JK, Mahoney KJ, Ruben KAD. Lessons from the Arkansas Cash and Counseling program: How the experiences of diverse older consumers and their caregivers address family policy concerns. *J Aging Soc Policy.* 2010;22(1):1–17. doi:10.1080/08959420903385544.

11. Ibid.

12. Benjamin AE, Matthias RE. Age, consumer direction, and outcomes of supportive services at home. *Gerontologist.* 2001;41(5):632–642. doi:10.1093/geront/41.5 .632.

13. Craig Hospital, Spinal Cord Injury Resource Library. Personal care assistants: How to find, hire and keep. Craig Hospital; Last revised January 2015. Accessed June 8, 2020. https://craighospital.org/resources/personal-care-assistants-how-to-find-hire -keep

14. AARP. How to hire a caregiver. AARP; Last updated November 7, 2019. Accessed June 12, 2020. https://www.aarp.org/caregiving/home-care/info-2018/hiring -caregiver.html

15. Family Caregiver Alliance. Hiring in-home help. Family Caregiver Alliance. Accessed June 12, 2020. https://www.caregiver.org/hiring-home-help

16. Hannay J, Feiden K, McKaughan M. *Better Jobs Better Care: Building a Strong Long-Term Care Workforce.* Robert Wood Johnson Foundation; 2011; U.S. Department of Labor Employment and Training Administration. Using registered apprenticeship to build and fill healthcare career paths: A response to critical healthcare workforce needs and healthcare reform. U.S. Department of Labor; 2011. https://www.doleta.gov/oa /pdf/apprenticeship_build_healthcare_paths.pdf

17. Foster L, Dale SB, Brown R. How caregivers and workers fared in cash and counseling. *Health Serv Res.* 2007;42(1 Pt 2):510–532. doi:10.1111/j.1475-6773.2006 .00672.x.

18. Ibid., 528.

19. Benjamin AE, Matthias RE. Work-life differences and outcomes for agency and consumer-directed home care workers. *Gerontologist.* 2004;44(4):479–488. doi:10.1093/geront/44.4.479.

20. Delp L, Wallace SP, Geiger-Brown J, Muntaner C. Job stress and job satisfaction: Home care workers in a consumer-directed model of care. *Health Serv Res.* 2010;45(4):922–940. doi:10.1111/j.1475-6773.2010.01112.x.

21. Howes C. Love, money, or flexibility: What motivates people to work in consumer-directed home care? *Gerontologist.* 2008;48(Spec No 1):46–59. doi:10.1093/ geront/48.supplement_1.46.

22. National Institute for Occupational Safety and Health, Centers for Disease Control and Prevention, U.S. Department of Health and Human Services. Occupational hazards in home healthcare. NIOSH Hazard Review. DHHS (NIOSH) Publication No. 2010–125. U.S. Department of Health and Human Services; 2010:49–51. Accessed March 9, 2020. https://www.cdc.gov/niosh/docs/2010-125/pdfs/2010-125 .pdf?id=10.26616/NIOSHPUB2010125

CHAPTER 14

1. U.S. Census Bureau. Older people expected to outnumber children for the first time in U.S. history. CB 18–41; Updated October 8, 2019. Accessed July 4, 2020. https://www.census.gov/newsroom/press-releases/2018/cb18-41-population-projec tions.html

2. Ibid.

3. Watts MO, Musumeci M, Chidambaram P. Medicaid home and community-based services enrollment and spending. Issue Brief. Henry J. Kaiser Family Foundation; 2020:2. http://files.kff.org/attachment/Issue-Brief-Medicaid-Home-and-Com munity-Based-Services-Enrollment-and-Spending

4. Scales K. *Envisioning the Future of Home Care: Trends and Opportunities in Workforce Policy and Practice.* PHI; 2019:20.

5. Ibid.

6. Campbell S. *We Can Do Better: How Our Broken Long-Term Care System Undermines Care.* PHI; 2020.

7. Scales K. *It's Time to Care: A Detailed Profile of America's Direct Care Workforce.* PHI; 2020.

8. Drake A. *Direct Care Work Is Real Work: Elevating the Role of the Direct Care Worker.* PHI; 2020.

9. Scales, *Envisioning the Future.*

10. Espinoza R. *Would You Stay? Rethinking Direct Care Job Quality.* PHI; 2020.

11. SCAN Foundation. Who provides long-term care in the U.S.? (Updated). SCAN Foundation; 2013:1. https://www.thescanfoundation.org/sites/default/files/us _who_provides_ltc_us_oct_12_fsrevised-10-10-13.pdf

12. AARP and National Alliance for Family Caregiving. Caregiving in the U.S. 2020 Report. AARP; 2020; 37. https://www.aarp.org/content/dam/aarp/ppi/2020/05 /full-report-caregiving-in-the-united-states.doi.10.26419-2Fppi.00103.001.pdf

13. Landers S, Madigan E, Leff B, et al. The future of home health care: A strategic framework for optimizing value. *Home Health Care Manage Pract.* 2016 Nov;28(4):266. doi:10.1177/1084822316666368.

14. AARP and National Alliance for Family Caregiving, Caregiving in the U.S., 16.

15. U.S. Census Bureau. One-person households on the rise. U.S. Census Bureau; Last revised November 21, 2019. Accessed July 5, 2020. https://www.census.gov/library /visualizations/2019/comm/one-person-households.html

16. Commission on Long-Term Care. Report to the Congress. Commission on Long-Term Care; 2013:10. http://ltccommission.org/ltccommission/wp-content/up loads/2013/12/Commission-on-Long-Term-Care-Final-Report-9-26-13.pdf

17. AARP and National Alliance for Family Caregiving, Caregiving in the U.S., 44–45.

18. Multi-disciplinary Research Team, U.S. Department of Housing and Urban Development. *Accessibility of America's Housing Stock: Analysis of the 2011 American Housing Survey.* U.S. Department of Housing and Urban Development; 2015:5.

19. Ibid., 2.

20. Ibid.

21. True S, Ochieng N, Cubanski J, Koma W, Neuman T. Under the radar: States vary in regulating and reporting COVID-19 in assisted living facilities. Henry J. Kaiser

Family Foundation; 2020. https://www.kff.org/coronavirus-covid-19/issue-brief/under-the-radar-states-vary-in-regulating-and-reporting-covid-19-in-assisted-living-facilities/

22. Yi SH, See I, Kent AG, et al. Characterization of COVID-19 in assisted living facilities—39 states, October 2020. *MMWR*. 2020;69:1730.

23. True et al., Under the radar.

24. Department of Housing and Urban Development. Supportive housing and services for the elderly and persons with disabilities: Implementing statutory reforms. Proposed rule. *Fed Regist*. 2014;79(194):60591.

25. Musumeci M, Chidambaram P, Watts MO. *Medicaid's Money Follows the Person Program: State progress and uncertainty pending federal funding reauthorization*. Issue Brief. Henry J. Kaiser Family Foundation; 2019:2. http://files.kff.org/attachment/Issue-Brief-Medicaids-Money-Follows-the-Person-Program-State-Progress-and-Uncertainty-Pending-Federal-Funding%20Reauthorization

26. Hargan ED. Report to the President and Congress: The Money Follows the Person (MFP) rebalancing demonstration. U.S. Department of Health and Human Services, Office of the Secretary; 2017:27. https://www.medicaid.gov/sites/default/files/2019-12/mfp-rtc.pdf

27. Fox-Grage W. Medicaid: A last resort for people needing long-term services and supports. AARP Public Policy Institute; 2017. https://www.aarp.org/content/dam/aarp/ppi/2017-01/Medicaid-A-Last-Resort-for-People-Needing-Long-Term-Services-and-Supports.pdf

28. Social Security Administration. Benefits for children with disabilities. Pub. No. 05-10026. Social Security Administration; 2020. https://www.ssa.gov/pubs/EN-05-10026.pdf

29. Commission on Long-Term Care. Report to the Congress.

30. Scales, *Envisioning the Future*, 6.

31. Watts et al., *Medicaid Home and Community-Based Services*, 11.

32. Eiken S, Sredl K, Burwell B, Amos A. Medicaid expenditures for long-term services and supports in FY 2016. Medicaid Innovation Accelerator Program; 2018:7. https://www.medicaid.gov/sites/default/files/2019-12/ltssexpenditures2016.pdf

33. Scales, *It's Time to Care*, 10.

34. Ibid., 2.

35. Leadership Council of Aging Organizations. The direct care workforce: A report on practices to promote quality long term care. Leadership Council of Aging Organizations; 2019. https://www.lcao.org/files/2012/12/LCAO-LTSS-REPORT.pdf

36. Scales, *It's Time to Care*, 19.

37. Glasmeier A. Living wage calculator. Massachusetts Institute of Technology; 2020. Accessed July 20, 2020. https://livingwage.mit.edu/

38. Guzman GG. Household income: 2018. American Community Survey Briefs. ACSBR/18–01. U.S. Department of Commerce, U.S. Census Bureau; 2019:8. https://www.census.gov/content/dam/Census/library/publications/2019/acs/acsbr18-01.pdf

39. U.S. Bureau of Labor Statistics. Occupational employment and wages, 2019: 25–1054, Physics teachers, postsecondary. Accessed July 12, 2020. https://www.bls.gov/oes/current/oes251054.htm

40. Morrisey M. The state of American retirement savings. Economic Policy Institute; 2019:8. https://files.epi.org/pdf/136219.pdf

41. Ibid., 1.

42. Ibid., 14.

43. Baughman RA, Smith K. The effect of Medicaid wage pass-through programs on the wages of direct care workers. *Med Care.* 2010;48(5):426–432. doi:10.1097 /MLR.0b013e3181d6888a.

44. Scales, *It's Time to Care*, 19.

45. Leadership Council of Aging Organizations, Direct care workforce, 9.

46. Ibid., 8.

47. Commission on Long-Term Care, Report to the Congress, 55.

48. Drake, *Direct Care Work Is Real Work*, 25.

49. Leadership Council of Aging Organizations, Direct care workforce, 18–19.

50. Scales, *Envisioning the Future*, 88.

51. Ibid.

52. Ibid., 89.

53. Ibid., 89–90.

54. Office of Civil Rights, U.S. Department of Justice. Questions and answers on the ADA's integration mandate and Olmstead enforcement. U.S. Department of Justice, Office of Civil Rights; Updated February 25, 2020. Accessed July 17, 2020. https://www.ada.gov/olmstead/q&a_olmstead.htm#_ftnref11

55. Watts M, Musumeci M. Medicaid home and community-based services: Results from a 50-state survey of enrollment, spending, and program policies. Kaiser Family Foundation; 2018:2. http://files.kff.org/attachment/Report-Medicaid-Home-and -Community-Based-Services

56. Buhler-Wilkinson K. Care of the chronically ill at home: An unresolved dilemma in health policy for the United States. *Milbank Q.* 2007;85(4):611–639. doi:10.1111/j .1468-0009.2007.00503.x.

57. Ibid., 612.

58. Commission on Long-Term Care, Report to the Congress, 63.

59. Ibid., 61.

60. Ibid., 27–28.

61. Iezzoni LI, Rao SR, Ressalem J, et al. Attitudes of physicians about people with disability and their health care. *Health Aff (Millwood).* 2021;40(2):297–306. doi:10.1377/hlthaff.2020.01452

62. Office of Civil Rights, Questions and answers on the ADA's integration mandate.

63. Ogg M. Remaining at home with severe disability. *Health Aff (Millwood)* 2019;38(6):1046–1049. doi:10.1377/hlthaff.2018.05532.

64. Ibid., 1047.

65. Iezzoni LI. A backstory to Michael Ogg's Narrative Matters essay: Why he needed to leave PACE. *Health Aff Blog.* July 18, 2019. Accessed July 20, 2020. https:// www.healthaffairs.org/do/10.1377/hblog20190717.505863/full/

66. Ibid.

67. Mukherjee D. Discharge decisions and the dignity of risk. *Hastings Cent Rep.* 2015;45(3):7–8. doi:10.1002/hast.441.

68. Iezzoni et al., Attitudes of physicians.

69. Buhler-Wilkinson, Care of the chronically ill at home, 632.

EPILOGUE

1. Centers for Disease Control and Prevention. CDC confirms possible instance of community spread of COVID-19 in U.S. Media statement. Centers for Disease Control and Prevention; February 26, 2020. Accessed July 31, 2020. https://www.cdc.gov/media/releases/2020/s0226-Covid-19-spread.html

2. Iezzoni LI, Ogg M. Hard lessons from a long hospital stay. *Am J Nurs.* 2012; 112(4):39–42. doi:10.1097/01.NAJ.0000413457.53110.3a.

3. Iezzoni LI. Dangers of diagnostic overshadowing. *N Engl J Med.* 2019;380(22): 2092–2093. doi:10.1056/NEJMp1903078.

Index

Lisa I. Iezzoni, MD, MSc, is a Professor of Medicine at Harvard Medical School and based at the Health Policy Research Center–Mongan Institute at Massachusetts General Hospital. She is the author or editor of several books, including *When Walking Fails: Mobility Problems of Adults with Chronic Conditions*, and is a member of the National Academy of Medicine in the National Academies of Sciences, Engineering, and Medicine.